The Philosophy Memos:

"If you have fundamental philosophies well ingrained, honestly believed and to which you are deeply committed, then it is not necessary to take each situation you face and re-think the basic guidelines within which you should take action."

Bill Weisz

Special Limited Edition
published in March 1993
by Motorola University Press.

Typeset in Adobe Trump Mediaeval
using Macintosh IIsi.
Fifteen thousand copies
Printing and binding by Kingsport Press,
Kingsport, Tennessee.

Hard cover: Permalin, Iris, Coffee
Soft cover: Carolina 15 point, coated 2 sides
End sheets: French Rayon, Flax Tan Text
Text stock: Lindenmeyr, Sebago, Eggshell

Design by Hayward Blake & Company,
Evanston, Illinois.

ISBN 1-56946-000-0 (cl)
ISBN 1-56946-001-9 (p)

The
Philosophy
Memos:
Articles,
Speeches &
Quotations

Bill Weisz

Motorola University Press
Schaumburg, Illinois
1993

*The
Philosophy
Memos:*

Contents

Contents

Introduction

This is Bill Weisz's book. But much more! It is a beacon of values. It vividly projects the character of the people of Motorola through the years.

In his foreword, Bill notes that only those principles that he deemed worthy were circulated in his periodic philosophy memos which make up this collective work. He knew what he stood for. He knew himself.

He also knew "his" people. He knew they would not stand for any lesser values than he. Thus, as he gathered and selected and circulated these thoughts and sayings, he was helping all of us echo a unifying theme without any of us having to mount a soap box.

Many were the times the words would be heard, "Did you read the quote in Bill's last philosophy memo? I couldn't agree more with the point it made. I only wish I could have said it as clearly."

Oh, there were die-hards who thought the memos too soft. Little did those few understand the power of ethics and expectations and quality and communication and the customer and ...

I compliment Bill for bringing this anthology to life— adding this vital book to the growing Motorola authored library. The able and the wise among us will be students of these Motorola lessons as we inspire and teach ourselves to earn our next achievements.

Robert W. Galvin
Chairman, Executive Committee
Motorola, Inc.

Preface

The Philosophy Memos collected and distributed by Bill Weisz over the years have indeed established themselves as part of the Motorola fabric. They are part of the creation of our beliefs and value systems, which indeed as practiced over time become part of our culture. To be sure, I believe that a person without philosophical underpinnings is an empty soul. Likewise, a corporation without a philosophical foundation to guide its daily behaviors is an empty collection of businesses. Motorola's culture, based on our key beliefs of respect for the dignity of the individual and uncompromising integrity in everything we do, has been strongly enhanced over these years by the continual reinforcement of the bits of wisdom collected and distributed by Bill Weisz in The Philosophy Memos. How great it is to now have a collection of these all in one place for each of us to glance at and reflect upon, to gain perspective, to challenge and to stimulate.

As a young manager at Motorola, I remember eagerly reading each of The Philosophy Memos and so many times being so impressed by the wisdom of the passages. To be sure, those periodic reminders made me a better person, and I think in aggregate they combined to make Motorola a better company. For a few brief moments, each one of those memos made us think more deeply and with greater perspective than we might have otherwise done. The cumulative effect has to have been a greater ability for all of us in Motorola to see the whole picture of business and life, and hence better anticipate the future, understand the present and learn from the past.

George M.C. Fisher
Chairman of the Board
Chief Executive Officer
Motorola, Inc.

Foreword

In the late 1960s, as Motorola's communications division grew in size, I became concerned as a general manager about the ability to accurately communicate my fundamental beliefs down through several layers of management. I wasn't worried that anyone would intentionally miscommunicate. Rather, I was worried that we would duplicate the old parlor game, where a group of people stand in a circle and a sentence whispered from ear to ear produces a totally different thought by the time it is said aloud by the last person. I wanted a way to communicate directly and accurately. The result was what I called my philosophy memo.

I decided to periodically send a philosophy memo to everybody in the communications division who was on the executive/professional briefing list. **I defined a philosophy to mean something a person believed so strongly that when a situation needed to be handled it was not necessary to rethink the fundamental principles that applied in that particular case.** Rather, because a person had deeply ingrained fundamental principles, he or she would approach each problem or opportunity in accordance with those philosophies—in the Motorola way, if you will.

Examples of such fundamental philosophies are Motorola's key beliefs: constant respect for people and uncompromising integrity. It was through the philosophy memo that I would reinforce those beliefs and tell others how I felt about a number of leadership and managerial issues.

Early philosophy memos expressed thoughts relating to a then-current business issue or simply circulated articles that covered an important leadership philosophy or business issue exceptionally well.

As time went on, the memos began including a number of quotations, all of which generally related to a specific thought. Because only those quotations with which I agreed were included, people who read the memo knew my personal belief on that particular subject.

I encouraged readers to write to me or call me if they wanted clarification, or if they disagreed with any quotation or philosophy. Many people did just that, and I was able to open correspondence with them, to further discuss and drive home the point that the quotation or memo had made. Eventually people started sending me quotations to use in future memos. If I agreed with the thought, I used it, identifying the submitter and his or her organization. A substantial backlog of quotations built up.

I continued the philosophy memo when I moved to corporate headquarters as assistant chief operating officer in April 1969, then mailing to the total corporate executive/professional briefing list. The memo was issued until January 1, 1988, when I passed the chief executive officership over to George Fisher. Throughout all of those years, it was gratifying to me to meet Motorolans from all over the world who had read the philosophy memos regularly and appreciated the direct communication from their top management.

I've added to this book some memos that were sent by me to other Motorola colleagues and a select number of the speeches I have given over the years, all representing my views on additional issues.

I hope you enjoy reading this book as much as I enjoyed making the statements throughout my 41 years as a Motorola employee.

Bill Weisz

Bill Weisz
Vice Chairman of the Board of Directors
Retired Chief Executive Officer
Motorola, Inc.

Biography

Bill Weisz began his career with Motorola as a junior development engineer in 1948, following receipt of his bachelor's degree in electrical engineering from the Massachusetts Institute of Technology and service with the U.S. Navy in 1945–46 as an electronic technician.

Among his first assignments was work on early versions of the company's Handie Talkie® FM Radiophone. He was named manager of the Portable Communications Product line in 1954. In 1956, he became chief engineer for all mobile and portable communications products and manager of these product lines in 1958.

Weisz was elected a Motorola vice president in 1961. He was named assistant general manager of the Communications Division in 1964, and general manager the following year. In 1968, he was elected to the Board of Directors, and the next year he became executive vice president and assistant chief operating officer. He was elected president and assistant chief operating officer in 1970, and, in 1972, became president and chief operating officer. He became chief executive officer in 1986. He was designated an officer of the board Jan. 1, 1988. On Dec. 28, 1989, Weisz retired from Motorola as an employee and operating officer. He remains as vice chairman and consultant to the company, in which role he teaches at Motorola University and represents Motorola in a number of senior executive, industry and government activities.

Weisz has been an active contributor to professional and civic organizations. In 1981 he was presented with the Electronic Industries Association's highest personal recognition, the Medal of Honor, by the EIA Board of Governors. The award recognizes outstanding contributions to the advancement of the electronics industry.

He has held a number of posts with the EIA from chairman of the Technical Committee on Land Mobile Services to chairman of the Association's Board of Governors. He was a member of the Special Committee on Telecommunications Policy of the Board, which served as Advisory Committee on the Department of Transportation. In that capacity, Weisz was the official EIA representative to the Federal Highway Administration.

He has served on the Federal Communications Commission Land Mobile Advisory Committee and the Land Mobile Communications Council. He was a member of the Business Roundtable and of the National Academy of Sciences Panel on Advanced Technology Competition between the Industrialized Allies. He has served on the Secretary of Commerce's EXPORT NOW Advisory Committee and on the Defense Policy Advisory Committee on Trade (DPACT) to the Secretary of Defense and the U.S. Trade Representative.

Other high posts have been held by Weisz in the national and Chicago chapters of the Institute of Radio Engineers and the Institute of Electrical and Electronics Engineers, including the chairmanship of the IEEE Professional Group on Vehicular Communication. He has authored numerous papers and received patents related to two-way radio communications.

Weisz became a Fellow of the Institute of Electrical and Electronics Engineers in 1966. He is also a fellow of The Radio Club of America, which awarded him the Sarnoff Citation in 1987. In 1970, he received the National Electronics Conference Award of Merit.

He is active in the affairs of his alma mater, the Massachusetts Institute of Technology. He is a member of the MIT Corporation (Board of Trustees). He is on the Investment Committee, a member of the Visiting Committee for the Sloan School of Management, and past chairman of the Visiting Committee for Electrical Engineering and Computer Sciences. He received the MIT Corporate Leadership Award in 1976.

He holds an honorary doctorate of business administration from St. Ambrose College, Davenport, Iowa, granted in 1976. The Freedoms Foundation at Valley Forge awarded Weisz an honor certificate in 1974 for his efforts on behalf of the private enterprise system.

Corporate Culture

April 28, 1985

The Motorola Corporate Culture

Presented to the Motorola Officers Meeting
Ft. Lauderdale, Florida.

*Corporate
Culture Speech*

For the last two days we have spent a lot of time talking about changes we are going to make to ensure our ability to serve the customer better than anyone else, and thus ensure the continued growth of Motorola. In periods of such change, it is absolutely necessary that we pull back for a moment to remember and reinforce the fundamental culture and policies of the corporation that must not be changed. The foreword of a book titled *Not Subject to Change*, published by IBM, discusses the balance between things that should change and things that should not:

"The job of the executive is to manage change in an environment of change. Products are continually changing to meet changing needs and tastes in markets, and the business environment is exploding with social and political change. However, some of the most important elements in the executive's life must not change. **No matter how dynamic the manager's approach to problems must be, ultimate success as a leader is based on an unchanging set of principles that direct the leader's purposes.***"*

Corporate culture is a mysterious thing to pin down, so I'd like to start by defining it. Corporate culture is the underlying set of assumptions that govern how people perceive themselves, their work, other people and the organization's goals. You might say culture is synonymous with operating philosophy. Many years ago when I started my philosophy memos, I defined the word "philosophy" to be a principle that you don't have to think about each time an issue comes up. If you have fundamental philosophies well ingrained, honestly believed and to which you are deeply committed, then it is not necessary to take each situation you face and rethink the basic guidelines within which you should take action. You will have an instant, correct reaction to each different issue because of your strong belief in the fundamental philosophies.

In Motorola's 57 years, it has had two chief executive officers and three other people as members of the chief executive office. It has had continuity of culture and basic beliefs, though each person had a different style of implementation. Edgar Schein of the Massachusetts Institute of Technology's Sloan School of Management contends that the prime role of top executives is culture management. Leaders must create and manage culture achievement. Sometimes they must destroy bad cultures in the process of rebuilding good ones. Our company's working environment is made up of myriad programs and procedures derived from the policies and principles codified in "For Which We Stand." However, no matter what is written, whether it is in "For Which We Stand" or in a "Quality of Performance" memo, our actions tell people in the organization what is expected of them.

Cultures must be 100 percent shared values. There can be no 90 percent agreement on such fundamental issues. Cultures don't occur randomly. They occur because leaders spend time on them, set examples and reward some behaviors and practices more than others. How we reward and punish tells our people how well we believe in the words we mouth as our "Motorola culture." In your organization, you are the CEO no matter what level of the company you are in. You are the leader who must live the culture, who must monitor where and how you spend your time, coaching and setting the example, encouraging and rewarding employees to behave in certain ways. If you do this well, then employees confronted with certain complex problems will "know" how to approach them the Motorola way.

You may be saying to yourself, "Why are we spending any time on this subject? I understand our culture and its importance. It's kind of an insult to even insinuate that I don't." Yes, we believe that you do understand our culture. But many times—when change occurs or when economic times are tough—expediency puts great pressure on how we all practice that culture. **Unfortunately, we too often tend to take shortcuts in order to achieve operational goals.**

In April 1969, I moved from the Communications Division to Corporate Headquarters, where I became the third man in the then chairman/president's office. I had the luxury of spending my first four or five months wandering all over the corporation, meeting people and learning how they operated. In September 1969, I gave a presentation titled "The Pursuit of Excellence in Management" to the Executive Conference. That talk was a direct result of my concern that in too many places we were becoming expedient in our living of the Motorola culture. My message at that time was basically the same message I am delivering today, or that Paul Galvin, Bob Galvin or Elmer Wavering delivered in one form or another during many periods of change in the corporation's history. Each time we reiterated, restated, reinvigorated and renewed our commitment to the Motorola culture, we propagated the proper tone into the future. Because of that, the corporation continued its growth, operating by the same fundamental standards and with the same atmosphere as it did years and years before. As we continue to implement the organizational effectiveness program—to decentralize even more, to create some form of additional Asia-Pacific thrust—it becomes more important than ever that we are absolutely sure we understand our Motorola corporate culture and that we recommit ourselves to living it.

After all that philosophy about the importance of continuity of the Motorola corporate culture, what is it? You all know, but let me reiterate the key tenets for all of us.

The single, most-important shared value at Motorola is the dignity of the individual. The book *Managers for Tomorrow* states it very succinctly:

"The challenge to the manager of tomorrow is to find ways by which individuals can be given opportunity for self-realization and will be valued for themselves. Every person within an organization should have the opportunity to grow. The purpose of management is neither to tend, nor to tame people, its purpose is to realize the power of people ... "

Our Motorola way of saying this is: "The most important job of management is to create the environment and the atmosphere in which each and every person can contribute to the maximum of his or her own capability." The best experts at managing people have to constantly work at developing this talent until they live and breathe the philosophy of the importance of people. Even then, they have to challenge themselves regularly to be sure that in the crush of current events they are still taking the time to pay proper attention to people motivation and management. Only by taking the time can the requirements for excellence in leadership be fulfilled. We in the chief executive office wish there to be a singular, worldwide philosophy regarding people. As we further decentralize organizationally, the responsibility for ensuring this, which is delegated to operating managers around the world, must become stronger, not weaker. Historically, the Personnel Department has reported directly to the chief executive office to underscore the importance of our belief in this element of corporate culture. While working as a fully supportive member of every operating team, the Personnel Department provides to our office a direct conduit for employee concerns.

Honesty, integrity and ethical conduct are no-compromise cultural precepts. Unfortunately, as in every large company, every once in a while we do find situations where a very few people bend or break these critical tenets—sometimes in the mistaken belief that it is for the good of the company. We do not tolerate such deviations. This responsibility is so important that the Board of Directors maintains personal cognizance of the company's activities through its Ethics Committee.

What are some of the other unchangeable Motorola tenets of culture? **We believe in communication between people and organizations, every which way—with no prerogatives about whether it is up, down or sideways—with no walls between sectors, groups, divisions or functions within an organization.** We believe in the open-door policy right up to the top. We believe in teamwork and expect cooperation, not confrontation, as the atmosphere for interactions between people and organizations. This means an atmosphere of objectivity on every issue. Since we believe that 99 $^{44}/_{100}$ percent of our people want to do the right things, we reject the demeaning of individual personalities and refuse to accept that ulterior motives are skulking behind any position taken. We believe in open and complete argument on controversial issues right up to the point where a decision is made. After that, we expect every manager to be an active supporter of a decision. We believe in the opportunity to privately re-argue a decision once more if new facts come on the scene.

We believe in the attitude of personal proprietorship and the entrepreneurial spirit so that every person involved can identify with the success of a particular product or business. Thus, we believe strongly in the decentralization of authority and responsibility. But that carries with it an even more strict requirement for extensive communications of all kinds. It mandates the volunteering of information that regularly gives other people above and below you a continuing feel for the business. It absolutely requires that a manager raise to higher visibility key issues, decisions and, particularly, bad news. We don't like surprises. While we expect teamwork and loyalty to your own organization, we require it even more to Motorola's overall greater good.

We believe in being non-union and dealing directly with our people. **We believe strongly in the need for more and more participation on the part of all employees, a culture many of you have lived but whose practice must be strengthened as a fundamental culture of Motorola.** We believe in the "we" approach, not "we vs. they." We believe in setting high standards, high expectations. We insist on a healthy spirit of discontent. We believe in creativity and innovation as being fundamental to our business. We believe in complete customer satisfaction—no ifs, ands or buts. That means the highest of quality and reliability in our products and services.

We believe that managers cannot manage from their offices. They must walk around and be intimately involved with their people. We believe in traveling widely throughout the organization, not staying in our—or your—ivory tower. We believe in talking freely at all levels of the company with big groups, small groups and individuals. We believe in knowing the businesses, in having the "feel." We believe in seeing that the details are accomplished, not just the big picture.

We believe in being a good corporate citizen, and in contributing to the economic and social well-being of every community and country in which we operate.

Actually, a key tenet of our culture has been the ability to adapt to an environment of dynamic change. In the past, we have generally acquitted ourselves well. Our environment changed from good to tough times. Our customers' requirements changed. We have developed new products and opened up new markets. We have gone from being an equipment business to encompassing components and processing. We have had the courage to divest ourselves of businesses that were improper, even though the corporation's short-term sales were reduced. We have constantly decentralized and shifted activities between sectors and groups. Our discussion here of the Asia-Pacific Task Force Report and our program of organizational effectiveness indicate our continual willingness to change. By design, we are further sophisticating our organization and evolving to a new level of decentralized operation. But we are not a holding company and do not intend to become one. We want no Motorola organization to be an island. We want to take full advantage of our broadly diversified competencies, of the skills that exist in one sector or group that complement those elsewhere in the corporation. These give Motorola a distinct advantage that makes two plus two equal six. Excellent examples of things that we have done in the past are the "Staccato" hand-held radio computer terminal, generated under a devolpment agreement for IBM, the NTT pager and our corporate thrust into Japan. To be successful in these types of endeavors means that, some few times, a decentralized operation's activities will be impinged upon in order to support the overall corporate good. **We expect you as decentralized managers not only to run your own businesses well, but also to be alert and reach out for synergistic opportunities and to be fully supportive of intersector/group activities—even if it does not seem to be to your own business's immediate direct advantage.**

These, then, are our fundamental, shared values—our Motorola corporate culture. You may say them in a slightly different way, or you may even think of another. I know that they are not new to you, but it is important to reiterate them in times of dynamic change. I said earlier that these must be 100 percent shared values, and we really mean 100 percent! Many years ago, Art Reese, a former executive vice president of Motorola and a member of its board of directors, developed an evaluation form for general managers. This form required that the chief executive officer, when measuring performance or evaluating candidates for a general manager's job, judge a series of performance characteristics over and above technical proficiency to do the job. These characteristics all related to how well the manager lived the Motorola culture. As we look over history, I think it is fair to say that in many areas where we failed it was because, in the selection of a senior manager, we rationalized away the lack of 100 percent adherence to some of our Motorola values and culture. In the future selection of senior managers, we intend, and we also wish you, to put increased emphasis on the requirement for enthusiastic belief in the Motorola culture, as demonstrated by daily perfomance. **Frankly, if a manager at any level isn't totally committed—if he or she does not practice the Motorola culture 100 percent—then no matter how good their technical or professional skill, we, and you, really should not want them in the corporation.** We cannot afford to have anyone in a leadership position who gives wrong signals to other employees—one who doesn't encourage them to tackle every problem in accordance with the fundamental principles with which we wish it to be tackled.

There is a bright future for Motorola and a bright future for all of you—notwithstanding the strong competition that we face—if we do two things very well. First, we must adapt rapidly to changing conditions to ensure that our service to customers is better than anyone else's. Second, no matter what else we change, we must truly live the Motorola corporate culture—every day in every way. If we do so, we will have guaranteed the end result, because all else flows from this.

We want you to leave this meeting with the absolute mandate to challenge everything we do, and the way we do it, if it does not help us beat the competition in serving the customer. But there is one overriding requirement: Whatever we do must be in accordance with the Motorola culture. These fundamental philosophies are "Not subject to change."

Bill Weisz (BW)

General Philosophy

April 15, 1974

The following is an excerpt from the autobiography of C.L. Burton,
former chairman of the board of Simpsons, Ltd., Canada.
Submitted by Art Murcott, Corporate Finance, Geneva, Illinois office.

General Philosophy Memos

Who Will Take the Initiative?

I find the world a better place to live in than when I entered it. To be sure, there are perils and hazards of a monstrous kind lurking in world politics and the world economy. But there is not only a rapidly expanding social conscience, but a furiously accelerating technological and scientific apparatus already on hand with which to face those hazards.

It all boils down to the ancient simple question: Who will take the initiative? Who has a sense of urgency? Which of us will take the lead? It is always a new day. And always, somebody is ready to go to work.

I hold no brief for private enterprise. But I have unshakable faith in individual enterprise.

Come on, you young fellows, whoever you are. Lead on.

September 15, 1976

The following is an excerpt from an issue of Horizons *magazine.*
Submitted by Dave Bartram, operations manager, Special Markets
Communications and Electronics, Inc.

A Refreshingly Reliable Business Forecast

Every year, business forecasts get more "iffy" and unreliable,
with hardly an observation that isn't hedged, or subject to
adjustment or conditional upon other unknown factors. So we
offer a refreshing change, a forecast guaranteed to be accurate:

1. Business will continue to go where invited and to return where appreciated.
2. Reputations will continue to be made by many acts and lost by one.
3. People will go on preferring to do business with those who give service.
4. Go-givers will continue to be the best go-getters.
5. The extra mile will have no traffic jams.
6. Performance will continue to outsell promises.
7. Enthusiasm will be as contagious as ever.
8. Know-how will surpass guess-how.
9. Trust, not tricks, will keep customers loyal.
10. Quality will be prized as a precious possession.
11. When the going gets tough, the tough will get going.

   author unknown

May 15, 1978

Submitted by Dan Noble, chairman, Science Advisory Board.

Basic Precepts of Science

Murphy's Law: If anything can go wrong, it will.

Patrick's Theorem: If the experiment works, you must be using the wrong equipment.

Skinner's Constant: That quantity which, when multiplied by, divided into, added to, or subtracted from the answer you got, gives the answer you should have obtained.

Horner's Five Thumb Postulate: Experience varies directly with the equipment ruined.

Flagle's Law of the Perversity of Inanimate Objects: Any inanimate object, regardless of its composition or configuration, may be expected to perform at any time in a totally unexpected manner for reasons that are either totally obscure or completely mysterious.

Allen's Axiom: When all else fails, read the instructions.

The Spare Parts Principle: The accessibility, during recovery, of small parts which fall from the work bench, varies directly with the size of the part … and inversely with its importance to the completion of the work under way.

The Compensation Corollary: The experiment may be considered a success if no more than 50 percent of the observed measurements must be discarded to obtain a correspondence with theory.

Gumperson's Law: The probability of a given event occurring is inversely proportional to its desirability.

The Ordering Principle: Those supplies necessary for yesterday's experiment must be ordered no later than tomorrow at noon.

The Ultimate Principle: By definition, when you are investigating the unknown, you do not know what you will find.

The Futility Factor: No experiment is ever a complete failure … it can always serve as a bad example.

Information-Source Contradictions: The quality of a committee decision will vary inversely as the square of the number of committee members.

March 4, 1983

Submitted by Frank Havlicek, corporate manager,
Recreation and Special Services.

The Quest for Excellence

There once was a land that launched freedom
And had prophets wise and bold
For they knew they must set standards
For their people to behold

But the populace had freedom now
For them … the goal achieved
So why not rest and contemplate
The laurels they'd received

They took their turns at looting
Their mental storage tank
For their urge for creativity
Had already closed its bank

But the prophets saw their duty
And 'roused a selected few
Who gathered that only competence
Would ever see them thru

Competence as a condition of freedom
Had widely been ignored
But now the lazy, slovenly and hazy
Would have to be explored

For those who do a slovenly job
Be they janitor, judge or of few
Lower the tone of society
And castigate anything new

So thc prophets asked for excellence
So all would get their due
For excellence asks more than competence
If their country was to arise anew

We need every form of excellence, they said
In all our creative life
To lead our people to new levels
Above the battle and strife

The idea for which our nation stands
Will not grow like a tree
If the highest goal set for ourselves
Is amiable mediocrity

It is easy for us to believe
All things come without buying
Like the air we breathe and the sights we see
And goals gained without trying

Nothing could be more dangerous
For the future of our generations
Than for us to live for evermore
Under the shadow of our stations

For we must set our own goals
When no one tells us what to do
With effort and performance
That makes us born anew

Then one rose from among the prophets
And stated for all to hear
'Tis the habitual vision of greatness
That we must see firm and clear

And they carved in rocks of granite
The words he held so dear
So each generation could rediscover
That excellence conquers fear.
Frank Havlicek

October 2, 1989

For many years now, I have had a 3"x 5" card in my desk drawer containing a quote by Arnold Glasow. I see it every morning as I pull out my calendar. I've read it and re-read it, and recommended it to a number of people. Together, with two other quotes, it makes up this philosophy memo.

"You'll break the worry habit the day you decide you can meet and master the worst that can happen to you."
Arnold Glasow

"Have no fear of failure. Just think of it as one of the many steps in the business of getting ahead in life."
John J. Rowlands

"Those who try to do something and fail are infinitely better than those who try to do nothing and succeed."
Richard Bird

November 15, 1976

Submitted by Walter Scott, Corporate Headquarters.

It Can't Happen Here

General Philosophy Articles

Have you ever faced the possibility that your country could cease to exist?

Nations richer and more powerful in their day than we are in this, have been sabotaged, defeated, enslaved.

Babylon was the largest and richest nation of its time, but its lust for luxury made it an easy mark for the Medes and Persians who overran it, and divided its land and enslaved people between them.

Rome was a greater military power than we ever were, but when free bread and circuses became more important to the people than hard work and patriotism, Rome was invaded and looted by the tougher vandals.

The Incas were the most civilized, richest people in the Americas, but ruthless, better-armed invaders destroyed them as a nation, and looted everything they owned and had spent generations in creating.

In every case it was the self-indulgent weakness of the victim which made the victory of the invader easy.

How strong is a nation which allows foreign competitors to capture the world leadership from one after another of its most vital industries?

How wise is a nation which gives away so much of its substance abroad and at home that it can no longer afford to keep up its own strength and protection?

How intelligent is a nation more careful to protect the criminal than his victim?

How weak is a nation which allows bureaucracy and a socialist philosophy to run riot and squander billions?

Undoubtedly there were Babylonians, Romans, Incas who warned against overindulgence and weakness, who warned that each citizen is responsible for his nation, and that that responsibility cannot be shrugged off onto officials. But to those who warned of impending trouble there was then as now the smug sneer, "It can't happen here."

But it did.

December 21, 1983

The attached information from Northwestern University was sent to me by Toni Dewey, corporate vice president, director of Public Relations and Advertising. Though I know you all "revel" in stress and strain, the comments might help you enjoy it even more.

Stress and Strain Reducers

by Harold M. Visotsky, M.D.
Owen L. Coon professor and chairman
Department of Psychiatry and Behavioral Sciences
Northwestern University Medical School.
Reprint permission granted.

Exercises and routines can reduce the stress and strain of our daily lives. While these alone do not correct a stressful life situation, they can reduce the accumulation of stress to a significant degree. Try them! But also remember to evaluate your entire spectrum of activities, relationships, habits and values.

› Take a walk. Try and walk briskly for five to 10 minutes each day.
› Take a break. Move away from your desk or work site.
› Take vacations. Short vacations are better than long ones.
› Eat a balanced diet. Check with your doctor if you are in doubt. Limit your alcohol intake.
› Exercise vigorously. Calisthenics, tennis, swimming, etc. If you are not sports-minded, at least walk rapidly for one mile three times a week.
› Sleep seven to eight hours. Or find out why you can't.
› Try and develop a sense of humor (if you don't have one). Use it if you do.
› Allow time for the unexpected. The unexpected is often caused by stressed and frustrated people.
› Learn to say, "NO." Do not over-schedule. Leave time for crisis solving.
› Set aside a quiet time and place every day. This does not necessarily mean a bar!

> Seek the help and advice of others you trust.
> Talk to your friends and relatives. Keep in touch.
> Become aware of tense muscles. Learn to relax them.
> Sit comfortably with head back and hands loosely upturned in lap. Then close your eyes for one minute. Don't try and clear your mind; let your thoughts flow.
> Admit your anger or frustration; take responsibility for your feelings. Let your anger cool; then express your views or feelings.
> Learn to redirect your anger or frustrations. Not at your wife, husband, friend or subordinates, but into a hobby or diverting activity such as needlework, carpentry, shopping—whatever "turns you on" and helps consume your creative energies.
> Face difficulties and difficult situations. Know your priorities. Take steps to change or solve what you can, and don't worry about the rest.

May 20, 1985

Submitted by Karl Burgess, vice president and Motorola director, Systems Communications and Computer Services.

The 10 Percent Difference

by Robert Forest, partner
Forest & Eyler Computer Communications
Reprint permission granted by *Infosystems*, April 1979.

I have a friend and sometime client who is a software consultant for a large, multinational corporation. He's been in the industry for a long time—25 years, I'd guess—and he's worked at many levels in many kinds of industries. He is, in addition, an extremely thoughtful and perceptive person. I'll call him Ron.

One of Ron's continuing concerns is with the quality of our industry's technical people—programmers, primarily. As part of his job, he's interested in helping his company to find, encourage and develop quality programmers—productive people who do good work.

One day he pointed out to me that at major professional golf tournaments, there is only about a 10 percent difference between the score of the winner and those who finish further back in the pack.

Perhaps, he wondered, that's true of life in general, and of programmers in particular. **Maybe there is only a 10 percent difference between the best programmers and the solid, professional programmers who could be thought of as good enough to qualify for a programming "tournament."**

What Ron would like to know is how you find the people who are that slim but critical 10 percent better. Find the people who will be "winners." How do you identify them early on, select those you'd like to work for you? (We'll ignore for right now the matters of how you provide the environment, the stimuli and the management that will bring out the best in such people.)

For starters, let's just think about what makes the difference between an outstanding leader and a solid, steady performer. We might be tempted to think that the 10 percent difference lies in some quality that we might call "technical." For golf that technical skill would be physical. For programming, it might be IQ.

I'd guess that these technical qualities would account for some of the 10 percent difference. After all, Jack Nicklaus and Arnold Palmer (in his prime) undoubtedly have (or had) superior physical skills. But then so do most of the golfers on the pro tour.

But you don't have to know much about golf to realize that it is a highly mental game. It requires immense doses of the ability to concentrate, for instance. That trait turns out to be important in programming, too. But then it's important to excel in almost any human activity.

By concentration I don't mean just the ability to shut out extraneous noises, sights or other distractions. I'm talking about evidence of the desire over a long period of time to do what needs to be done to become extra good at whatever it is you do for a living.

For golfers and other athletes, that means not only practicing but staying in good physical condition. For activities that place more emphasis upon mental abilities, excellence comes not only from "practicing"—or doing—but keeping your mind in sound condition.

Another aspect of the ability to concentrate is what could be called "cool"—the ability to ignore pressure. Some people can program well under ordinary circumstances: when it's quiet, when there is no tight deadline, when they are not tired. But being able to produce under an opposite set of circumstances is one of the traits that separates the women from the girls and the men from the boys.

It's not quite that simple, of course. Some golfers play better under pressure, and have trouble maintaining their concentration when they're "safely" in the lead. I suspect that this is true of programmers, too.

There are plenty of other "non-technical" traits that separate the leader, the winner, from the pack. (Remember, we're talking about professionals, now.) There is hunger, the desire to excel. And there's ambition, the desire to get ahead, which can sometimes get in the way of excellence. In programming, we look for the ability to communicate (including listening carefully and intelligently), sensitivity to others, imagination; we could build a long, long list.

I'm not trying to establish an analogy between programming and golf. I'm trying to establish that what makes the difference between excellence and above average—in any profession—lies not merely in what may appear to be the primary "technical" skill. In programming, we need more than the ability to think logically and manipulate abstract symbols.

The more important attributes may just be psychological. They include the desire to excel, the willingness to work hard, the ability to concentrate and to produce in what may be an unsympathetic environment, or under pressure—time and time again. That's what makes a professional ... and proves excellence.

General Philosophy Quotations, Poems and Lists

"Nobody will use other people's experience, nor have any of his own 'til it is too late to use it."
Nathaniel Hawthorne

"To make astute people believe one is what one is not is, in most cases, harder than actually to become what one wishes to appear."
George Lichtenberg

"The darkest hour in the history of any young man is when he sits down to study how to get money without honestly earning it."
Horace Greeley

"Too many people's virtue consists chiefly in repenting faults, not in avoiding them."
George Lichtenberg

"Time is like money; the less of it we have to spare, the further we make it go."
Henry Wheeler Shaw

"With most people unbelief in one thing is founded upon blind belief in another."
George Lichtenberg

"Few of us get anything without working for it."
William Feather

"It is the triumph of reason to get on well with those who possess none."
Voltaire

"Everybody is a bit right; nobody is completely right or completely wrong."
Eugene Rosenstock-Huessy

"The readiest and surest way to get rid of censure, is to correct ourselves."
Demosthenes

"A clash of doctrines is not a disaster—it is an opportunity."
Alfred North Whitehead

"Courage, considered in itself or without reference to its causes, is no virtue, and deserves no esteem. It is found in the best and worst, and is to be judged according to the qualities from which it springs and with which it is conjoined."
William Ellery Channing

"The best evidence of merit is the cordial recognition of it whenever and wherever it may be found."
Christian Bovee

"Ignorance and impudence always go together; for in proportion as we are unacquainted with other things, must we feel a want of respect for them."
William Hazlitt

"Only madmen and fools are pleased with themselves; no wise man is good enough for his own satisfaction."
Benjamin Whichcote

"Before you criticize someone on failure to fulfill their own responsibilities, better first look in the mirror to determine your own degree of perfection."
author unknown

"Difficulties strengthen the mind as labor does the body."
Seneca

"We know accurately only when we know little; with knowledge doubt increases."
Goethe

"I have no secret of success but hard work."
Edward Turner

"I believe in the dignity of labor, whether with head or hand; that the world owes no man a living but that it owes every man an opportunity to make a living."
John D. Rockefeller, Jr.

"I am a great believer in luck, and I find the harder I work the more I have of it."
Stephen Leacock

"Thought must be a guide to action, not a substitute for it."
author unknown

"Ideals are the most powerful force known to man. No nation's greatness long survives the lowering of the greatness of its ideals. And, as with nations, so with individuals. Low ideals and high station cannot long retain company. We all must have ideals unless we are content to drift along aimlessly, ambitionless, ineffectually. Ideals vitalize. Ideals energize."
B. C. Forbes

"Prejudice is being down on something you're not up on. It is essentially an outgrowth of ignorance."
Judd Marmor

"If nobody spoke unless he had something to say, the human race would very soon lose the use of speech."
Somerset Maugham

"It is better to say I don't know than to lie about it."
Ignas Bernstein

"God gave us two ears but only one mouth … does that tell you something?"
author unknown

"He that will not reason is a bigot; he that cannot reason is a fool; he that does not reason is a slave."
William Drummond

"Patriotism is that love for country in the hearts of the people which shall make that country strong to resist foreign oppression and domestic intrigue—which impresses each and every individual with a sense of the inalienable rights of others and prepares him to accept the responsibility of protecting those rights."
American Tribune, March 7, 1890

"Take heart again; put your dismal fears away. One day, who knows? Even these hardships will be grand things to look back on."
Vergil

"Real evils can be either cured or endured; it is only imaginary evils that make people anxiety-ridden for a lifetime."
Earl Nightingale

"Life is too short for mean anxieties."
Charles Kingsley

"Perhaps wisdom is to be found in people who have suffered greatly but have surmounted it."
Louis Jolyon West

"Shallow wits censure everything that is beyond their depth."
author unknown

The Lombardi Credo
"It is becoming increasingly difficult to be tolerant of a society that has sympathy only for the misfit, only for the maladjusted, only for the criminal, only for the loser. Have sympathy for them, help them, but I think it's also a time for all of us to stand up

for and to cheer for the doer, the achiever, one who recognizes a problem and does something about it, one who looks at something extra to do for his country—the winner, the leader!"
Vince Lombardi
Former coach, Green Bay Packers

"The man whose authority is recent is always stern."
Aeschylus

"A man should never be ashamed to own he has been in the wrong, which is but saying in other words that he is wiser today than he was yesterday."
Alexander Pope

"Men tinged with sovereignty can easily feel that the king can do no wrong."
Paul Douglas

"To know one's ignorance is the best part of knowledge."
Lao-tsu, circa 604 B.C.

"We must be doing something to be happy. Action is no less necessary to us than thought."
William Hazlitt

"We are confronted with insurmountable opportunities."
Walt Kelley

"Man's mind stretched to a new idea never goes back to its original dimensions."
Oliver Wendell Holmes

"Strange how much you've got to know before you know how little you know."
Duncan Stuart

"If there is any such thing as a wise compromise, it is not likely to be reached by a refusal to think."
Joseph Wood Krutch

"What splendid heights many people attain by merely keeping on the level."
John Newton Baker

"I testify that the privilege to work is a gift, the power to work is a blessing, and the love to work is success."
author unknown

"When in doubt, tell the truth."
Mark Twain

"It takes two to speak the truth—one to speak and another to hear."
Henry David Thoreau

"Truth must be repeated again and again, because error is constantly being preached round about."
Goethe

"All truth is safe, and nothing else is safe; and he who keeps back the truth, or withholds it from men for motives of expediency is either a coward or a criminal or both."
Max Muller

"There is nothing so easy but that it becomes difficult when you do it with reluctance."
author unknown

"To be nothing is the result of doing nothing."
Harry F. Banks

"Blessed is the man who, having nothing to say, abstains from giving us wordy evidence of the fact."
George Elliott

"Depend on this one fact: The future of mankind, peace, progress and prosperity must be finally determined by the extent to which men can be brought to a state of common and honest understanding."
Ralph C. Smedley

Take Time
Take time to think ... it is the
  source of power
Take time to play ... it is the
  secret of perpetual youth
Take time to read ... it is the
  fountain of wisdom
Take time to pray ... it is the
  greatest power on earth

Take time to love … it is a God-given privilege
Take time to be friendly … it is the road to happiness
Take time to laugh … it is the music of the soul
Take time to give … it is too short a day to be selfish
Take time to work … it is the price of success.
author unknown

Press On
"Nothing in the world can take the place of persistence. Talent will not; nothing is more common than unsuccessful men with talent. Genius will not; unrewarded genius is almost a proverb. Education will not; the world is full of educated derelicts. Persistence and determination alone are omnipotent."
author unknown

"Failure is often the path of least persistence."
author unknown

"Tension strangles and suffocates creativity. Don't expect a flow of ideas if you let yourself get tied in a knot."
Arnold Glasow

"Let well enough alone and there will be no progress."
William Feather

"If you say what you think, don't expect to hear only what you like."
author unknown

"The biggest men with the biggest ideas can be shot down by the smallest men with the smallest idea. Think big anyway!"
author unknown

"Ulcers come from mountain-climbing—molehills."
author unknown

"Don't fight a fact. Deal with it!"
Hugh Prather

"It is not in doing what you like but in liking what you do that is the secret of happiness."
James Barrie

The Man in the Glass
When you get what you want in your struggle for self,
And the world makes you king for a day,
Just go to a mirror and look at yourself,
*And see what **That Man** has to say,*

For it isn't your father or mother or wife,
Whose judgment upon you must pass,
The fellow whose verdict counts most in your life,
Is the one staring back from the glass.

Some people may think you a straight-shooting chum,
And call you a wonderful guy,
But the man in the glass says you're only a bum,
If you can't look him straight in the eye.

He's the fellow to please, never mind all the rest,
For he's with you clear to the end,
And you have passed your most difficult test,
If the man in the glass is your friend.

You can fool the whole world down the pathway of life,
And get pats on your back as you pass,
But your final reward will be heartaches and fears,
If you cheat the man in the glass.
author unknown

"You have not converted a man because you have silenced him."
John Morley

"What you do not use yourself, do not give to others. For example: advice."
Sri Chinmoy

"Nothing gives one person so much advantage over another as to remain cool and unruffled under all circumstances."
Thomas Jefferson

"Listening to advice often accomplishes far more than heeding it."
Malcom Forbes

"You can often profit from being at a loss for words."
Frank Tyger

"Tact is the great ability to see other people as they think you see them."
Carl Zuckmayer

"There is no such thing as a good excuse."
B.C. Forbes

"To be conscious that you are ignorant of the facts is a great step to knowledge."
Benjamin Disraeli

"Resting brains create rusting minds."
Bill Tomlinson

"There are no simple solutions. Only intelligent choices."
author unknown

"Honesty and frankness make you vulnerable. Be honest and frank anyway!"
author unknown

Food for Thought
The greatest sin—fear
The biggest day—today
The biggest fool—the boy who will not go to school
The best town—where you succeed

The most agreeable companion—one who would not have you any different from who you are
The greatest bore—one who will not come to the point
The still greater bore—one who keeps on talking after he has made his point
The greatest deceiver—one who deceives himself
The greatest invention of the Devil—war
The greatest secret of production—saving waste
The best work—what you like
The best play—work
The greatest comfort—the knowledge that you have done your work well
The greatest mistake—giving up
The most expensive indulgence—hate
The cheapest, stupidest and easiest thing to do—find fault
The greatest troublemaker—one who talks too much
The greatest stumbling block—egotism
The most ridiculous asset—pride
The worst bankrupt—the soul that has lost its enthusiasm
The cleverest man—one who always does what he thinks is right
The most dangerous person—the liar
The most disagreeable person—the complainer

The best teacher—one who makes you want to learn
The meanest feeling of which any human being is capable—feeling bad at another's success
The greatest need—common sense
The greatest puzzle—life
The greatest mystery—death
The greatest thought—God
The greatest thing, bar none, in all the world—love
author unknown

"The acid test of intelligence is its ability to cope with unintelligence."
William Feather

"The trouble with too many people is they believe the realm of truth always lies within their vision."
Abraham Lincoln

Anything you can do, they can do, too
While you flex your muscles in front of your morning mirror and congratulate yourself on your nimble brain, consider this: The light over your mirror was perfected by a deaf man. While your morning radio plays, remember the hunchback who helped invent it. If you listen to contemporary music, you may hear an artist who is blind. If you prefer classical, you may enjoy a symphony written by a composer who couldn't hear. The President who set an unbeatable American

political record could hardly walk. A woman born unable to see, speak or hear stands as a great achiever in American history. The handicapped can enrich our lives. Let's enrich theirs.

© **United Technologies Corporation, 1980**

"Perfection of means and confusion of goals seem, in my opinion, to characterize our age."
Albert Einstein

He who knows not and knows
    not he knows not,
He is a fool—shun him.

He who knows not and knows
    he knows not,
He is simple—teach him.

He who knows and knows not
    he knows,
He is asleep—wake him.

He who knows and knows he
    knows,
He is wise—follow him.
author unknown

On Patriotism

True patriotism is more than getting a lump in your throat when the flag passes by. It involves determination on your part to see that America remains free. It involves your willingness to put the best interest of the nation ahead of your own self-interest. Single interests may be important. But the art of democracy is the ability to recognize the common good. The ability to

give, not just to take. 231 million people can pull our nation apart or pull it together. Which way did you pull today?

© **United Technologies Corporation, 1982**

"Our conduct is influenced not by our experience, but by our expectations."
George Bernard Shaw

"You can do very little with faith, but you can do nothing without it."
Samuel Butler

"Judgment can be acquired only by acute observation; by actual experience in the school of life; by ceaseless alertness to learn from others; by study of the activities of men who have made notable marks; by striving to analyze the everyday play of causes and effects; by constant study of human nature; by the cultivation of a spirit of fairness, even generosity, to all."
B.C. Forbes

"Sometimes a fool has talent, but never judgment."
La Rochefoucauld

"He has a good judgment that relieth not wholly on his own."
Thomas Fuller

Ten Secrets of Success

1. Keep your temper to yourself
2. Give your enthusiasm to everyone
3. Make others feel important
4. Stamp out self-pity
5. Put your smile to work
6. Keep trying
7. Give a good start to anything you do
8. Forgive yourself … if you fail
9. Overwhelm people with charm, not power
10. Keep promises

author unknown

"What kind of man would live where there is no daring? I don't believe in taking foolish chances, but nothing can be accomplished without taking any chances at all."
Charles A. Lindbergh

"Experience without learning is better than learning without experience."
H. G. Bohn

"Education is to get you where you can start to learn."
George Aiken

"Every person who pursues a career, as distinct from a jobholder, should expect to continue his education for the rest of his professional life."
Harry Levinson

Don't be Afraid to Fail

You've failed many times, although you may not remember. You fell down the first time you tried to walk. You almost drowned the first time you tried to swim, didn't you? Did you hit the ball the first time you swung a bat? Heavy hitters, the ones who hit the most home runs, also strike out a lot. R.H. Macy failed seven times before his store in New York caught on. English novelist John Creasey got 753 rejection slips before he published 564 books. Babe Ruth struck out 1,330 times, but he also hit 714 home runs. Don't worry about failure. Worry about the chances you miss when you don't even try.

© **United Technologies Corporation, 1986**

Reach Out

"Do not fear mistakes. Wisdom is often born of mistakes. You will know failure. Determine now to acquire the confidence to overcome it. Reach out!"
P.V. Galvin

"The most agreeable recompense which we can receive for things which we have done is to see them known, to have them applauded with praises which honor us."
Jean Molière

"My observation and investigation have convinced me that nine times in ten success is won by those who deserve to win it. Dame Fortune is not so capricious as superficial indications sometimes would suggest: Fame, responsibility and (uninherited) wealth usually seek shoulders broad enough to bear them worthily."
B.C. Forbes

"Luck follows those who are trained to see the opportunity."
Wilbur M. McFeeley

"Every new opinion at its starting is precisely in the minority of one."
Thomas Carlyle
Great Ideas of Western Man

"There are three kinds of people— those who make things happen, those who watch things happen, and those who have no idea what happened."
author unknown

"The real danger is not that machines will begin to think like men, but that men will begin to think like machines."
Sydney J. Harris

"Men are wise in proportion, not to their experience, but to their capacity for experience."
George Bernard Shaw

"One cool judgment is worth a thousand hasty counsels. The thing to do is to supply light and not heat."
Woodrow Wilson

"To make sacrifices in big things is easy, but to make sacrifices in little things is what we are seldom capable of."
Goethe

"We judge ourselves by what we feel capable of doing while others judge us by what we have already done."
Henry Wadsworth Longfellow

"Shallow men believe in luck; wise and strong men in cause and effect."
Ralph Waldo Emerson

"An optimist sees an opportunity in every calamity. A pessimist sees a calamity in every opportunity."
author unknown

"A problem is like a pebble. If one holds it close to the eyes, it fills the whole world and puts everything out of focus.

If the pebble is held at a proper distance, it can be examined objectively for what it is worth.

If the pebble is thrown on the ground, it is seen in its true setting—a tiny bump in one's path."
author unknown

"If your job was less difficult, someone with less ability would be doing it."
author unknown

"The highest reward for man's toil is not what he gets for it but what he becomes by it."
John Ruskin

The Glory-Giver
And in those days, behold there came through the gates of the city a worker from afar off, and it came to pass as the weeks went by that he earned plenty and kept moving ahead.

And in that city were they that were the belly-achers and they that spent their days in adding to the alibi ghosts. Mightily were they astonished. They said one to the other, "What the hell; how doth he getteth away with it?" And it came to pass that many were gathered in a back room and a soothsayer came among them. And he was a pretty smart guy. And they spoke, and questioned him, saying; "How is it that this stranger accomplished the impossible?"

Whereupon the prophet made answer: "He of whom you speak is one hustler. He ariseth very early in the morning and goeth forth full of pep. He complaineth not, neither doth he know despair. He giveth heartily of good effort and welcome cheer."

"While ye gather here and say one to the other, 'Verily this is a terrible day to work', he is already finding things that needeth doing and doing them. And when the eleventh hour cometh he needeth no alibis. He knoweth his abilities and they that would stave him off discover he diggeth up work to profit his company and getteth at it. He maketh his own opportunities to grow and prosper, Men say unto him 'nay' when he cometh in, yet just a short time later he hath the approval of the brass, enjoys their favor and earns promotions aplenty."

"He taketh with him the two angels 'inspiration' and 'perspiration' and worketh to beat hell."

"Verily I say unto you, go and do likewise."
James Munton ©1967
Success/Sharing/Speaker
Associate Sponsor, Midwest Institute;
Dale Carnegie Sales Course

Products

Product Memos

Philosophies of Product Leadership

In the last few months I have participated in a number of review sessions of various product lines. In addition, I have paid particular attention to products as they come out of engineering or the factory, and to the technological state of the art that leads to these products.

I have met many good people who have grown rapidly in our organization to positions of importance, due to the substantial broadening of our product activities these past years. I have become a little concerned that because we have grown so rapidly, some of the key philosophies we have had over the years may lose a little in the translation. I don't like to refer to the "good old days," because I don't think the "good old days" hold a candle to the kind of sophisticated demands that are being placed on all of you today. However, I do believe that there are certain basic philosophies that always apply. I am aware of activities that will yield component parts books, checklists of various tests and procedures, etc., but let me tell you some of the basic philosophies relating to product that I believe were rather universally followed in the past and that we should review and insist upon in the future.

1. It has always been our philosophy to remain years ahead in technology and product in the marketplace. I would always like to see us two years ahead of our nearest competitors. By ahead I mean employing state-of-the-art techniques in product that we are actually selling when our competitors are only thinking about them. Of course, these techniques

must meet an important criterion, and that is that they really do something for the customer. We must be doing development work in new arts and building prototype products long before the art is stabilized and the cost for new components is practical. **If we wait until the costs are right and everything works perfectly before we start our development, then we will truly lose our leadership.** Our history has been just the opposite. We have worked years in advance; transistorization is a key example. We have developed product in anticipation of the bugs being worked out of the components and the costs coming down, and we were there when our competitors were just waking up. We have continually offered more and better products to the customer years in advance of the competition, and thus have maintained our leadership and kept our competitors off-balance. This basic philosophy is mandatory.

2. New product development can never cease. The day we decide we have a complete product line and pull back on the amount of effort, money and time placed in engineering effort, is the day that we have sealed our own doom.

3. Cost-reduction efforts on a product start the day we introduce it. We all know that regardless of how well a product is designed for low cost, there are always substantial cost reductions that may be implemented. Therefore, formal cost-reduction programs must be implemented on all major items on a regular basis. We must continually lower our costs, so that we

do not create a price umbrella in the marketplace that allows competition to come in way under us. This does not mean we must always be low in price. It does mean that we must give true value for our price, whatever it is.

I heard the other day that one of our key automotive radio customers has offered to give Motorola's automotive division an automobile to dissect, with a view toward new product ideas and cost reduction in existing ones. Here is another idea that we might use: How about our giving a radio, or parts of a radio, to some of our key suppliers for them to work on? It certainly would be an inexpensive way to encourage cost-reduction suggestions from a broad scope of experts in the field.

4. We must always be striving to achieve a broad market for our products. The Motrac/Motran market is akin to the Continental, the Cadillac or the Buick market. There is nothing wrong with this market, let me assure you. It is profitable and it will always be a major market, but as in the case of motorcar manufacturers or anyone else, the market may be substantially broadened, and sales and profits raised, by attacking large segments of potential customers with products they can buy. Our Mocom-30 and Mocom-10 products are aimed at doing just that. Of course, the products in your areas follow the same pattern. **When a business is built only on high-priced product, it is extremely susceptible to losing large segments of its market to competitors at the lower price levels unless it gives demonstrable value for the price.** An intelligent management organization is one that maximizes its sales and profits by presenting a broad enough product line, consistent with its internal capabilities for manufacturing that product line, so that it is not vulnerable and is simultaneously reaching the broadest possible market segment.

"In business, the competition will bite you if you keep running; if you stand still, they will swallow you."
Semon Knudsen

5. **It is becoming increasingly evident that there will be a substantial shortage of various critical talents, ranging from analyzers and testers on a production line to competent maintenance personnel in the field.** This puts an ever-increasing demand on our engineering people, in both development and production, to design product that can be made with high quality, tested quickly and easily, and installed and maintained by people of lesser skills. This means automation and mechanization in our factories, smarter engineering and broader tolerances in our design factors, and possibly modular construction in our products. But whatever it means specifically to any given product, the generality is true. We must re-emphasize our efforts in these directions. At this point, I might congratulate the engineering group that designed the Detroit Edison radio switch. Key manufacturing personnel from all divisions of the company have told us that this was a well-designed unit for production. I don't mean to single these people out as exceptions—others of you have performed in the same manner.

Two last philosophies, though very specific to design and engineering, are very critical to successful product. There should always be a complete operating breadboard of a total unit. In other words, while different design groups may be working on IF's or RF's for a receiver, there should always be a complete receiver operating, so that when a change is made by any individual group it can be immediately incorporated in the complete breadboard to ensure there are no interacting effects. Unfortunately, we have seen situations where individual modules are designed very well, but when put together just don't play. This complete operating breadboard should be an inviolate part of every engineering project and should be put together at the earliest possible time.

Of equal concern is ensuring that the costs of a product end up meeting design objectives. There is only one way I know to ensure this. The very first complete breadboard or prototype is costed carefully at the earliest point in the program. It is then brought up to date once a week by adds and omits of cost resulting from changes made by the design engineers that week. In this way, the current cost of a unit under development is always available. No surprises occur when a unit is ready to go into production, because the cost has been known every week since the date of the first prototype.

I have said a lot of things in this memo, and I suspect some of you are sitting back and saying, "Two years ahead—he's crazy," or "It is impossible to always beat competition and still get the units out with quality, on time and make money," or "It is better to be out six months late or a year late and really have the right product with no problems."

I suspect that you can persuade yourself to believe any one of these comments, or a dozen more just like it. However, it is possible to do both. It is possible to be a leader, to be years ahead, to have product that works and is reliable and built with quality, and to make money in the process. I agree it is not easy. **Leadership in anything is not easy, but it can be done.** We have done it in the past, and it is my directive to you that you run your businesses with these philosophies in the future. You can do it, and if you do, the rewards are tremendous.

BW

A copy of Dan's book titled Noble Comments *appears in various Motorola libraries. Dan Noble was a senior Motorola Executive for many years, the founder of Motorola's Government Electronic, Semiconductor and Communication Businesses, and Chief Technical Officer of the Corporation.*

I am enclosing for your reading a copy of the selected philoso-phies, if you will, of Dan Noble, regarding equipment design and many other important things. These highlights have been pulled from many of Dan's works throughout the last 20 years. The thoughts expressed in *Noble Comments* have been one of the reasons that a number of Motorola Divisions have risen to the top of the heap in their areas of endeavor. I suggest that you re-read these thoughts now, or read them for the first time if you have not been exposed to them personally in the past. Freely pass the book around amongst your associates and those who work with you in your various projects. I think the thoughts expressed are as applicable and important today as they were when Dan first wrote them.

BW

Innovation and Technology

During the last month I have heard a couple of people say that we have to be careful that we don't "use technology for technology's sake."

I would like to suggest that we stop saying this to ourselves or to anybody else. When we at high levels say that, we all understand what we mean: Don't use a new technology that does not work well and does not do very much for the customer, but use technology as soon as it is ready to ensure product leadership.

Unfortunately, when we use the shorthand term without all of the qualifiers and it is repeated throughout the organization, mid-managers and technical people can interpret this as, "Don't reach out to put new technology in the product, particularly if there is some risk involved." Whether we like to admit it or not, I think that this attitude has been prevalent in a number of places in Motorola. Too often the result is a far too conservative use of technology and a de-emphasis on high technology in developing products.

You all know that we started technology reviews to counter this effect. One of the top 10 corporate goals is: "Technology—

"We must not ask where science and technology are taking us, but rather how we can manage science and technology so that they can help us get where we want to go."
René Dubos

be the product leader through timely, appropriate use of technology and by designing for optimum reliability and automated manufacturing."

When the Board of Directors' strategy committee reviewed the goals, they unanimously suggested that we change the word "timely" to "early" to further emphasize the importance of technology in our products and to let everyone throughout the company know that we really do mean to be a technology leader.

I know that certain technologies may be too high in cost to be put into a broad line of products. But the early use of technology in some of our products, at a premium price if necessary, will drive us down the experience curve and enable us to make very broad use of that technology a lot sooner.

So please, let's stop saying to each other that we should not use technology for technology's sake. Of course we should not. Let's have a reach-out philosophy on the use of technology, not a riskless, conservative posture. And let's have all of our people who are involved in designing products know that the earliest possible intelligent use of technology is a major cornerstone of our strategy.

BW

Using the Technology Review in Product Planning

The fundamental purpose of the technology review and the technology road map is to ensure that we put in motion today what is necessary to have the right technology, processes, components and experience in place to meet the future needs for products and services. Most of Motorola's businesses depend on technology for their leadership positions. With this definition of the objective, the technology review cannot be just a "show and tell" of products developed since the last review or a description of the products to be available in the future. The technology review must be a searching and challenging evaluation of our different sector and group plans to make sure that we indeed are doing the right things to ensure future leadership.

Two types of product programs must be considered. The first is the "ELM Program," which uses existing technology to fill a product opportunity, and where time to market may be especially critical. This is generally between six months and two years. No new technology is employed here, but products are defined very accurately and specifications agreed to in advance and not changed during the life of the program, thus allowing the products with riskless technology to be brought to market as quickly as possible, on schedule and with very accurate cost results.

The second major type of product development meets projected, long-term product needs. To fill market opportunities we believe will develop requires the development and, possibly, the invention of new technologies, so the product can come to mar-

"Everything now being done is going to be done differently, it's going to be done better, and if you don't do it, your competitor will." from **Joe Powell's** management motion picture, ***The Real Security.***

ket. Here, marketing research and other information on customer wants and needs must be synthesized with engineering's projection of coming technologies to determine what new products can be developed. In fact, customers may not even know what they need, or can have, because of their lack of knowledge about potential technologies.

We wish to lay out a leadership product plan, or to leapfrog the product leader in the field. This must be supported by a technology road map that indicates what we need and when we need it in order to have a product available at a particular time. It forces us to consider whether we can develop new technology internally to meet the product plan or if we must seek it elsewhere. There might be other suppliers of the technology. There might be other opportunities to license the technology from someone else. There might be opportunities to have third parties develop the technology for our use. **But the responsibility of the product operations involved is to seek the technology from anywhere in the world in order to meet their product requirements.** Certainly, we wish to do our own original work and maintain a proprietary position. However, rather than duplicating effort that is costly, we should practice the philosophy that it is "better to receive than to give," as long as we receive technology by legal, ethical and moral methods.

We must constantly ask ourselves who in the world is best in a given technology. We must constantly compare technologies available in the marketplace so we never lose sight of what

"Advertising and salesmanship are time savers in the promotion of products. They are essential tools in meeting competition. At the foundation of every successful business, however, is a product which thoroughly satisfies a real need on the part of the buyer, and from which he profits and knows that he profits."
William Feather

is going on. The very first technology review, 15 years ago at SPS, highlighted new semiconductor technologies on a matrix listed by their developer. For this review we developed the little matrix that scaled our capability from one to five, showing past capability, present capability and future capability. When we were forced to catalog all the known technologies being used by our competitors, we were surprised at how little we knew about competitors' fundamental processes in many cases. We knew what the resulting product performance was, but we were not good at identifying processes that related semiconductor production to defects per centimeter, or to quality, etc.

Technology road maps should be prepared in the following fashion. In addition to marketing studies of customer requirements, studies of competitors' past and current product introductions, their research and development, and their introduction patterns allow us to predict their future courses of action. Having integrated all of these things into a desired product plan, the products are called out along the bottom of a sheet of paper that is graduated in years. The "technologies required" are listed vertically along the left side of the paper and the "schedule for their development" is shown horizontally so that it can be easily matched with the product requirements along the bottom, or time scale. The technology road map should be on one piece of paper for each business operation. It should not have products on one sheet and technologies on another.

The technology road map is one of the fundamental tools by which performance can be evaluated each year. **A searching analysis of what was supposed to have been done in the past year versus what actually was done should be made at the review.** Where schedules have been missed, the reasons for the miss should be evaluated so it can be determined what must be done to get back on schedule or to ensure that we end up with the right technology at the right time. Of course, road maps must not be cast in concrete. They are allowed to be modified as major new technological events occur or as new facts become apparent. Thus, the technology road map indeed becomes a living, working document.

The following additional questions should be asked at a technology review:

1. Are there any technologies that ought to be on the road map that are not there?
2. Have you identified the programs that are not currently planned to be funded in the five-year plan?
3. Have you searched the world for a technological answer to your requirements and not just looked internally at Motorola?
4. Are there products or assistance that must come from other sectors and groups of Motorola? (This is important so that they may be put on a corporate-level road map, thus ensuring that visibility by corporate management is not lost.)
5. Are there minority reports? In other words, are there people who disagree with the road map as proposed, and if so, why?

Other tools that have been developed should continue to be used. These include product life-cycle charts and cost-and-price experience charts with 70 percent experience slopes. Regular cost-reduction programs are important and should be on the chart, not just fundamentally new technologies. Technologies relating to excellent manufacturing and superb quality should also be on the chart. In some cases, technologies such as our ability to operate computer-aided design systems should be on the chart.

A certain amount of "show and tell" is always necessary at a review, but it should not be out of balance with the fundamental objective of the review. Possibly people should be invited from other organizations to enhance information transfer. But too many people or other visitors inhibit strong challenges.

Perhaps meetings should have two segments, one with a large group of people, and the second with a much smaller group of corporate, sector or group management, where critical issues can be discussed openly.

In looking at where the best technology resides, i.e., benchmarking the best in class of a given level of technology, we should consider hiring people from these organizations. This of course must be done in an ethical and legal manner and not by stealing the technology owned by others.

BW

October 14, 1988

We have all breathed a sigh of relief as the value of the dollar versus the yen has changed dramatically over the last year and a half. Certainly this has made our competitive business better than it was before. But lest we believe that the currency changes have won the ball game for us, I would like to repeat some comments made by a recent visitor to Japan. They were printed in the Washington Post.

Japan and Currency Changes

By the standard calculations of free market economics, Japan should be worried by now. The dramatic fall of the dollar and the corresponding rise of the yen over the past three years were supposed to make things tough for its export-led economy. In fact, this is not the case at all. On my most recent trip to Japan last month, I found an unprecedented level of self-confidence in Tokyo. Indeed, many forecasters are predicting that after a slight dip, Japan's trade surplus will begin to rise next year as exports boom again.

"Anybody can cut prices, but it takes brains to make a better article."
Alice Hubbard

One industrialist told me, "Foreign competitors could not easily enter our market. Now we have cut our costs by 30 percent over the past two years and we are aiming for another 20 percent. We will be able to compete with the yen at 90 to the dollar."

In response to the fall of the dollar, the Japanese government stimulated the domestic economy to maintain growth while businesses drove to make needed adjustments. For the first time in modern history, Japan's fear of losing overseas markets has been replaced by a realization that the country is less dependent on others than anyone ever thought. Moreover,

Japan has found that being the only significant supplier of many critical items makes it difficult for foreign customers to switch to other, less costly suppliers.

The feelings expressed by the author are corroborated by my own experiences. In my view, the change in the yen's value has just made the Japanese much more efficient, and combined with the excellent Japanese economy, provided a sound base for their products. The net result of these and other factors is to make the Japanese more competitive, not less. So our challenge continues on a higher plane of performance for customer satisfaction.

BW

May 7, 1987

"The Swing Shift" reprinted with permission from Don Kite, Editor of Parts Pups, *Originally printed in* Parts Pups, *November 1971 as the "Slobborian Swing," and the* Readers Digest, *October, 1973.*

The Swing Shift

As marketing requested it

As sales ordered it

As engineering designed it

As production manufactured it

As plant installed it

What customer wanted

Product Article

One of the most important things to be able to do is to understand how your competitors think. From such an understanding comes the ability to project their actions and to plan proactive or reactive moves to counter their competitive thrusts.

In the last few weeks, a number of people have commented on the Japanese thinking pattern. Attached is an article from The Japan Times Weekly, *with comments by Dr. Hisashi Shinto, president of Nippon Telegraph & Telephone. It gives the perspectives of a very successful Japanese businessman.*

An extremely significant quote from a senior General Motors executive appeared in The Wall Street Journal *recently: "There is no great mystery about what the Japanese do. It's almost a question of learning to think Japanese, and I guess that is what we are really trying to accomplish."*

One of the problems of typical American businessmen is that we extrapolate our best history when we think about doing something differently. Many times this is matched with the statement that the Japanese are not creative or innovative. This allows us to greatly underestimate what Japanese competition will do because they do not have our historic mentality. We will only beat Japanese competition if we learn to understand how they think. It is important to know what they have done, what they do now, what their thinking pattern is and how they will apply it to our markets.

BW

Japan's Secret Is More, Better Engineers

by Hobart Rowen

TOKYO—Nippon Telegraph & Telephone Public Corporation (NTT) is the Japanese government telecommunications monopoly. At $17 billion in annual sales and $40 billion in assets, it is a leader among giant Japanese conglomerates.

For years, American and European communications and electronics manufacturers have been trying to break open NTT's tightly locked door to foreign high-quality imports, and for the first time, the Japanese bureaucracy—which regards internal telecommunications as the equivalent of national defense—is yielding a bit.

A key change has been brought about by the arrival two years ago of a new man at the top, 72-year-old Hisashi Shinto, the first NTT president to come from the private sector. Shinto, an engineer and shipbuilding expert who knows the United States well, was president of the Ishikawajima-Harima Heavy Industries (IHI) from 1972 to 1979, when Japanese shipbuilding (now in decline) was at its peak.

But what makes Dr. Shinto especially interesting to American businessmen these days—beyond his effort to open up NTT procurement—is that he has specific ideas on why some American industries have fallen behind in the competitive race with Japan.

"From 1950 to about 1963, when I was working in the shipyards," Shinto told me, "the United States had higher productivity even though your wages then were five times higher than they were in Japan. Your side was extremely competitive in turbines and main generators—and they were of such high quality!"

To discover the American secret, Shinto visited American shipyards and factories, and he thinks he found the answer:

"Your young engineers who graduated from the university were working in the workshops along with the (production) workers. The engineers knew the production program, and they knew how to use machine tools. Because they knew the production process in detail, they were able to get greater productivity and higher quality."

It's that simple, says Shinto. "High intelligence is the only source of competitiveness." So by 1956, Shinto installed this American practice in his Japanese shipyards, and other Japanese manufacturers did the same thing; not only was engineering stressed as a high calling to Japan's young people, but once a graduate engineer came out of the university with his degree, he was put to work, initially, on the shop floor.

At the same time, something was changing in the United States—and Shinto doesn't quite know why. But the fact is that after graduation, most American engineers now "get into computerization, not into the workshop. When I visited (the States) in 1980, I didn't find the same kind of intelligence (as before) in the workshop. I don't know why, but the fact is that it has disappeared, and I am quite astonished.

"My impression is that a young engineer in the United States attaches himself to a computer keyboard, not to the robot in the shop."

There is a growing view among critics of the American industrial establishment that the American industrial decline was coincident with the mid-1960s drive for mergers, acquisition and immediate financial gains. Bright kids turned away from engineering to law schools and to the schools of business administration.

Now, in terms of numbers of engineering graduates, the United States has fallen behind Japan, which turns out 15,000 to 20,000 electronic engineers a year. That is more than the U.S. total, even though the American population is twice that of Japan.

Shinto's advice to American chief executive officers competing with Japan is to take young engineers and increase their salaries by 50 to 100 percent as an inducement to move them onto the workshop floors. "Your people are so intelligent, that if you do this, within three to four years, your productivity and quality will go up. The United States has a high potential in most areas and can recover."

But how about American complaints of unfair Japanese competition, the highly publicized "Japan, Inc." syndrome, which allows industry to "target" an export market with government help? I asked Shinto to deal with the charge that Japanese semiconductor firms had unfairly grabbed off a big share of the market for 64K RAM semiconductors, currently the most popular micro-processor used in a variety of home computers and electronic equipment.

"If you talk about the 64K RAM," Shinto responded, "the competitiveness of the Japanese product depends almost entirely on quality control. The production process in Japanese factories and yours is quite different. The basis of quality control (here) is not to depend on the human (worker). Quality is determined by the environmental control of the workshop, supervised by the intelligent engineers."

What will Japan do if the United States does in fact start churning out engineers instead of lawyers and MBAs, and regains its old skills and productivity? Shinto's answer: "We would just have to work harder, that's all. We can never argue against better productivity on your side. All we could do is work harder."

Japanese Competition: American Straight Talk

Presented upon acceptance of the Medal of Honor from the Electronic Industries Association, Washington, D.C.

Product Speeches

Almost everywhere I go today, I am asked a question that goes something like this: "What are you people in the electronics business going to do about the Japanese competition?" Many times it is said with a feeling of desperation or a feeling of the inevitable. My answer to each questioner is that our company has made up its mind to win. For our part, winning means that long ago we committed to just plain running our business better than they run theirs. We haven't reached our expectation levels in all functions, but we can and will. By the way, when I say "win" I don't mean that we desire to push the Japanese competitors into the Pacific Ocean. **We can all win in the ever-increasing worldwide electronics market, as long as we compete fairly under the same rules, here and everywhere in the world. Good competitors always broaden the market, and as always, customers will make the final choice based on excellent products, value, quality, reliability and features.**

The Japanese competitors of today are creative, innovative and competent. They make excellent products with high manufacturing skill, good quality and fine marketing. They needed to crack a U.S. market that was highly sophisticated and inhabited by strong competitors. In some fields they did it successfully. The extent to which they were helped by their highly leveraged debt-equity positions (because a different financial environment allowed companies to earn profits of 1 percent to 2 percent with no penalty), by the dumping of products at low prices, by government support of industry, or by cartelization, is a matter of great contention. These factors cannot be ignored in determining how they achieved their results. But the result—good quality at attractive prices—allowed them to capture significant market shares in some fields.

The Japanese competitors have a good reputation and are steadily building momentum. In fact, they have a reputation much bigger than the actual facts warrant. They have consciously merchandised that reputation in a well-coordinated campaign. I congratulate them. If I were they, I would be doing exactly the same thing. They are the worldwide competitor in all of our businesses, targeting the semiconductor, computer and communications markets as the next places for attack. They have openly told us so in their government and industry pronouncements. I believe them.

But they do not walk on water. They did not invent creativity and innovation. They did not pioneer quality, mass production, marketing or customer service. Americans did. But they have done a good job of implementing what they continually tell us we taught them.

Unfortunately, some in America were complacent. They were not sensitive to what was going on and were not listening to customers who reported how well the Japanese competitors were doing. The signs were ignored. Many preferred to believe that it was merely propaganda. I don't think anyone in our industry is complacent anymore. We know that we must not only meet the Japanese competitors, but go them one better in every category in which the customer measures us. I know we *can* do it because we *are* doing it in many places.

U.S. electronic companies make high-quality products. We have competed, and do successfully compete, with Japanese companies — here and in the rest of the world. There are many examples at my company. For instance, Ford Motor Company's electronic ignition control business, Generation IV, has just been awarded to Motorola over Toshiba. Our Government Electronics Division equipment transmitted all the signals and pictures from Saturn recently, and that is a repeat of the Motorola story on every major U.S. space shot. The Japanese Women's Mountain Climbing Team that conquered Mt. Everest wanted reliable communications equipment. They used Motorola Handie-Talkie® units. Among awards won by our company, the Semiconductor Group received an award from the Hitachi Computer Division, *in Japan*, for being one of their best suppliers. I'm sure that each of you can come up with similar examples of where your quality and customer service is best, bar none. The success of the space shuttle Columbia, whose landing we cheered today, is due in large part to the high-quality work and sophisticated technology of the people in our companies.

Yet today we find countless newspaper articles, seminars and speeches by a wide variety of people, including some self-styled opportunists, who tell us how good the Japanese competitors are. We are bombarded from all sides by counterproductive sensationalism that reinforces the misperception that the Japanese competitors are inevitable victors in any economic contest. **We have to get the observer and the spectator to see that the American electronics competitor in many**

instances is outperforming the Japanese competition right now, and can, in most remaining areas, achieve equivalence or outperform them.

A couple of months ago, I talked to a large group of our employees who had just completed and delivered a quantity of prototype radio paging units designed specially for the Nippon Telegraph and Telephone Corporation. They had the highest morale of any organization I have ever been exposed to, even though many of them had worked 70- and 80-hour weeks for months on end, culminating in 24-hour days in order to meet the delivery commitment. That night I said many of the things I am saying to you tonight. I was literally interrupted a dozen times by applause and cheers. I've given many speeches to many groups of people, and except for some gung-ho sales meetings, I have never had the spontaneous reaction I got that night. I've had the exact same reaction at other external functions; from business people of all types, not just electronics people; from college students; from university faculties. **The message is clear. They want to be led in a positive, enthusiastic fashion. No one wants to be a loser. They want to work hard. They want to win, and they want to be united in that single purpose. We've got to get excited—get back our pride.** As a nation, we've been apologetic on a wide variety of subjects far too long. Thank God that's changing in our country today. We've got nothing to be apologetic about. We've got plenty to be proud about.

One of the things commonly attributed to the Japanese is the ability to develop a consensus. They've cranked up their whole industry and teamed with their government to be successful worldwide. I'm not sure they understand why we in America haven't yet done the same thing. I think I understand. It has to do with one of our fundamental traits. We encourage individual entrepreneurship, and as a result, we don't develop total consensus, except on major, critical issues. It takes a long, long time to get consensus in this country, but when it comes, the power that is released is awesome. **America has a unique spirit and capability. When we elevate anything to the proper sense of urgency, we have the ability, knowledge and willingness to do the job.** I think the Japanese competitors are just as worried about our getting our act together as some people here are about their conquering the world economically.

In my opinion, notwithstanding all that has been said and written, the Japanese have no unique culture that preordains their success. They have certain excellent strengths. We have certain of the same, and many others that are different. We must build on our success and our strengths, deal with the positives and stop the doomsayers and the opportunists.

We must set high expectations, with reach-out goals, and show substantive accomplishments. But we must also tell our story. You and I must talk with people inside our companies— all our employees, not just our executives. Our people are very astute. They want to work hard, to help and to win. We must talk to people outside. We must tell our quality and service story. American products are still the most in-demand products around the world.

We can take on the Japanese competitors, or anyone else, and be winners. Let's take them on across a broad front: product, service, government and the press. We can win as long as the conditions of competition are equal and fair for all, not skewed to help one more than the other. This means that government and industry here must be much more supportive of each other, though not necessarily in the same way that the Japanese are. It also means enforcing all laws relating to fair trade, or creating new ones where equity requires. The Japanese expect us to do so, and we know they do. I know that you and your people have pride and the capability to support that pride. Let's tell our story of quality and service, not just by words but by performance. And wherever we aren't performing well enough, let's set the highest of expectation levels, and let's produce. We know how to do the job.

For more than 50 years, one of the central themes of my company has been "reach out." We have a "can do" attitude, but it must be followed by "do it" performance. Let's all get on the same positive team. Let's stop the demeaning of our own competence. Let's get on the offensive. Let's work as hard as we can, and do what we know we can do—satisfy the customer better than anyone else in the world.

BW

October 12, 1988

Technology Leadership and Challenge

Presented to the Motorola Science Advisory Board Associates
Orlando, Florida.

As politicians say, "I'll try to be as brief as possible for as long
as it takes."

This is a year of anniversaries. I've just returned from my
40th college reunion at Massachusetts Institute of Technology.
There I observed a superb course that teaches creativity in
design and manufacturing to freshmen, and does it in a way
that's a lot of fun. By the way, MIT just started NCAA inter-
collegiate football and the story goes that they won their first
game against Cal Tech—the score was π to e!

In six days, I will celebrate my 40th anniversary with
Motorola. That qualifies me to be what Herman Miller Co.'s
chief executive officer, Max Depree, calls a tribal storyteller.
That's not a position that's supposed to continually tell you
about how excellent things were "in the good old days," but,
rather, one that can relate the company history, its key philosophies, the reasons why we did what we did, and how we arrived
where we are today, to current Motorolans. It's a role I take
very seriously.

On September 25, Motorola was 60 years old, and on
Monday I participated in the groundbreaking ceremony for the
Motorola Museum of Electronics. The museum will connect to
the Galvin Education and Training Center on our Schaumburg
campus. Sixty years of Motorola technology leadership will be
showcased in the Motorola Museum. On display is a history of
our company that highlights key events and products to which
many here have contributed.

I'm an agitator, and, I hope, a creator of dissatisfaction with the status quo. I'll talk about some negatives today. They can be classified as generalities, and not all true in all places. We need your help, not as technologists only, but as leaders to turn these negatives into opportunities that can yield technological leadership.

Let me state my two major points right now. First, the need for technological leadership. I'll question whether, at Motorola, we all really believe this. And second, even when we have technological leadership, it takes too long to get that technology to the marketplace in the form of products and services. This is not an indictment of any specific group or function. It's a systems problem that happens to almost all large, growing companies.

Motorola's fundamental objective is total customer satisfaction. Our technical objective to support that is "Leading technology converted to do valuable things for our customers in the shortest time possible—faster and better than our competitors."

One of the original top 10 corporate goals, circa 1981, stated the following: "Be the product leader through timely, appropriate use of technology and by designing for optimum reliability and automated manufacturing." Timely use! The strategy committee of the board of directors insisted that we change the word "timely" to "early."

The early use of technology at a premium price, if necessary, in certain leadership products, will drive us down the experience curve and enable us to make very broad use of that technology across the board much sooner. It unquestionably establishes a leadership image in our customers' minds. **We can't wait until technology and price are all just right. If we do, we'll have no advantage over our competitors.**

When the Motrac® radio, the first all-transistorized mobile radio, was being designed at Motorola, there were many at high levels in the company who advised against doing so because they thought it was too early. But Dan Noble overruled them, and we designed version after version, learning more about semiconductors all the time. When we finally went to market, we beat General Electric by three years with a superbly performing, well-designed unit. GE then crashed out a product that had no end of trouble.

The fountain-pen-sized Sensar® radio pager is another example of leadership, brought to market at a premium price that told all our customers that we were indeed the leaders in converting state-of-the-art technology into value for the customer.

Today, as stated in our key goals, we aspire to be "best in class" in technology and products. We often hear that Motorola is a product/technology-driven company, and should be more marketing-oriented. It is true that we have had many failures due to poor marketing. But I also know of no substantial successes without product leadership in performance and quality. **We certainly should be better at marketing, but our customers tell us that leadership technology is also a mandatory requirement.** In a recent Semiconductor Products Sector task force study on share of market, our customers told us that they want suppliers who lead in technology, so that they can apply that technology to develop their own leadership products and systems, thereby serving their customers better than their competitors do.

Too many of our people have a mindset that can be simply stated as, "Don't use technology for technology's sake" or, "Don't ever design a product with any technology reach-out because of the risk of using new technology." Certainly it is true that many products must be brought to market quickly and should use existing technology to minimize potential problems and delays. However, we must also have a balanced share of more advanced programs that must have reach-out goals in order for us to push the state-of-the-art, and appropriately convert it to valuable product and services. That's technology and product leadership that means something to our customers.

At a recent meeting of the Corporate Technology Steering Committee, Hector Ruiz, vice president and director of technology for the Semiconductor Products Sector, made a very astute but disturbing comment. As he reviewed the recommendations made by some of the company-wide technology study committees, he found that in too many cases where we are behind competition, almost no committee came up with suggestions that would make us a leader in three to five years. They seemed to suggest actions that would only bring us up to the average. The technology study committees should ask, "How do we get to be a No. 5 in our technology matrix— the best in class?" Committees must come up with these types of recommendations, not ones that yield 3's, which are average results.

Attitude may be a large part of the problem where reach-out leadership does not exist. The process of gradual improvement, i.e. 10 percent per year, versus dramatic improvements, deserves some discussion. Because reach-out dramatic improvement cannot be achieved by old techniques, fundamental, new creative approaches are required. One example is the "10 times quality improvement in five years" corporate quality goal, which demanded and achieved new attacks on the quality and reliability problem.

So what should we do to become "best in class"? Set high expectation levels. Identify programs and propose them to be "best in class," not average. Hire the best people. Ask for support and budget. Don't give up, even if you are rebuffed at first. You can't always get where you want to go in one fell swoop. Bootleg at times. I don't like to advise violating the rules, but some of our best products were designed hidden away in labs by creative, enthusiastic engineers, until they could be exposed to senior managers when they were proven to be successful. Of course, this must be done while doing all the things you're supposed to do.

There must be no N.I.H., or "not invented here." **You must scour the world for technology wherever it exists: at competitors, at universities, at research labs, in the government; always ethically and legally.** Use the Government Electronics group's eye into advanced military technology. We must hire new people who bring us excellent technological skills. Are we taking advantage of good technical people all over the world, and not just in the United States? Most particularly, know all there is to legally know about competitors' technology. Project the technological future and the competitors' future products by a study of their past technological and product introductions.

Make the regular technology review a useful tool. The fundamental purpose of the technology review and the technology road map is to ensure that we plan regularly, so that we will have the right technology, processes, components and experience to meet the needs of products and services in the future. The technology review must be a searching and challenging evaluation of our various sector and group plans to ensure that we are doing the right things to maintain leadership in the future.

The technology road map should be constructed in large part by marketing organizations' projections of future product needs, and also by technologists who can project the next major steps in technology that marketing people can't foresee. **We will not be limited by running out of new technologies. Rather, we will be limited by our ability to take total advantage of them.** The following additional questions should be asked at a technology review:

1. Are there any technologies that should be on the road map that are not there?
2. Have you identified the programs that are not currently planned to be funded in the five-year plan?
3. Have you searched the world for a technological answer to your requirements, and not just looked internally at Motorola?
4. Are there products and/or assistance that must come from other sectors and groups of Motorola? This is important so that they may be put on a corporate-level road map and ensure that visibility by corporate management is not lost.
5. Are there minority reports? In other words, are there people who disagree with the road map as proposed? If so, why?

Technology reviews are your opportunity to demonstrate capability, to showcase your opinions and to help force faster implementation of the technology into deliverable product and services.

Who determines what the research departments work on? How about handling research department funding like this: 75 percent allocated to work for products three to five years out at the direction of the product lines, and 25 percent to be allocated at the discretion of the research department, as long as it's within the general confines of our business charters.

What is a better way to measure the performance of research organizations, technologists and product development teams? Can you help define a way to measure performance better than what we do today, that is encouraging of technological leadership?

When you feel strongly about a technology or product development that will give your business a distinctive edge, be a pain in the neck. Don't take no as an answer from your manager. **Agitate, rabble-rouse, march on sector or group headquarters until the technology or product idea is moving into the deliverable state.**

Just as important as having technology leadership is shortening the time to get it into deliverable products. Our competitors are getting to market more quickly than ever before, many before we are. Short cycle time is another key Motorola goal. Get educated at MTEC on design for manufacturing and short cycle time techniques. Shortening the cycle time from conception to production means minimizing redundant effort. "It is better to receive than to give." Search out other places in Motorola to see if work has already been done, or can be done to help you. Use the best tools—computer design techniques, etc. Plan well and identify critical paths. Problem-solve until fundamental solutions are found. Team-design with other functional organizations: purchasing, manufacturing, marketing, quality, order processing, etc.

It is not a necessity that every technological venture be a complete success. If we have no failures, we will not have reached out far enough. But whether success or failure, you as the technologists must have performed well, and the ratio of successes to failures must be reasonably high. **A success means that a technology has been converted to a product that is successful in the marketplace.**

You here today are the key technologists of Motorola. Help us! Take the initiative! You must be the leaders in reinvigorating, renewing and maintaining our thinking on the importance of technology. You must be a salesperson and sell your technology if you believe in it. You must come up with technological advances that are easy for the business managers and marketers to view as critical to their ability to maintain distinctive competence over our competitors. Assume personal responsibility for helping to lead your organization and Motorola to technological leadership. **You have much more power to effect change than you can imagine. Develop a sense of urgency!**

We have stated over and over again that our key goals require us to be "best in class" in technology and products. We mean it! We are counting on you, the Science Advisory Board Associates, to take the lead and help all of us achieve that goal by setting high expectation levels, by living daily as appropriate examples and by achieving reach-out results. **BW**

November 10, 1992

Competitive Success Requires Participation, Teamwork and Quality

Presented to the MIT Sloan School of Management, Senior Executive Program.

I'm going to start today by setting the stage for three key points. Over 40 years ago, when Motorola was making monstrously large mobile radio telephone units with big klunky stepping switches, a group of engineers had a vision—or at that time, really, a dream. The dream was this. We believed that when a person made a telephone call, they wanted to talk to another person, wherever that person was, not just when he or she was in a vehicle. Therefore, sometime in the future whenever a baby was born, he or she would be given a miniature portable telephone and assigned a personal telephone number for use anywhere in the world. If you dialed that number and it rang six times without being answered, you could assume that the party being called was dead!

A wild dream to have in those days. We knew then that it was not currently possible and had no idea when it would be. All sorts of research and development and invention had to occur to make it so.

But that vision was a driving force for 40 years to work constantly for miniaturization, to design for lower current to reduce battery drain and extend operating life, and to reduce weight. And so we did—for years. **Over the years, we developed whole lines of radio pagers, and Handie Talkie® units and pack sets for public safety and business organizations — each line of products becoming smaller and lighter, and working longer on its built-in batteries.**

Among these products was a radio pager that allowed you to be paged anywhere in the United States; a wrist watch in combination with a pager; and recently a credit card-sized pager for complete U.S. coverage. About 10 years ago, Motorola introduced the Dynatac® portable cellular telephone, which was the first part of the dream coming true—but still brief case sized and with cellular coverage only in major metropolitan areas. Three years ago, the MicroTAC® portable cellular telephone, the flip phone, was introduced, which really did fit in a pocket. Then came the MicroTAC Lite® and just a couple of months ago, the MicroTAC® Ultralite™, weighing only 5.9 ounces.

And then in 1990, Motorola announced the Iridium™ Satellite system, which will really make that crazy original dream come true. **Sixty-six satellites in non-synchronous orbit, 400-plus miles above the earth, integrated with today's terrestrial cellular systems, will provide cellular-type coverage literally to every place on the globe.** Iridium™ is a $4 billion program with satellite launch starting in 1996 and the whole system in commercial service in 1998. The portable units themselves are today the size of our original Dynatac® units, but will eventually resemble the MicroTAC® pocket-sized unit.

Our vision over 40 years ago, no matter how general and crazy it may have seemed at the time, was an important driving force for technological development. But in order to pull off the realization of that vision—a successful worldwide Iridium™

cellular system—there are three other required ingredients. They are the three points that I am going to cover today. Let me telegraph them to you very directly.

› Mandatory for Iridium™ success—and for that matter, any commercial success today—is perfect quality. We can't have failures in space or in portable units operating in the African jungle. We have a good start on this with no failures in any of the Motorola equipment that has been on all U.S. space shots, and with Malcolm Baldrige award quality in our current cellular portables.

› Because of high development cost and high subsequent operating cost, we must have maximum efficiency in design, manufacturing and operating the system. This means cooperation and teamwork within and between very diverse types of organizations.

› To win competitively, we must have highly motivated people contributing their best effort all the time.

BW

————

Note to the reader: *Find the complete speech on page 350.*

The Philosophy Memos

Product Quotations

"If a business is to grow, it must continually improve its products and formulate new ones."
Henry G. Lazell

"If you don't obsolete your own products, your competition will."
author unknown

"What's shoddy and cheap, in the long run is expensive."
Ignas Bernstein

"If you would create something, you must be something."
Goethe

"I never did anything worth doing by accident, nor did any of my inventions come by accident; they came by work."
Thomas Edison

"But innovation is more than a new method. It is a new view of the universe, as one of risk rather than of chance or of certainty. It is a new view of man's role in the universe; he creates order by taking risks. And this means that innovation, rather than being an assertion of human power, is an acceptance of human responsibility."
Peter Drucker

How to Kill Ideas
Don't be ridiculous
We tried that before
It cost too much
It can't be done
That's beyond our responsibility
It's too radical a change
We don't have the time
That will make other equipment obsolete
We're too small for it
That's not our problem
We've never done it before
Let's get back to reality
Why change it, it's still working OK
You're two years ahead of your time
We're not ready for that
It isn't in the budget
Can't teach an old dog new tricks
Let's form a committee
Too hard to sell
If it was good, we'd already be doing it
We'll be the laughingstock
That doesn't apply to us
We're doing the best we can
We did all right without it
Has anyone else ever tried it?
It won't work in our industry
author unknown

"The man with a new idea is a crank until the idea succeeds."
Mark Twain

Leadership

*Leadership
Memos*

Planning for Change

It has always been my philosophy to create enthusiasm, improve attitude, challenge people and encourage new, uninhibited outlooks by reviewing organizational structures on a regular basis. Throughout the years I have attempted to make major changes in the organization to meet growing opportunities. Other times I have made minor changes to redefine jobs and allow movement and experience-broadening. I have tried to adhere to a program that makes such changes about every three years. There is, of course, no magic in the number three—many times people should be changed in one year, and other times the continual broadening of their existing job presents such challenges that three years is insufficient.

We certainly have had some important changes in our division in the last few years. As a part of the continuing process of "self-renewal," such changes are healthy, assuming they are not disruptive, or that they do not occur so often that we lose more than we gain. I believe, however, that there may be some organizations down below the division staff level that have remained relatively stagnant for long periods of time. In these situations I think we always find some demoralization, and less than best attitude and performance. There, the people might well be excellent performers if they were put into a new situation. May I suggest that each of you review your organizations to determine whether or not you are continuing to meet the challenge of people motivation.

During last year's objectives and goals review, I asked that each key manager prepare a five-year organization chart showing boxes and the names of people to go in these boxes. I fully recognize that each year this chart may change and look dramatically different. However, the exercise of formalizing your organizational goals on paper will alert you to the need for more key managers, the necessity of moving people around in advance so they are prepared for additional responsibility, and the need for outside recruitment.

As a part of your goal package there should be interim organization charts showing the organization as it evolves through the five-year period. As an example, any given key manager may submit four or five charts, one which he plans to implement in mid-June of 1968, another in March of 1969, and so on until he has achieved his five-year objective.

This five-year organization chart submittal will be a mandatory goal in every future objectives and goals program. **BW**

"An idealist believes the short run doesn't count. A cynic believes the long run doesn't matter. A realist believes that what is done or left undone in the short run, determines the long run." **Sidney J. Harris**

July 15, 1976

Submitted by Pete Simonis, manager, Consumer Products Division.
Reprint permission granted by Supervisory Management.

Everyone Likes the Sweet Smell of Success

When a man makes a worthwhile contribution, he expects to share in the recognition that goes with it.

Unfortunately, not all managers are sensitive to this need in people. Some think that, because they are in charge, it automatically entitles them to all the credit for everything that goes on. They only kid themselves. Who can possibly enjoy working for a boss like that?

Denying people credit makes them bitter. That's why it pays to check up once in a while. Whom have you neglected to tell recently what a good job he's doing and how rough things would be without him? Look at any really successful executive and you'll find he's always ready, willing and anxious to share his successes with the people who work for him.

Andrew Carnegie, the famous steel maker, always maintained that there were many men in his organization who had more ability than he. They worked their hearts out for him because he was so willing to share the thrill of planning, the credit for achievement and the tangible rewards as well.

There's more to sharing success than just a fatter paycheck. It involves other important items like:

› Recognizing latent abilities and giving people a chance to develop them;
› Asking opinions and advice instead of just telling people to do things;
› A pat on the back when the going is rough;
› Passing the credit for achievement along to everyone who had a part in it.

Andrew Carnegie wasn't the first to use these tactics— nor will he be the last. The alert executive, whether he is a first-level supervisor or company president, soon learns that people will work a lot harder because they really want to than they will because he is trying to pressure them. And they'll work hardest of all for someone who gives them a real sense of sharing in the planning, achievement, credit and rewards.

author unknown

June 15, 1978

Submitted by Bill Drake and Ed Bales,
Communications Division.

The Penalty of Leadership

In every field of human endeavor, he who is first must perpetually live in the white light of publicity. Whether the leadership be vested in a man or in a manufactured product, emulation and envy are ever at work.

In art, in literature, in music, in industry, the reward and the punishment are always the same.

The reward is widespread recognition; the punishment, fierce denial and detraction.

When a man's work becomes a standard for the whole world, it also becomes a target for the shafts of the envious few. If his work be merely mediocre, he will be left severely alone— if he achieves a masterpiece, it will set a million tongues a-wagging.

Jealousy does not protrude its forked tongue at the artist who produces a commonplace painting.

Whatsoever you write, or paint, or play, or sing, or build, no one will strive to surpass or to slander you, unless your work be stamped with the seal of genius.

Long, long after a great work or a good work has been done, those who are disappointed or envious continue to cry out that it cannot be done.

Spiteful little voices in the domain of art were raised against our own Whistler as a mountebank, long after the big world had acclaimed him its greatest artistic genius.

Multitudes flocked to Bayreuth to worship at the musical shrine of Wagner, while the little group of those whom he had dethroned and displaced argued angrily that he was no musician at all.

The little world continued to protest that Fulton could never build a steamboat, while the big world flocked to the river banks to see his boat steam by.

The leader is assailed because he is a leader, and the effort to equal him is merely added proof of that leadership.

Failing to equal or to excel, the follower seeks to depreciate and to destroy—but only confirms once more the superiority of that which he strives to supplant.

There is nothing new in this. It is as old as the world and as old as the human passions—envy, fear, greed, ambition and the desire to surpass.

And it all avails nothing.

If the leader truly leads, he remains—the leader.

Master-poet, master-painter, master-workman, each in his turn is assailed, and each holds his laurels through the ages.

That which is good or great makes itself known, no matter how loud the clamor of denial.

That which deserves to live, lives.

author unknown

January 5, 1971

I was reading the TWA *magazine on a recent airplane trip and came across this article. I tore it out for circulation to key Motorola managers. When I got back to Chicago, a number of people had sent me the same article for circulation. I think when you read it you will agree that it really hits the nail on the head in terms of some common problems in big business today. I recommend your careful reading of it.*

*Leadership
Articles*

Decisions

by Charles H. Ford

You're managing a team locked in a pennant race. It's the crucial game, with two out in the ninth inning. You're losing, 1 to 0. Count on the batter: 3 and 2.

The pitcher grooves a home-run ball right down the middle. Your batter lets it go by.

Strike 3! Game's over.

Head down, defeated, the batter shuffles back to the dugout. You yell, "Why didn't you hit it?" He mutters, "I was afraid I'd miss it."

If you're a business executive, you know the manager's frustration. You go through it every day, waiting for other people to make decisions—waiting and waiting, because they're afraid if they do "swing," they'll "miss."

The rude truth is: *Decisions are hard to get in business today.*

There are some obvious reasons, such as improper delegation, an ill-defined table of organization, and corporate policy uncertainties.

But another reason is not so obvious: We have become increasingly infatuated with the principle of "scientific management," which holds that management (and decision-making) has become a precise science. Credence is lent to this myth by the computer, which deals in exacting measurements. The result is a gradual depersonalization of people—particularly lower and middle management—who become mere impersonal cogs in the corporate machine.

Increasingly, it is felt that anyone making a wrong decision in this machine is a malfunctioning part to be expunged regardless of his rationale for making the decision, or the problem he tried to solve.

The result? *Executive timidity.*

We can mask this with business school theories to prove it doesn't exist, explain it with delightful-sounding acronyms when we find it does, but the simple truth is: Most executives are scared to death to make a decision because it may result in a mistake and they may seriously impair their careers or get fired.

This has produced the play-it-safe attitude that if you don't make a decision, you can't make a wrong one—a patterned acceptance of the concept that if one waits long enough, time will eliminate the necessity to lay one's head on the block.

As a result, even the most routine decisions go begging. Corporate tempo slows to a crawl.

In the past, when an executive initiated a new approach or a well-thought-out decision that resulted in a mistake, he was consoled with a pat on the back and reassured, "You can't win 'em all." He went back to work wiser, and with undiminished enthusiasm to make new decisions.

No longer. More and more, the attitude is, "One mistake and good-bye to the guy who made it."

Unfortunately, this is the most tragic mistake of all, breeding timidity as an overriding part of executive life.

Even the ability to make those fast, everyday, "gut" decisions that keep a business moving and functioning—decisions based on a minimum amount of data, but with a "feel" of what is right—is fast becoming a lost art through disuse.

"I'm waiting for so-and-so."

"I need more information."

"We're still thinking about it."

"These things take time."

All are symptoms of executive indecision.

Timidity has polluted even the committee system—originally designed to tap and correlate the knowledge of many heads. Committees now are rife with fence-straddlers, who protect themselves with vague recommendations, flocks of alternatives and an after-the-fact nimbleness in associating with right decisions, or ducking one that turns out wrong.

When decisions are made, they tend to be those carrying the smallest risk, both to the company and the person making them, and, if successful, they carry the smallest rewards.

Enthusiasm is replaced with boredom, as more and more executives mechanically perform their daily routine tasks and avoid making the waves that come with making decisions.

Analyze the successful new companies of the past decade and you'll find most started with a high level of tolerance for mistakes. Decisions were made and mistakes corrected with the same decisive speed.

Still-growing companies engender a tolerance for mistakes—placing a premium on decisiveness and discouraging the false security of doing and risking nothing, which can only result in a continuation of existing problems and lost opportunities. Some conglomerates ran into trouble when they reined in the innovative and decisive talents of executives in the companies they acquired, and introduced "scientific" management to keep those executives spending as much time avoiding personal onus for mistakes as they formerly spent in making decisions.

Obviously, mistakes are not going to enhance a company's growth and profitability. No one looks forward to them. And an executive who has a consistent pattern of poor judgment is misplaced. But the old corporate idea, "the more we try, the more mistakes we'll make, but the more we'll succeed," is giving way to the individual attitude: "Let's not rush into this. Let's not goof up. Let someone else make the decision. Don't involve me if it goes wrong."

All managements must take a hard look at the character and personality of their organizations to determine if—and to what degree —timidity is prevalent. The '70s, with a promise of tougher competition, abrupt changes in marketing patterns, product and business climates, will not be kind to the timid and indecisive.

This is no clarion call to managerial chaos—freewheeling, undisciplined decision-making. (Decisive, unafraid executives require *more* management and support than the timid.)

Instead, it is a call to retune business organizations to the needs of the times. Paradoxically, tomorrow's business climate demands more imagination, aggressiveness, flexibility and decisiveness, yet today's management is heading the other way.

Steps *must* be taken to rekindle the decision-making process. To highlight but a few:

> Introduce a policy of time limits, even for routine decisions. Strictly enforced deadlines will not only "force" decisions, but encourage innovation to meet them.

"The job of a manager is somewhat like that of a symphony conductor. There is absolutely no reason why the conductor should try to be a better instrumentalist than each member of the orchestra. Conductors must understand the music and what the instruments are capable of doing.

They must recognize when mistakes are being made. Their job is to motivate people to play together and to play better. This should be done by setting an example rather than by issuing edicts. A good leader should give people the freedom to fail once in a while. The main point is that in this company we all need each other. None of us accomplishes anything big ourselves"
William Hewitt,
retired CEO of John Deere, From *Image At The Top* by Richard C. Ruch and Ronald Goodman. ©1983 by Richard C Ruch and Ronald Goodman. Reprinted with the permission of The Free Press, a Division of Macmillan, Inc.

> Give the person closest to the problem a "no-excuse" responsibility for making the decision, and arm him with authority to place time limits on any help he needs—*up and down the chain of command!*

> Develop a mistake-sharing (and credit-sharing) attitude by requiring those who provide the decision-maker with information to state, at the same time, what they would do if the decision were theirs.

> Refine your organization table so responsibility for making a decision involving several departments clearly falls on one man. This will prevent the "out" used by many executives to avoid or delay making a decision because others are involved.

There are many ways to structure timidity out of an organization. But correction starts first with recognition of the problem and a feeling of urgency to do something about it.

It must be recognized that management is *not* a precise science. When you crank people into the management equation, you also crank in their ambitions, imaginations, fears, frailties and strengths. **Marshaling their efforts to best advantage calls for tolerance, encouragement and leadership—not fear—and an environment where people will function from their strengths, not their weaknesses.**

It requires effort and imagination. But if you don't make the effort and your competition does, it can be good-bye to growth and profits in the '70s.

And, perhaps, good-bye to you.

January 31, 1973

Submitted by Pete Simonis, manager, Consumer Products Division.

No man is a robot. All of us have personal feelings. But the executive who lets personal feelings and emotions color his thinking isn't doing the job he's paid for.

An executive is expected to think—not emote. When a man moves up to the management level, he's supposed to be at least a fair cut above average. His superiors have a right to expect that he'll have the good sense to keep his feelings under control. They also expect him to consider the welfare of the company—not just his own personal future.

Unfortunately, it doesn't always work out that way. And when it doesn't, the result is friction, feuds and politics—none of which does a company one bit of good.

How frequently, for example, do you have to step into some sort of dispute or disagreement between your subordinates that they really should have been able to settle for themselves? If they had kept their heads ... if one of them hadn't gotten his personal feelings aroused and, in turn, antagonized the other's ... if they had considered the company's welfare first instead of their own personal ambitions ... the answer should have been obvious.

And how often do you find yourself involved in similar disputes at your own level?

When a fellow executive or employee does something that you have every reason to resent, he's wrong—he's made a mistake. But if you actually do resent it, and let that resentment affect the way you act in return, you've made a worse mistake—a serious management error.

An executive is paid to think, to make sensible decisions. He isn't paid to satisfy his own personal resentments at the expense of the company.

In case this seems like a strange viewpoint, we'll bet a silver dollar it's exactly the way your company president feels about senseless, petty rivalries among your executives. The men he'd most like to promote are those who know how to avoid needless friction rather than create it.

November 15, 1973

Submitted by Pete Simonis, manager, Consumer Products Division.

Authority is a Poor Substitute for Leadership

Every management job has a certain amount of authority that goes with it. One of the fine arts of management is to use it sparingly and wisely.

Everybody likes to have authority—it make us feel important. But when we use it unnecessarily—or in a way that makes other people feel unimportant—it isn't good management.

Sometimes it's incredible what a little bit of power does to people. Move some men up a notch or two and they act so superior you can hardly talk to them anymore. They give the orders and that's that.

This may seem the fastest way to get people to respond, and, in situations requiring instant reaction, perhaps it's justified. But it's no way to build a lasting feeling of cooperation and loyalty in people.

Actually, can real authority be just handed to a man anyhow? We doubt it. To be really effective, it must be earned. It's not so much the authority of a man's position or title that gets people to perform well as their regard for his competence and ability.

The more able your subordinates sense you are, the more willingly they will follow your direction. A man's competence automatically gives him a certain measure of authority. If people look upon you, for instance, as an authority on the subject, they will normally let you exercise all the authority you need to get the job done.

On the other hand, people who don't respect the competence or judgment of their boss will follow his lead grudgingly, no mater how much he pressures them. They'll be more apt to drag their feet, resist what he wants done, maybe even throw sand or a monkey wrench in the gears.

Competent managers rarely feel the need to "pull rank" or throw their weight around. The man who is confident that he can handle his job will find no necessity to impress everyone that he's boss. He'll get better results and be better liked by relying on reason and persuasion rather than by just ordering people to do things.

April 15, 1979

Submitted by Ed Porrett, Communications Division.

Yes, No or Maybe

by Jerry Goldstein

Those are your three choices in virtually every situation. In fact, I can't think of a fourth choice. However, only two of the above are true decisions. A *maybe* is not a decision. It's a put-off. Neither here nor there. It's not a yes or a no. It's a stall. It's a cop-out.

It's not what success is made of.

Successful people in all professions are decision-makers. They gather as many facts as is possible and then they reach a conclusion. They make a decision. What's more, successful people are prepared to live with their decisions.

"Sure," the average person says, "that's what I'm afraid of … living with my decisions. What if I make the wrong decision?"

You are incapable of making a wrong decision.

That's true. Think back. You have never, consciously or intentionally, made a decision that would hurt you. It is actually against human nature to do so. No matter what the decision was, you made that decision in your best interest. You made that decision based on the facts at hand.

Of course, later on you may have found new information which would have altered your decision. But the point is: At the time, you made the best decision you could. We all do. So, why be afraid of making a decision?

Actually, your life—both personal and business—is the result of a number of decisions. Some will be right and some will be wrong. Even the wrong decisions can be corrected, overcome, altered and of use in finally accomplishing the overall objective.

Most everyone will agree that a guided missile is a very accurate instrument. But did you know that it never travels directly toward a target? Never. What it does is constantly correct for the errors it is making. When it moves slightly off course to the left—it overcompensates and moves slightly off to the right. It does this constantly.

You do exactly the same thing when you drive a car. You move the steering wheel a little to the left, then back to the right. You are correcting your mistakes.

You do exactly the same thing throughout your life. You compensate for slight errors as they occur. Each of these errors is the result of mini-decisions. And the same principle applies to major decisions. **If you have gathered as many of the facts as possible—go ahead and make that decision.** Say yes … say no … but don't stall … don't cop out. If need be, you'll alter your decision in the future.

You will not be remembered for your mistakes, if your accomplishments are great enough. For instance, who holds the record for the most strike-outs in major league baseball? It happens to be the same man who is best remembered for his ability to hit home runs. That's right. Babe Ruth.

I love the Mark Twain story about the cat that jumped on a hot stove. He certainly learned a lesson. It is a pretty safe bet that the same cat will never jump on a hot stove again. Unfortunately, that same cat will never jump on a cold stove either.

Decisions. What a marvelous thing they are. How fortunate you are to have the ability to make them. Use that ability. Use if often. However, know that decisions alone will not give you success. There is something more. There is something which follows.

Do you remember the story about the three frogs sitting on a lily pad. One decided to jump. How many frogs were left?

If you said two frogs—you were wrong. There were still three. You see, I said one frog decided to jump. I didn't say he did. Once a decision is made, it must be followed by action. And it is this combination—decisions followed by action which will bring you closer and closer to success.

Don't be afraid of decisions. You won't make the wrong one. You *will* make the right one at the time. And later, if need be, you can make another decision. **Decision-makers are people who cause things to happen.** People who always say, "Maybe—I'll think it over," are people who watch things happen. Others, who refuse to make any decision, are people who say "what happened?"

Be a decision-maker.

July 15, 1979

Submitted by Jack Dean, Automotive Sound Products.

Sales Talk ... Management by Responsible Example

by Jacob Weisberg, eastern regional sales manager,
Professional Division, West Chemical Products
Reprint permission granted by Penetone Corporation.

You're a manager. Your title tells you that. The job description spells out your duties, responsibilities and areas of authority. Your superior tells you a manager "gets things done through other people."

You're a leader. That's your responsibility, but more than that, it's your opportunity to influence people and events in selling and the wider world it thrives in.

When you're a manager, a leader, your subordinates look to you for direction, help and example. It's in your power to set the responsible example. You're on display every day, in your business and far beyond your business.

The managers who start the day late and end it early can expect even less work from their subordinates. But the managers who set the responsible example of starting early and working a fair full day will get the same from their sales representatives. More than that, their subordinates will get in the habit of "giving a fair shake" to all others.

The managers who knock their company can't expect loyalty from their subordinates. But the managers who set the responsible example of honestly analyzing the strengths and limitations of their company will gain the respect of their representatives. More than that, their subordinates will get in the habit of examining both sides of a question.

The managers who shortchange customers can expect to be shortchanged themselves in times to come. But the managers who set the responsible examples of seeing to it that the customers get their "full measure" regardless of *caveat emptor* will win the respect of customers and sales representatives alike. More than that, their subordinates get in the habit of being fair to those people they sell to.

The managers who renege on a promise can't expect subordinates to have confidence in their words, nor should they believe theirs. But the managers who set the responsible example of living up to their word can expect their subordinates to weigh their commitments carefully because they will want to meet them. More than that, they get into the habit of demonstrating integrity to all those around them.

It can start with one manager setting a responsible example. Others will follow suit. Ultimately managers must take a leadership role and teach their subordinates the ethics of selling and living: a full day's work and pride in achievement, an honest loyalty to employer and satisfaction in being at work, a concern that the customers get full value because they have paid for it, and living up to commitments because it's the honorable thing to do.

Morality in business can lead to a revitalized climate in the nation, for a country is the reflection of its business community. It starts with you.

Business Sin and Its Forgiveness

by Bill Lifka, President/CEO of ITT Courier
(a "sermon" delivered to a meeting of his management group)
Reprint permission granted.

The theme of today's sermon is derived from the writings of Luke, Chapter 15. "I tell you there will be more rejoicing in heaven over one repentant sinner than over 99 virtuous men who have no need of repentance."

Over the years I have been exposed to much sin, have forgiven many sins and have even sinned a bit myself. The tale of sin and forgiveness level that I shall now reveal is extracted from all my exposure to evil. The sins I refer to are management mistakes and the forgiveness level is my response to each category of sin.

Situational—always. When a mistake is made because of conditions legitimately outside the area of control, responsibility or knowledge, I tend to forgive always. Examples of this category are changes in economic conditions, unreasonable acts of competitors, acts of God. Although this type of sin is readily forgivable, we sinners tend to rationalize more severe sins into this category. This rationalization is usually made evident in a confession prefaced with words like this: Forgive me, Father, but how was I to know that the competitor was intelligent, or, with inflation being what it is, how can I have any control over margins, and so forth.

Commission—usually. When a person conscientiously collects data, postulates a decision on the data, considers the effects of the decision and acts within the scope of his authority, he seldom makes a mistake. But no one bats 1,000. Therefore, mistakes will be made. After awarding an A for effort, I usually forgive these, especially if it's the first time for any specific mistake. I'd sooner have a group of managers who often try and sometimes fail than ones who never fail because they seldom try.

Omission—occasionally. Some people think that doing nothing prevents mistakes. Not in my book. If the situation calls for a decision or action within the manager's scope of responsibility and he doesn't act, it's a mistake. He should have done something, but didn't. It's not too often I can forgive that. If I have to be for sin at all, I'm in favor of sins of commission.

Ignorance—hardly ever. You all recognize this one. How was I to know? I just didn't have time to collect the facts. How could I know they'd take the decision away from the friendly buyer? And so forth. I can't eliminate the possibility of forgiveness here because I forgave one once—back in 1959, I recall.

Fear—never. You know the rationale. I was afraid of the reaction of my people. The personal risks are too great. If I'm wrong, the boss will chew me out. What will people say? We've never done it that way before. I don't want to take responsibility for it.

I can't think of a single reason why sins of fear should be forgiven. In a successful organization there is no room for fear. Nowhere.

By the power given me in my appointment, I now grant you general absolution. Go and sin no more. But if you do, remember that we can tolerate any number of sins. What we can't tolerate are sins that are not admitted, not confessed quickly or covered up with additional sin.

I have not experienced a single mistake that couldn't be turned into an opportunity, provided only that it was recognized and dealt with promptly and openly. And that is the key point of today's sermon.

The Pursuit of Excellence in Management

Presented to the Motorola Executive Conferences.
September/October 1969

Leadership Speeches

Over the last four months I have visited all of the divisions. I have had the opportunity to meet many of you I didn't know before. My first impression was that we have some very fine people in all of our operations. My second is that everybody is as busy as the devil. It is this busyness, and some of the side effects of the busyness, upon which my comments are based.

Some years ago, I had some very bad personal experiences that taught me an important lesson. That lesson can be stated very simply: Whenever you're tremendously busy with day-to-day operational activities, it's very easy to forget to pay attention to some other very important things.

I think it is proper to occasionally pull back and look at ourselves, our philosophies of management and our methods of implementing those philosophies. Today, I'm going to talk about only one philosophy of management, but it's the one I think is the major one. I'm going to talk about people and their motivation.

Clarence Randall, in his forward to the book *Managers for Tomorrow*, writes, "We hear much these days about the technological revolution which has transformed American industry in this generation, but altogether too little is being said about the human revolution, which has made this possible. The second is as significant as the first."

The book goes on:

"The challenge to the manager of tomorrow is to find ways by which each individual can be given opportunity for self-realization and will be valued for himself. Every person within an organization should have the opportunity to grow. The purpose of management is neither to tend nor to tame men, its purpose is to realize the power of men."

I am convinced that, as in the past, in the future people will make the difference, not machines or technology. The right people in the right places will create the technology and design and operate the machines. I am also convinced that in the press of getting product out the door, we haven't paid enough attention to this fact. And I don't mean in the way of salary, or insurance, or bowling clubs or the like. I mean in the basic fundamentals of motivation and concern for the personal enthusiasm and growth of our people. If we are to be excellent managers, I suggest that we stop now—all of us, without exception—and pull back from the day-to-day hectic scene to review and evaluate our performance in this regard.

The criteria for measuring excellence can be very simple. In every one of our divisions, and in every one of our departments, people should be very "gung-ho" about the importance of their jobs, the company and their opportunity to reach out and grow with Motorola. If they are not—if people aren't so enthusiastic that they can't wait to get to work each day—then we don't have the kind of spirit and morale that will ensure a leadership position. Given such spirit, average people can do fantastic things. Without it, excellent people turn in second-rate performances.

My question for critical self-evaluation is—do we have it? Do we have it everywhere? If not, we've got a lot of homework to do.

Today, many managers blame poor performance and a lackadaisical attitude on our present state of economic affluence. They say that people don't want to work hard anymore, and that people aren't interested in giving that little bit of extra effort for perfection. I don't believe any of that. I believe that 99 $^{44}/_{100}$ percent of the people want to do a good job. Actually, they want to do the best possible job. The problem is not poor people, it is poor management. There is an occasional bad apple, but that is the exception, not the rule.

People want to be proud of their performance, proud of their company's activities and proud of their personal contributions to the success of those activities. The challenge to us as managers is to find the ways to ensure that all of our people can feel that pride in whatever they do, and in the achievements of Motorola, regardless of who did it. Every one of our 40,000 employees should be proud of the role our company played in the success of Apollo XI, whether they work in the Government Electronics Division or anywhere else in the corporation. Motorola is a hell of a good company. I'm proud to be associated with it. I want every employee to feel the same way.

How do you get pride and enthusiasm? Well, it starts with a deep and abiding concern about people. Each individual, no matter how small a cog in the operation, must feel that he or she is important to the success of the business. A woman on the line in the Communications Division must believe that she fights crime every time she makes a perfect solder joint in a Handie-

Talkie® unit—that the quality of her work may save a police-man's life some day when he calls for help over that radio. A janitor in the Consumer Products Division must know that he contributed to the quality of the Quasar television set in a meaningful way, and helped make it the set that both the Holiday Inn and the Marriott chains selected for its fine performance and reliability.

There is no big razzle-dazzle program you can put on to get pride. Yes, there are a lot of things that can be done to help. Plant open houses, bulletin boards highlighting product usage and personal contribution, customer congratulatory let-ters, news clippings of all Motorola's divisional achievements, visits from astronauts or Medal of Honor winners to our pro-duction lines all help. But you only build pride and spirit by your everyday personal leadership, which must set the exam-ple for your people.

Handshakes at Christmas by the division manager show that top management cares, but nobody says that is the only time the big wheels ought to visit the production lines or the engineering labs. Regular visits to congratulate people on spe-cific performance, or to inquire about a particular problem, show that management cares and that they aren't people in an ivory tower who send down directives, but real human beings interested in their employees doing a good job. Don't limit this comment to cover division managers only—it means all of us.

But all these things mean nothing without one other. Art Reese taught me this critical philosophy: The most important job of management is to create the environment and the atmos-phere in which each and every person can contribute to the maximum of his or her own capability.

Every individual must feel that Motorola truly does offer all the opportunities for his or her own self-fulfillment. We must ensure that personal challenge and opportunity for growth exists for all who are capable, and that it is clearly understood that such growth is tied to the success of the corporation.

Participative management techniques—continuous, fair, objective employee evaluation and development programs that help a person to become more proficient in his or her work, and to reach out and take on more and varied responsibility— are mandatory. By the way, I'm not just talking about direct labor or lower-level supervisors. Department heads and key managers are people, too, and they should get the same concern and treatment.

Proper reward tied to personal contribution is mandatory. Promotions, patent awards and suggestion system payouts are all ways in which our people can share in the fruits of their own labor, and in the success of Motorola as a corporation. Many tools are available. Other tools tailored to your specific situation must be created by each of you. The challenge and opportunity are there. View it as your responsibility, not anyone else's.

I have said nothing profound, nor do I intimate here that we have a serious crisis that will blow up tomorrow. In some areas we are superb in our actions. Maybe in others we already have problems. In every operation, we must ensure that we never lose those basic Paul Galvin fundamentals that built the business. Even an expert in the management of people has to constantly work at developing a proficiency at this talent until he lives and breathes the philosophy of the importance of people. Even then, he has to challenge himself regularly to be sure that in the crush of current events he is still taking the time to pay proper attention to people motivation and management, because only by taking the time can he fulfill the requirements for excellence in leadership.

Yes, it takes time and effort to build team spirit, morale and enthusiasm. We must work at it for our own departments, and for Motorola. To those who say they haven't got the time it takes to do this, there is only one reply—you can't afford not to take the time.

Ladies and gentlemen, I bring to you an abiding faith in people and their importance.

I ask of you a continuous concern at all levels for superb performance in the motivation and management of those people.

I insist that you build and maintain unbeatable teams bursting with enthusiasm and pride in all parts of the corporation.

I place upon you the requirement that you must achieve excellence in management, the mandatory results of which must be the success of your organization in fulfilling its business role.

Nothing less is acceptable!

BW

February 4, 1971

Excerpts from remarks at the Motorola Executive Institute, Vail, Colorado and Oracle, Arizona, about the responsibilities of the Chief Executive Officer.

As you may know, I am an alumnus of the Institute, having been through in November of 1969. So I know what you are going through from first-hand knowledge.

I first gave this presentation as a substitute for Bob Galvin in July of 1969, about two months after I moved into the job of executive vice president and assistant chief operating officer. I remember saying then that here I was—with no experience in my new job, let alone as the chief executive officer—yet talking to you as an expert. However, as I talked with Bob in preparation for that date, and as I began to get into my job, I was surprised at how similar what he had to say was to my definition of the job of a division general manager—something I really did know something about. After all, a large division is a big company itself. I've now been the chief operating officer for almost two years, and I've reconfirmed that thinking. I don't think you'll be surprised that Bob's description and mine may almost describe your job, because you are the CEO of your organization. The principles are the same—only the names and magnitude of the problems and opportunities are different. But your problems are as important to you as the chief executive officer's are to him.

While Motorola may have different people leading it, we have been blessed with a continuity of management philosophy, though specific implementation may be different. So what you hear will be a combination of some of Bob's thoughts, some of mine, some of P.V. Galvin's and some of many other good Motorola managers. I don't take the credit for their origination, but I do for embracing them. I'll try to give them to you in my own words and with my own experiences.

Today, I'll be saying "the chief executive officer" throughout my talk. I really mean the chief executive/chief operating office—the chairman/president's office.

The purpose of a business is to honorably serve the needs of the community at a profit. The purpose of the chief executive officer is to see that the purpose of the business is fulfilled. The basic role of the chief executive officer is leadership—the leadership of people and plans.

Bob Galvin tells this story: P.V. called him in when the company was considering two possible paths—one of which was substantial growth. He said to Bob, "You will lead us in the future if you have the zest for such leadership. Do you?" Obviously Bob said yes, and a decision was made for growth.

Emerson said, "Nothing great was ever accomplished without enthusiasm."

Someone else said, "The person without enthusiasm is like the motor without gasoline. It may be a fine machine, but it won't go anywhere."

Walter Lippmann said, "The final test of a leader is that he leaves behind him in other men the conviction and the will to carry on."

The major job of top management is to create the atmosphere and environment in which each and every individual can contribute to the maximum of his or her own capability. Then to put the right people in the right job, set broad parameters for them, and give them as much authority and responsibility as they are capable of handling.

The chief executive officer is all at once a planner, a recruiter, a trainer, a motivator, an inspirer, a challenger, a rewarder.

The chief executive officer sets the philosophical standards of operation. He or she must set the highest standards of integrity, honesty, concern for the individual and customer satisfaction. We believe in excellent performance delivered by excellent people. Average people will do an average job and the result will be an average company. Ask for perfection in all that you do. Don't settle for average performance. Don't believe that you can't win 'em all.

The chief executive officer sets the expectation level.

The chief executive officer must be an example. Dean Edward Pennell Brooks of MIT's Sloan School of Management is the former senior executive at Sears, Roebuck and Co. He has said:

"There are some qualities absolutely indispensable to an industrial manager or administrator that are beyond the reach of formal education as such. How does one teach boldness, initiative, imagination, willingness to bear responsibility—above all the desire to manage? How does one teach judgment or character or develop a sense of timing—the first essentials of leadership? These qualities all contribute to the intangibles that make up, in varying degrees, management action. If they can be taught at all, one effective means of doing so is by the examples of men who have them."

Chief executive officers get people involved and set the whole tone of dealing with people. They live participative management—but don't manage by committee; listen to their people—let them show off even when they know the answer; believe in people—99 $^{44}/_{100}$ percent want to do the right thing, so give them the chance; believe in fairness—absolutely; encourage risk-taking, and reward for accomplishment.

Chief executive officers set the major corporate policies. They plan—they're the visionaries. They define priorities when there are limited resources. They relate individual programs to the total capability of the corporation in terms of the return to the corporation. They do the really important things first.

The chief executive officer must stay informed so that he or she may coordinate. He or she is not necessarily an expert in all of the corporation's businesses, but is an expert in leading people and motivating them to see and solve their own problems.

The chief executive officer contributes leading questions, thoughts and ideas. He or she: identifies opportunities and problems; uses wild, odd-ball suggestions as a catalyst; challenges fairly, properly and diplomatically; offers solutions, but backs away from making most decisions.

Bob Galvin generally takes the position: "You come up with a recommendation. We'll help challenge and evaluate it, but you make the decision. We'll back you up."

But the chief executive officer must make the critical decisions—the ones that no one else can make because they cut across organizational lines or because of divergent opinions in the company.

The chief executive officer is a corporate spokesperson to the public, the community, the customer, the government and the industry.

I'd like to offer a special note of caution that is true whether you're the chief executive officer or a division manager: You must understand the power and limitations of your office. You must not get overly impressed with your personal contributions or importance. You must not unintentionally redirect effort.

Well, that's basically the job. How close is it to yours? Probably pretty darned close.

Now what about the trials and tribulations of the job, the frustrations and the things that bother me or Bob—some of the pet peeves, if you will. Yes, there are some. I'll tell you about them, although of course, they are far outweighed by the positives of accomplishment and satisfaction.

Pet Peeves and Big Frustrations:
Those who don't face the truth or can't admit mistakes.

Failure to volunteer major problems or mistakes to me so I can help before the ship sinks. I have additional degrees of freedom.

People who always note problems in somebody else's department, but never in theirs.

People who play games and are not frank.

People who don't speak up when they disagree with me.

People who don't want to bother me because I'm too busy. (It's their job to protect me.)

People who are afraid to come directly to me because of the layers of command.

Failure of middle managers to pass on the philosophies and intents of top managers.

I'm perturbed by those who can't stick to the essentials or go to the heart of the problem—those who can't see the whole picture, can't find the critical determinant.

I'm concerned about those who can't listen to anyone on the thing they think they are the most knowledgeable about, or those who feel they must talk with equal time.

I'm frustrated when my comments—not intended as directives—are overinterpreted or misinterpreted.

I am bothered by managers who succumb to decisions that they disagree with—against their better judgment—without protesting, because the chief proclaimed it! There are too many times when people think we're making a wrong decision but fail to speak up.

There is never enough time; too many meetings, too many ceremonial requirements, too many speeches and too many committees.

Is there loneliness at the top? Sometimes, but it is often more lonely at the division general management level than at the CEO level, because with decentralized responsibility, "you make the decision."

So, sure, there are all these problems, but the rewards outweigh them by an order of magnitude. The biggest rewards are not money and prestige—they are personal satisfaction and pride of accomplishment, the thrill of beating the competition and the development of people.

I used to worry that I had to know the answer to everything and always had to be right. How wrong that thought was. Sure, I must be right a large percentage of the time, but the biggest thrill is to see people I've helped train and develop do a better job than I did. I get a kick out of out-thinking you. But each time one of you out-thinks me or outdoes me, I know I've done my job well.

BW

November 15, 1988

Business Leadership in a Dynamic Environment

Presentation to the School of Business and Industry,
Florida A&M University, Tallahassee, Florida.

Some years ago, an advertising executive named Tom Dillon
pointedly noted that:

**"Business has generally evolved along Darwinian lines.
Like all living things, a business sought to adapt itself to its
environment, and when it failed to adapt itself to changes in
that environment, it died.**

*The business that died out was much like the dinosaur.
The dinosaur presumably made good day-to-day adaptations to
its environment. It probably made a pretty good choice of what
leaves to eat off what trees, and selected the most desirable
swamps in which to slosh. At a tactical level of decision, we
have no reason to believe that these giant beasts were not reasonably competent.*

*But when faced with major changes in Earth's climate
and the competitive behavior of other animal and plant life,
the dinosaur was unable to make a strategic adaptation to its
new environment.*

*For centuries, business organizations have lived and died
much as the dinosaur, unable to adapt themselves strategically to
their environment with the speed necessary to maintain survival.*

*The environment of a business is the market, the technology,
the competition, the customer's attitude toward business in general and a company in particular. If it chooses to do so, a business
can continually make strategic adaptations to these changing*

environments. It can change its organization, its products and services to maximum adaptation, thereby avoiding the necessary fatalities of the Darwinian system of natural selection."

In its growth from a $500 investment in 1928 to sales of $6.7 billion last year, Motorola has changed from a small, totally domestic U.S. automobile radio manufacturer to a broadly diversified, high-technology global electronics company. To accomplish this, senior management had to do two fundamental things. First, ensure the long-term growth and health of the company, notwithstanding any major changes or short-term perturbations. And second, react positively and quickly to the unforeseen opportunities or problems that inevitably occur in a dynamic environment. To do both of these, there are four key attributes that any business organization must have:

1. A reasonable idea of long-term strategic direction;
2. A corporate culture that encourages change where appropriate, but whose fundamental principles are so ingrained that they never change;
3. Excellent intelligence-gathering and objective analysis; and
4. The flexibility to implement change when needed.

Notwithstanding any short-term dynamics, the chief executive officer must correctly set the long-term strategic direction.

The CEO must be the "big thinker" setting the focus appropriately based on his analysis of the world around him. In the words of author Alvin Toffler, "You've got to think about big things while you're doing small things so that all the small things go in the right direction."

In doing this, the CEO must evaluate the major trends affecting the company in many areas: the economy, technology, the marketplace, competition, the government and others. The CEO must determine whether the company can affect the outcome or whether it must react to it. He or she must ensure that the correct strategy is developed to guarantee successful execution and achievement of the end objectives. That means picking the key people who will be responsible for successful implementation. All this must be done while the internal problems that come with growth are handled. I do not want to imply that the CEO operates totally alone. **Participative management and teamwork are just as important at the leadership level as on the factory floor. But final responsibility and decision are the leader's, not a committee's.**

For a company to change effectively whenever required, it must have a *fundamental* culture that creates a *continuous* atmosphere in which constructive change is encouraged. Edgar Schein of MIT's Sloan School of Management said, "The most important job of the CEO is culture management. Cultures don't occur randomly. The CEO must establish the right corporate culture, set the appropriate example and audit the organization at all levels regularly to be sure that the culture is being adhered to. Leaders must create and manage culture achievement, and sometimes they must destroy bad cultures in the process of rebuilding good ones."

How we reward some behaviors and practices more than others tells our people how well we believe in the words we mouth as our company culture.

Beyond the absolutely required basics of honesty, integrity and ethics, you must reinforce, or build and manage, the culture of your organization to ensure that all managers reach out, assume responsibility and take action. **You must continually inculcate a strong belief in the dignity of the individual. Insist on teamwork and expect cooperation, not confrontation, as the atmosphere for interaction between people and organizations.** This means an atmosphere of objectivity on every issue. The norm should be open and complete argument on controversial issues right up to the point where a decision is made. Even then, re-argument should be allowed if fundamentally new evidence becomes available. Insist on a healthy spirit of discontent. Believe in creativity and innovation as being fundamental to business success, and believe in total customer satisfaction—no ifs, ands or buts. You must give a mandate to everyone to challenge anything that your organization does, and the way it does it, if it does not help beat the competition in serving the customer.

Frankly, if one of our managers at any level isn't totally committed to the Motorola culture, then no matter how good his or her technical or professional skill, we really do not want that manager in our company. We cannot afford to have anyone in a leadership position who gives wrong signals to other employees—who doesn't encourage them to tackle every problem in accordance with the fundamental principles with which we wish it to be tackled.

The management of a multi-business corporation like Motorola requires:
1. Support of the best strategy for each of its businesses,
2. Identification and selection of new market and product opportunities and establishment of the strategy for each new business so selected, and

3. Appropriate deployment of resources to each business, to maximize the corporation's objectives.

To do all this requires an understanding and analysis of the outside economic, technological, social and political environment with its consequent opportunities, threats and levels of risks. This must be matched to a consideration of the inside environment, including shareholder and personnel expectations as well as evaluation of the size, strengths and weaknesses of existing or acquirable resources. It follows that accurate intelligence about outside and inside environmental issues is mandatory. Objectivity in analysis is a prerequisite to correct decision-making and execution. **Well done, timely intelligence-gathering and analysis forces you to ask how you can take advantage of the opportunities created; how you can protect your company from the adverse effects of potential negatives; and how you can posture your organization to be the long-term winner in the competitive battle.**

At Motorola, in addition to all the normal marketing intelligence activities going on in our operating divisions, we have a small, corporate-level intelligence office whose job is to constantly scan the broad environment and synthesize information into a composite picture. Simple, extrapolation-type forecasting misses big environmental changes. As Toffler said, "decision-makers ought to be thinking more about 'high impact' events, even though they may seem very unlikely to occur. Obviously, you can't scan everything and imagine everything. But if you consciously devote some of your attention to lower-probability, high-impact changes, you may be prepared for the biggest changes of all. **Leadership and managerial excellence depends on having a sense of the big changes and acting on them before they're obvious to everyone else.**"

The process of thinking through such issues will result in putting an organization in the most flexible position possible to take advantage of the big opportunities, or avert catastrophe as the situation plays out.

No matter how dynamic the environment is, we know that there are certain problems in a growing company that must be planned for and successfully handled. A major factor in growth is size, and that usually means loss of flexibility and slow decision-making: How to effectively manage the company as it gets bigger and bigger? How to get quick reaction and flexibility? How to retain the enthusiasm of the people? How to take advantage of bigness, yet not strangle in bureaucracy in the process?

Motorola's fundamental philosophy has been and will continue to be decentralization of authority and responsibility to the lowest practical level. This decentralization must be combined with centralized corporate policy-making, and excellent coordination and control procedures. We constantly subdivide our organization, creating a large number of product operations, each with its own profit-and-loss statement. We give the product operations manager total control of everything that affects success. **This decentralization reinforces flexibility and allows quicker action and reaction to environmental changes as they relate to each product line, not just to the company as a whole.** We try to keep the small-company, entrepreneurial proprietorship atmosphere in view of all employees, even though the sum of hundreds of such product operations will approach $8 billion this year.

A very important prerequisite for continued growth and its funding is maintaining the basic financial strength of the company during bad times. We have long ago given up trying to be precise about the economy. The frequency and depth of economic slowdowns are different, with the potential for serious problems higher than ever before. We study the economic cycles intensely. We correlate our businesses to different economic and market indices. But we have no way of predicting accurately what's going to happen in any specific year. Our conclusion is to plan on growth in the long term, but be able to react quickly to recession in any given year. We prepare a number of contingency plans for all our operating organizations — not just downward alternatives, but also upward possibilities. We find that if you recognize the distinct possibility of variation in either direction in long-range planning and in yearly budgeting, people act just a little differently as they make decisions throughout the year.

With the increasing capital intensity of industry, very particularly for us in the electronics business, we must continue to fund our regular growth yet also afford front-end expensing of new businesses. While *capability* to succeed will be a crucial ingredient in the future for many companies, *affordability* to pioneer will be critical. **The institution must live through whatever the economic conditions are. That means a conservative balance sheet to protect the financial strength of the company while taking all those calculated risks for continued growth.**

As well as we may think we've served our customers, improvement in the '90s will be mandatory. An absolutely certain characteristic of the future is that competition will be tougher, much tougher. The Motorola strategy is very simple: Give customers what they want when they want it in a better fashion than any competitor! Know the customers' businesses better than the customers know it themselves. Know what the customer thinks is needed and wanted. Beyond that, know what your company's new technologies or processes can do for the customer, even when they don't know themselves. "Total customer satisfaction" is a simply stated strategy, but the question is not just strategy, it's how to ensure perfect execution of the strategy. We believe that the key to getting maximum focus on serving the customer is to get all of the employees involved in that single focus. Employee participation is a clear trend. Every time we get a group of our managers together, we tell them that the most important job of management is to create the environment in which every person can contribute the maximum of his or her capability. The book *Managers for Tomorrow*, by Rohrer, Hibler and Replogle, puts it as follows:

"The challenge to the manager of tomorrow is to find ways by which each individual can be given opportunity for self-realization and will be valued for him/herself. Every person within an organization should have the opportunity to grow; the purpose of management is neither to tend nor to tame people, its purpose is to realize the power of people."

At Motorola, we have been using a management system for some time called the participative management process (PMP), which breaks organizations into logical teams whose sole purpose is to get every employee working as part of a team to make key contributions to serving the customer better, thus improving the success of the business. We've been involved with the program for 20 years, long before Japanese quality circles were the "in" thing. It is different from the quality circle, because it involves all levels of the organization from the production line right up to the officers. It is horizontal as well, involving all functional departments. As employees functioning in a team make improvements in quality, delivery, productivity, inventory, market penetration and other areas, it pays a cash incentive. We continue to be amazed by the improvements that occur when the management and all the employees really unite in a PMP group with a single purpose. I believe that companies that survive in the '90s and beyond will be the ones whose employees are motivated and deliver 150 percent effort.

We believe that participative management combined with our fundamental policy of continuous decentralization will make it possible to lead and work our behemoth flexibly, artfully and successfully in the '90s and beyond. PMP is a counterbalancing force to size, breaking challenges down to where individual employees can see the results of their participation. It helps provide some of that "small company" atmosphere I talked about earlier, while releasing individual potential and fulfilling the needs for intimate business communications and involvement.

Our world is constantly changing, and for any given generation of management, not all the proposed directions will be determined. As Tom Dillon said years ago, carefully thought-out strategic planning for the long term with quick tactical reaction in the short term is mandatory. Failure to recognize, adapt to and help shape the major long-term trends while taking advantage of the big-impact events will make dinosaurs of us all. **But a continual sensing of the environment, analyzed appropriately in a culture that encourages reach-out decision-making and change, will put you in control of your organization's destiny and ensure a consistently successful future. BW**

Leadership Quotations

"There are some qualities absolutely indispensable to an industrial manager or administrator which are beyond the reach of formal education as such. How does one teach boldness, initiative, imagination, willingness to bear responsibility—above all, the desire to manage? How does one teach judgment or character, or develop a sense of timing—the first essentials of leadership? These qualities all contribute to the intangibles which make up, in varying degrees, management action. If they can be taught at all, one effective means of doing so is by the examples of men who have them."
Dean Edward Pennell Brooks
Massachusetts Institute
of Technology

"People ask the difference between a leader and a boss …
The leader works in the open and the boss in covert. The leader leads and the boss drives."
Theodore Roosevelt

"I'd define coaching as the job of getting men to play up to the best of their natural endowments."
Fritzy Crisler

"The most valuable gift you can give another is a good example."
author unknown

"The essence of business is how people relate to people—whoever improves these relations exercises business leadership."
William Cooper Procter

"The leadership and other processes of the organization must be such as to ensure a maximum probability that in all interactions and all relationships with the organization each member will, in the light of his background, values and expectations, view the experience as supportive and one which builds and maintains his sense of personal worth and importance."
Rensis Likert

"The genius of a good leader is to leave behind him a situation which common sense, without the grace of genius, can deal with successfully."
Walter Lippmann

"The goal of criticism should be to leave the person with the feeling that he or she has been helped."
author unknown

"Being the boss doesn't make you right, it only makes you the boss."
Milton Metz

Sermons to See

I'd rather see a sermon than hear
   one any day,
I'd rather one should walk with
   me than merely show the way.
The eye's a better pupil and more
   willing than the ear;
Fine counsel is confusing, but
   example's always clear;
And the best of all the preachers
   are the men who live their
   creeds,
For to see the good in action is
   what everybody needs.
I can soon learn how to do it if
   you'll let me see it done.
I can watch your hands in action,
   but your tongue too fast
   may run.
And the lectures you deliver may
   be very wise and true;
But I'd rather get my lesson by
   observing what you do.
For I may misunderstand you
   and the high advice you give,
But there's no misunderstanding
   how you act and how you live.
Edgar A. Guest

"Leaders have two important
characteristics: first, they are
going somewhere; second, they
are able to persuade other people
to go with them."
taken from **"Bits & Pieces"**

A Supervisor's Prayer

Dear Lord, please help me—
To accept human beings as
   they are—not yearn for perfect
   creatures;

To recognize ability—and
   encourage it;
To understand shortcomings—
   and make allowance for them;
To work patiently for improvement—and not expect too
   much too quickly;
To appreciate what people do
   right—not just criticize what
   they do wrong;
To be slow to anger and hard to
   discourage;
To have the hide of an elephant
   and the patience of Job;
In short, Lord, please help me be
   a better boss!
author unknown

"A good boss is someone who
takes a little more than his share
of the blame and a little less than
his share of the credit."
taken from **"Bits & Pieces"**

"Leaders are best when people
barely know that they exist;
Not so good when people obey
and acclaim them;
Worse when they despise them.
Fail to honor people
They will fail to honor you;

But of good leaders, who talk
little, when their work is done,
their aims fulfilled,

They all will say
'We did this ourselves.'"
Lao-tzu, circa 604 B.C.

"Strong leaders know that if they
develop their associates, they will
be even stronger."
James F. Lincoln

"In order to be a leader, an individual must have followers. And
to have followers, one must have
their confidence. Hence the
supreme quality for a leader is
unquestionably integrity. Without
it, no real success is possible, no
matter whether it is on a section
gang, a football field, in an army
or in an office. If an individual's
associates find he or she lacks
forthright integrity, he or she fails.
One's teachings and actions must
square with each other. The first
great need, therefore, is integrity
and high purpose."
Dwight D. Eisenhower

"If the modern leader doesn't know
the facts, he is in grave trouble,
but rarely do the facts provide
unqualified guidance."
John W. Gardner

"Keep cool and you command
everybody."
St. Just

"Leaders are made, they are not
born; and they are made just like
anything else has ever been made
in this country—by hard effort.
And that's the price that we all
have to pay to achieve that goal,
or any goal."
Vince Lombardi
Former coach, Green Bay Packers

Management

Management Memos

"The wisdom of the wise is an uncommon degree of common sense."
William R. Inge

The Common Sense Check

I thought I would pass on to you a little tool that I try to use on almost everything I do, whether it is making basic policy decisions or producing a report. I am sure that most of you do the same thing, but I think it is worthwhile to stress. A small number of you have already been exposed to these thoughts. Please excuse the redundancy.

As we compile financial budgets, objectives and goals, five-year forecasts, daily and weekly reports, and as we make a myriad of daily decisions, this tool is particularly important. I call it "the common sense check." Any complicated report, project, forecast or decision is usually constructed by using a step-by-step process, adding many parts to make a whole. Upon completion of such a task, which yields a final answer—a number, a report, a decision—step back from the details and just ask yourself, "Does this answer make sense in light of the particular situation?" In other words, forget about all of the minute calculations you used to get the final solution. Does the answer, when viewed in light of your experiences and intuition, sound like a right answer? Many times, I find that when I ask myself that question in this detached manner, and relate the answer to outside factors that may not have been considered when constructing the document, my answer to the question is no. This signals danger and forces a careful re-evaluation of how the answer was formulated. Sometimes this check has revealed simple mathematical mistakes. Sometimes it has revealed a lack of consideration of people's feelings. But whatever the situation, the common sense check puts the answer into perspective.

In an organization as large and complex as Motorola, where much depends upon accurate communications, our reports and correspondence must be correct. Our decisions must be as good as we can make them. If they are not, then we start a chain reaction of errors where people make incorrect decisions because of wrong inputs.

I think the common sense check is a valuable, important and simple last-chance procedure by which everyone, not just key managers, can help ensure against mistakes. I recommend the technique to you. As we prepare to review five-year forecasts, it becomes increasingly important.

BW

"A great number of people think they are thinking when they are merely rearranging their prejudices."
William James

"It takes less time to do a thing right than to explain why you did it wrong."
Henry Wadsworth Longfellow

"Why is it that there's seldom enough time to do things right ... and so much time to correct mistakes which result?"
author unknown

Setting and Achieving Corporate Goals

As most of you know, the corporate objectives committee has made, over the last year and a half, detailed studies of our company's performance, comparisons to other companies in our industry, and projections of trends in the electronics industry and other industries. These studies were made so our board of directors could set meaningful goals for the future—goals that looked out not only five years, but also 15 years.

At the December board of directors meeting, the board set a very definitive goal for the corporation to achieve by 1976. The chairman/president's office of the corporation has thus been directed by the board to run the corporation to meet this requirement.

Over the past year and a half, in anticipation of those tight but meaningful goals, the chairman/president's office, together with other senior executives, studied the organization's structural needs as Motorola grows in complexity and size. As you know, we have made major changes in the company's organization, including the implementation of a new ventures and acquisition program. Along with this reorganization there will no doubt come a number of changes in methods of operation, which will evolve over a period of time.

As we reviewed and evaluated our past performance and future hopes, it became apparent that rededication to the importance of goal achievement is necessary by all key managers, including corporate management.

"People don't fail in life because they planned to fail. They fail because they failed to plan."
author unknown

This will be the first of a number of memos you will receive from me over the next few days, weeks and months, discussing this general philosophy as it affects operations, budgets, five-year forecasts, etc.

I am sure the comments in this particular memo are known and understood by all of you. However, I wish to put them down on paper so you understand how strongly I feel about them and how I intend to conduct myself in terms of their achievement. The statements are not limited to division-corporate relationships. I hope you will re-emphasize them in your divisions and departments.

In order for us to achieve the goals set by the board, the divisions and corporate departments will have to realistically forecast their plans, programs, strategies, goals and financial results. Only by doing so can we integrate the expected divisional results with our new ventures activity in a manner that will allow us to meet the board's requirements. I would like to re-emphasize that the proper definition of the word "goal" is meant to cover all types of goals, not merely financial ones. **Obviously, financial goals can only be reached if you succeed in a host of non-financial goals.**

We are, as a corporation, only the sum of our parts. Each operating organization must believe in the validity of its goals, whether they are product leadership, customer value and service, yearly budgets or five-year forecasts, and be fully committed to meeting those goals.

We have gone through some very rough economic times in the past few years, and the effect of these outside influences on an organization's ability to perform must be taken into account. Each division is affected differently by these circumstances, but each division's achievement will also be affected by their own attitude and determination to achieve in spite of adverse conditions, and by the attitude of corporate management in insisting on such achievement.

In order to attain the desired result, whether yearly or over five years, financial or non-financial, an organization must have regular milestones of achievement and must meet each result called for at that point. If it falls behind at any milestone, it must take steps to get back on plan. Whether the missed milestone is a new product introduction or the budget for profit, it must change its plan only when the original plan is exhaustively proved to be improper.

In 1970, the reactions of our divisions to the economic conditions and the implementation of alternate plans was well done. Indeed, the recession called for a major re-look at our long-range plans.

In 1971, the achievement of most divisions to their plan was excellent.

In 1972, you have set some very high goals of all kinds. You and your divisions must achieve each of your milestones throughout the year in order for the corporation to achieve its target.

Over the next five years, each division must achieve its five-year goals if the corporation is to achieve the ones set for it by the board. In order to do this, both the divisions and the corporation must perform properly year by year. On the other hand, the five-year forecast is not to be "cast in concrete" in a fashion that doesn't allow us to take advantage of opportunities or consider unpredictable conditions. I'll talk more about the five-year forecast in a later memo.

Many times the comment is made that we are too "numbers oriented." Let's not confuse the words "financial" and "numerical." We use numbers in many areas to measure achievement of non-financial goals such as quality, delinquencies, customer satisfaction, share of market, etc. Therefore, my attitude and yours should not be to look down on numerical goals as "too much emphasis on the numbers," nor to equate them with financial results. Numbers are only used as a unit of relative measure of performance of some of the important things about a business. If numerical milestones are properly determined, they can and should be used to measure progress and performance within those parameters. Obviously, the "feel" of the experienced manager about what should be done, when and how, is of major importance.

But in the final analysis, the determination of our success or failure over a longer period of time is measured by the financial numbers, assuring that we maintain high standards of ethics, honesty, social consciousness and concern for our employees' welfare. **The disciplining of ourselves and our organizations to achieve all of our goals will result in the achievement of our financial goals.** Corporate management will ever more strongly insist on the meeting of our milestones and plans in the months and years to come. We hope you will adopt this attitude in your organization. We can only achieve our corporate results if your organization achieves its results.
BW

January 14, 1977

Submitted by Pete Simonis, manager, Consumer Products Division.

Learning to Listen

You can learn more by listening than you can by talking. That's a fact worth remembering no matter how far you move up the executive ladder.

The higher a man goes in management and the more authority he wields, the less he is needed to listen to others. Yet his need to listen is greater than ever. The further he gets down the firing line, the more he has to depend on others for the accurate information so necessary for correct decisions. If he hasn't formed the habit of listening—carefully and diligently—he isn't going to get the facts he needs.

There's another good reason for listening carefully, especially to your subordinates. They want to talk to you about their problems. And it's important to their effectiveness and job satisfaction to know that you are really listening, not just going through the motions.

Why do some executives tend to become such impatient listeners?

Partly it's a matter of pressure. We hate to waste time listening to something that might not be worth hearing. Yet the very act of listening to people, regardless of the significance of what they are saying, is important in itself.

Sometimes we get impatient and interrupt because we think we already know what a person is going to say. But how can you be sure—and how can the talker be satisfied—if you don't give him a chance to finish?

Other times we cut people off because we're sure we've heard the story before. But how can you be sure? And were the circumstances exactly the same? The executive who isn't willing to reconsider a decision in the light of new facts may be a stumbling block in the way of progress.

Occasionally, we hesitate to listen because we doubt the competence of the man doing the talking and are overly sure of our own. Yet the executive who listens might learn something—you never can tell for sure where a good idea will come from. If you refuse to listen, you definitely won't hear anything.

Last, but not least, some of us hate to listen because we much prefer the sound of our own voice to someone else's.

Nothing stops progress faster than people in managerial positions who won't listen, people you can't communicate with. Hardening of management opinions is as detrimental to a company's health as hardening of the arteries is to an individual.

Listen—and keep on listening—with your ears and mind open.

author unknown

September 15, 1981

*Submitted by Jim Mikulski, member of the technical staff,
Chicago Corporate R&D Center.*

    Ted Frank/David Ray, Basic Business & Professional Speech
Communication, ©*1979, pp.113-114. Reprinted by permission
of Prentice Hall, Englewood Cliffs, New Jersey.*

What do some people do that makes others call them professionals?

1. Professionals trust and so cause others to trust themselves.
2. They know that others want to know what is happening on the job.
3. They assume that others want to learn more, work harder and earn higher pay.
4. They talk with others as people first and as holders of rank second.
5. They pass beyond petty cliques in the office to support the company's mission.
6. They prefer to get along well with others than to cause pain.
7. They are pleased without being jealous when others excel.
8. They let bad humor in others go by as only momentary outbursts.
9. They gamble that others will work hard and succeed.
10. They praise, admire and instill pride to make others feel good.
11. They expect others to respect and admire their bosses.
12. They reduce fear between workers and bosses.
13. They teach others to lead.
14. They set goals that allow others to grow within themselves and to improve their lives and humanity in general.
15. They add new ideas to egg others on to work.
16. They assume that others know what they are doing and choose to do well.

November 1, 1982

Submitted by Jon Rodgers, High Frequency and Optical Products Division, Semiconductor Products Sector.

James K. Van Fleet, The 22 Biggest Mistakes Managers Make, ©*1973. Reprinted by permission of Prentice Hall, Englewood Cliffs, New Jersey.*

The 22 Biggest Mistakes Managers Make

1. Failing to keep abreast of developments in your own field.
2. Confining yourself to your own specialty.
3. Refusing to seek higher responsibility or take responsibility for actions.
4. Failure to make sound and timely decisions.
5. Neglecting to conduct personal inspections properly.
6. Failing to make sure the job is understood, supervised and accomplished.
7. Wasting time on details or work that belongs to others.
8. Refusing to assess your own performance realistically.
9. Accepting the minimum instead of going for the maximum.
10. Using your management position for personal gain.
11. Failure to tell the truth ... to always keep your word.
12. Not setting the personal example for your people to follow.
13. Trying to be liked rather than respected.
14. Failing to give cooperation to your employees.
15. Failing to ask your subordinates for their advice and help.
16. Failing to develop a sense of responsibility in your subordinates.
17. Emphasizing rules rather than skills.
18. Failing to keep your criticism constructive.
19. Not paying attention to employee gripes and complaints.
20. Failure to keep your people informed.
21. Failing to treat your subordinates as equals.
22. Refusing to train an assistant to take your place.

by James K. Van Fleet

"We don't want geniuses for managers,"
says a well-known company president.
"We want men and women who can motivate
other people to do good work."

Do you think you're a little brighter (maybe a lot brighter) than the people who work for you? Perhaps a little brighter than your boss?

And do you feel a need to have other people recognize this fact?

If so, you've got ego problems. Because a good boss is the kind of person who goes around passing out the credit and encouragement—not trying to scoop up all he can for himself. He or she recognizes the importance of other people's contributions and soft-peddles his own.

Good managers like to get individual recognition just as much as everyone else—maybe more so. But they're also smart enough to realize that the only kind of credit really worth having comes without asking. They also recognize the tremendous gains in goodwill and encouragement that come from passing credit along to others.

Good executives are big enough not to compete for personal credit with their own people. They identify subordinates' suggestions when they pass them up the ladder, aren't afraid to let their people step into the limelight now and then, and refrain from putting their own name on another person's work or ideas.

In short, they let their people shine and are content to shine as their manager. After all, isn't being able to get good work out of people what being a manager is all about? That's what you're there for.

Real leaders want all their people to stand out. They know that when their people look good, they do, too.

author unknown

In November 1982, I sent out a philosophy memo called "The 22 Biggest Mistakes Managers Make." I have heard from a number of you on this issue, each of whom has had a thought here and there. The best overall list of additional items was sent by Dave Long and Jim Sorenson from the Research and Development Operation at Four Phase. I pass them on to you.

11 More Biggest Mistakes Managers Make

1. Failure to recognize one's own strengths and limitations.
2. Insistence on treating one's limitations as excuses, not as opportunities to improve.
3. Failure to exercise the judgment to choose between difficult alternatives.
4. Refusal to adjudicate disputes between subordinates impartially.
5. Refusal to delegate.
6. Failure to delegate authority and responsibility in roughly equal measures.
7. Placing the perceived good of one's own group above the greater good of the entire organization.
8. Thinking small—being overly concerned with details to the point of losing sight of the big picture or overemphasizing short-term goals to the detriment of longer-term considerations.
9. Parochial attitude—insistence on applying one's own narrow expertise to broader issues. Typically appears as forcing technical judgments into organizational or marketplace issues.
10. Insistence on "reinventing the wheel" regardless of delay or costs involved.
11. Killing the bearer of bad tidings—i.e., being unwilling to listen to negatives, no matter how accurate, important or timely they may be.

by Dave Long and Jim Sorenson

November 25, 1986

*From The Bradley Printing Company, 2170 S. Mannheim Road,
Des Plaines, Illinois 60018, submitted by David Weisz, manager,
Public Relations, Communications Sector. Reprint permission
granted by Linda Kelen.*

Either You Accept Change or You Expect It

Winners Expect Change

One of the things I like about my philosophy memos is that they often develop into ongoing personal correspondence with someone who writes to me or calls me to comment on a particular subject.

I have received two comments on the November 25, 1986 memo, which was titled "Either You Accept Change ... or You Expect It." If you remember, this particular memo displayed the picture of a sad group of people who were left on one side of a ravine that had been crossed by an individual carrying a plank. The first comment was negative! The writer indicated that I gave the wrong message about participative management because the person who crossed the ravine should have laid his plank across it and helped those left on the other side. This is an interesting observation. Teamwork is important, and we should all help one another to cross the ravines and obstacles we face. So, my thanks to this writer.

However, the fundamental message in that cartoon was the importance of being ready for change, and that it is everybody's responsibility to be capable of facing and surmounting change because that's the name of the game in our competitive world. In fact, another writer modified the words "Either You Accept Change ... or You Expect It" to "Accept Change and Always Expect It ... or Plan It." That particular person, Tom Rollins, of the Paging Division, Boynton Beach, Fla., modified the cartoon by labeling the man with the plank as the total

"It ought to be remembered that there is nothing more difficult to take in hand, more perilous to conduct, or more uncertain in its success, than to take the lead in the introduction of a new order of things. Because the innovator has for enemies all those who have done well under the old conditions, and lukewarm defenders in those who may do well under the new."
The Prince, by Niccolò Machiavelli

Motorola company and the poor souls on the other side as our competitors. That would be the best of all worlds.

All of these viewpoints are correct. They are good additions to the fundamental one—that change is inevitable, both in our business and personal lives—and being flexible enough to face change really makes the difference.

There is another set of philosophical notes that come to my mind on the same subject. Far too many people say that certain things are beyond their control, and therefore they can be excused for the effects of those things. Statements from the Old Testament relate that there are two kinds of reactions to change. The first group of people excuse the results because the change was beyond their control. The second group acknowledges that certain changes are outside their control, but understands that they do control how they react to those things, and therefore, can do something about the end result. These are the winners!

BW

"Experience has repeatedly shown that a change is accepted best when employees understand, participate, and are given a stake in its success. Therein lies the real difference between a change that works or one that goes down the drain. People may accept change willingly—or resist it bitterly. It depends a great deal on how the change is introduced."
author unknown

August 22, 1988

Encouraging Innovation

On the last day of the five-day Motorola Training and Education Center course titled "Manager of Managers," I usually spend a substantial amount of time discussing with the group the need for constructive, proactive change. A major issue always raised by the attendees deals with their enthusiasm to go back to work and experiment with new technologies. They tell me they are too often prohibited from doing so because their managers are not receptive to implementing new things that have been learned at MTEC. I hope all of you will create an atmosphere that encourages the use of new techniques and experiments so that none of you fit the mold of the "Executive in Trouble" outlined on the next two pages.

BW

"If you keep doing what you've always done, you'll keep getting what you've always gotten."
Boy Scouts of America Leaders Conference

"The Executive in Trouble"

He Fights Change
He struggles to maintain the status quo, to defend what is, to oppose the new. He strives to repeat the past.

He Becomes Defensive
He guards against attack of any kind. He wants not to be questioned or challenged. He never moves forward or sticks his neck out.

He is Disorganized
He jumps irrationally from job to job and is fragmented, wasted. He begins a job at the middle, works on two jobs at a time. Does unimportant work first.

He Flies Into Rages
Fails to exercise emotional control. He rants and raves and insults his subordinates. He intimidates his superiors. He is himself upset and unproductive.

He is "Fixed" Inflexible
He takes a position ... refuses to move from it. He will not bend. He is incapable of compromise.

He Has No Team Spirit
He wants to "do it all by himself." He wants no suggestions, no criticism, no help of any kind. Even a helper is a threat to him.

He Won't Take a Risk
To enter into competition of any kind, to suggest a new system ... these actions present hazards too great to bear.

He Passes the Buck
Whether it's a minor mistake or a colossal catastrophe, he either can't or won't accept responsibility or even casual involvement in it.

He Has Poor Understanding of People
He lacks the ability to listen and to hear the people with whom he works. He can't be sympathetic ... or kind ... and, therefore, is rarely helpful.

He is Without Imagination
He cannot or will not think creatively. He refuses to reach out and stretch his mind to the broad horizons.

November 17, 1969

Submitted by Pete Simonis, manager, Consumer Products Division.

Everyone Would Like to Be Looked Up To, To Be Somebody

Human beings, no matter what size or shape the package, have one thing in common: a need to feel important.

Management Articles

Nobody enjoys being treated like a push-button, a payroll number, or a perforation in an IBM card. The employee who scrawled across his time card, "Do not fold, bend or mutilate—I am a human being," was telling us something worth listening to.

Some of the most troublesome problems industry faces today are a direct result of failing to satisfy this fundamental human need. Too much of what we do has become highly impersonal. In our push to get the job done, it's been hard to find time to get to know each employee personally and to give each one some special attention.

How can we make people feel important?

The best way to start is by believing people are important. In this day and age, you'd better believe it. The manager who doesn't handicaps his effectiveness in everything he attempts. If you sincerely believe a subordinate is important, you'll find yourself showing it in lots of ways:

› by giving him all the responsibility and authority he can handle
› by including him in what's going on
› by assigning him work that is important in his eyes and that he can take pride in doing
› by letting him share the limelight now and then
› by taking a sincere interest in him as an individual
› by never belittling or ridiculing him
› by asking for and listening to his advice
› by confiding in him once in a while
› by letting him know "things would be rough without him."

Most people are starved for personal recognition. Not necessarily to become a celebrity or have their picture on the front pages, but to be looked up to in their own circle—in their jobs, among their friends and fellow-workers, in the eyes of their boss.

Any boss who, unknowingly or otherwise, destroys a man's self-importance also destroys the man. Build a subordinate's self-esteem, on the other hand, and you'll make a new man out of him. Don't worry about his getting swell-headed. That's a small price to pay for unlocking his full talents and putting them to work.

author unknown

The Difference Lies in Their "Follow-Through"

Lots of executives have good ideas. Not nearly as many achieve good results.

A supervisor who liked to keep track of every little detail handed a job to a subordinate and immediately asked how long it would take.

"About two hours," the man replied, "but if you stand over me, it may take two days."

His answer probably contained more truth than fiction. No man is an effective manager until he has learned the art of giving someone a job, then getting out of his way and letting him do it. But the fact remains that you can't just delegate work to people, then forget about it. Some kind of follow-through is essential for best results.

It's surprising how many otherwise capable executives fall down at this crucial point. They think well, plan well and delegate intelligently. Then they relax on the oars, and are surprised when things don't work out the way they planned.

Following up, carefully and methodically, to check on how something is actually working out isn't nearly as glamorous as planning it. But it happens to be an essential part of being an effective executive. It's a quality you notice quickly in subordinates—whether or not they really follow through, or tend to let things ride and hope for the best. Your own boss is equally aware of the same quality—or lack of it—in your efforts.

A good manager lets people alone to do a job. But having delegated the work, he doesn't simply fade out of the picture. He stays in touch—and keeps control—by following progress.

On routine jobs, all he may do is to stop by now and then to make sure the man hasn't run into any difficulties. On larger jobs, he may ask a subordinate to figure out the best method, then keep him posted on how things are going. He always knows the score because he's keeping score.

There's many a slip between the cup and the lip—and a good manager learns to expect them. He knows that good plans, by themselves, don't ensure good results, that the job that gets followed up is less apt to get fouled up. So he gets out of his chair and does it.

author unknown

25 Ways to Spot the Perfect Executive

by Ted Pollock
Reprinted permission granted by *Production Magazine.*

1. He makes his people want to do things.
2. He is a good listener.
3. He plays up the positive, constantly building up the self-esteem of his subordinates.
4. He sets a good example.
5. He gives effective work assignments, fitting jobs to the abilities of people to do them.
6. He is receptive to new ideas and supports worthy changes.
7. When he goofs, he admits it.
8. He helps his people grow and fights for them when it's necessary.
9. He never belittles a subordinate, regardless of the temptation.
10. He never plays favorites.
11. He gives his people his undivided attention when they come to him.
12. He avoids domination of subordinates, knowing that this can only breed a crew of yes-men.
13. He communicates, is brief but thorough, gets his message across.
14. He follows up and follows through on new ideas, new programs.
15. He anticipates change, understands, welcomes and cooperates with innovation.
16. He pinpoints priorities.
17. He is flexible, when flexibility is called for.

18. When in doubt, he asks questions. He doesn't pretend to know everything.
19. He looks beyond his company and is a responsible, concerned citizen.
20. He is decisive, willing to assume responsibility for his assessment of the facts in any given situation.
21. He never appears preoccupied with his own interests.
22. He exercises time-management.
23. He structures solitude for himself, giving himself the chance to know himself.
24. He concentrates on the cardinal responsibilities.
25. He has a sense of humor.

June 12, 1970

Submitted by Pete Simonis, manager, Consumer Products Division.

Little Talk and Big Do

The value of an executive is measured by the results he produces, not the amount of time he spends talking things over.

The golfer who never bothers to keep his score may get a lot of exercise, but it's a poor way to improve his game. **There's nothing like an accurately kept score card to show whether you're playing a better game or just talking it.**

In business it's vital to know that you're playing a good game, not just talking it. The best way to check is to look at the results. What have you accomplished lately? What have you failed to do? What are you planning to accomplish next?

Try writing down what you actually accomplished last week. It may surprise you how few tangible achievements you have to show for the week's work. You may have done a lot of talking and listening in conferences, committee meetings, etc., but what came out of it? What actually got done?

A good executive doesn't confuse talk with action. He knows the importance of analyzing problems carefully, but he also knows that talk by itself isn't worth very much. The pay-off lies in action and results.

One of the best ways to encourage action—by yourself and those who work for you—is to keep score. Review regularly what you have done or failed to do recently. Set goals for what you and they intend to accomplish tomorrow, next week or next month. At your next review, see who succeeded in meeting his goals ... who failed and why.

And don't kid yourself—or let anyone else kid himself—into thinking that talking about a problem is the same as doing something about it. No amount of words can make up for a lack of results.

The best kind of reputation to have is for what one company president calls "little talk and big do." Keeping score is a good way to get it.

author unknown

April 15, 1978

Submitted by Jim Moncada.

Open Letter to an Employer

Dear Employer:

You see me every day ... with many faces
In many jobs ... possessing many skills
I am your employee.

I am employee number 584736,
Occupying a full-time position
Allocated to cost center 4938864.
But I have a name and distinct personality too,
Just like you.

If I complain about a petty thing,
Maybe I am saying more than you hear;
That I am a human being, with feelings.
And just like you,
I want attention too.

I'll accept criticism when I've done wrong,
But how I wish you would praise me
When I've done right.
I'm just like you,
I like compliments too.

When I belabor a point that seems
    unimportant,

Maybe what I am really saying
Is that I consider my opinion important.
And I'm just like you,
I want someone to listen to me too.

And when a new policy is announced
And I rebel against the change,
Maybe I honestly don't know why.
You see, I'm just like you,
I want my questions answered too.

Some days you smile and some days
    you frown,
And I understand:
Your life is full of good days and bad days.
Do you understand? I have good and bad
    days too.
I'm just like you.

And when I gripe about this or that,
Please don't write me off as a "troublemaker."
Haven't you ever griped before?
I'm just like you,
I need to let off steam too.
And if I ask something of you
And you know it can't be done,
Please don't try to "con" me.

Remember, I'm just like you,
I'd rather hear "no" than a "maybe" that
    never comes true.

If sometimes I don't show initiative, there
    may be a reason.
Maybe I'm confused and really don't
    understand
What you want me to do.
I'm just like you,
At times I need direction too.

Sometimes I rebel when you criticize me
For something I've done wrong—and you're
    probably right—
But the tone of your voice can destroy
    my day.
Remember, I'm just like you,
I want respect too.

If this letter sounds like I place all
    the blame on you,
Then I've failed to say what I mean.
I just wanted to tell you,
From my point of view:
All in all, I'm just like you.

September 15, 1979

Submitted by Bill Parrish, Communications Group/Schaumburg.

Humanagement

by Perry Pascarella
Reprint with permission from *IndustryWeek*, May 14, 1979.
Copyright, Penton Publishing, Inc. Cleveland, Ohio.

Management. That's perhaps the most misunderstood word in the dictionary.

Maybe if we called it "humanagement" we could better understand the managerial role. The term would remind us of what it is that is managed, for whom, by whom, and in what manner.

The successful organization of the future is going to depend increasingly on humanagement. People's rising expectations for themselves as workers, customers, stockholders, and members of the community will demand it. Those who lead our organization, therefore, will have to:

> Deal in all aspects of the business in ways that reflect their appreciation for people as whole persons.
> Find ways to enable workers to put more of themselves into the job and derive meaning and personal growth from it.
> Appreciate the human relationships that give an organization vitality and make it relevant to the outside world.
> Take an optimistic view of people, building on cooperation rather than conflict.
> Permit managers and executives to reveal themselves as human beings with fears, wants, and the need for growth.

Humanagement might sound like a soft style of managing—or not managing at all. This could not be further from the truth. Responding to people as people is far more difficult than following rules that treat them as simple reaction mechanisms. Acting as a complete person—and regarding others as such—is far more demanding than settling for distant relationships between two-dimensional figures.

The role of management was simpler when people were not a factor to be concerned with; when they were merely something to manipulate. But the equation for effective management is changing. With the need for more attention to the "people factor" the complexity of the managerial function increases exponentially.

Humanagement is a tougher challenge. But the executive who shifts to that role will find it matched with greater opportunity to express more of himself at work and derive more satisfaction from it.

May 15, 1980

Submitted by Brent Fox, Semiconductor Group.

Eleven Ways to Kill an Idea

Are you pestered by idea men? Have you longed for an effective way to get rid of them? Do you resent attempts to drag you out of the status quo? Rest easy. Here is a foolproof set of rules for dealing with do-gooders and their rest-disturbing ideas.

Let's organize what we know about *ideocide*. Daily, we have to kill ideas that may develop too far and cause us to think and work along unfamiliar paths. Here are the 11 most successful methods used to quash concepts and throttle thought. Do not try to think of other ways. It doesn't pay. They've probably been tried before, won't help, or are a waste of your precious time.

1. **Don't be ridiculous.** After all, if a new idea sounds absurd, why continue? If someone else thought of it first, the odds are that the idea is ridiculous anyway. (This concept is also known as Quasher's Law, named after Dr. Emil Quasher, who, as new products director for a large conglomerate, has so far turned down xerography, the hula hoop, microcircuits and radar.)

2. **We tried that before.** Beware of these defenses—"It was not used in the best way previously." "A new means of utilizing the idea has been thought of." Reply that it is just wasteful to repeat a past failure. Bellow loudly that no upstart could possibly think of a new way to use an old, probably ridiculous idea.

3. **We've never done it before.** Simple. If it has not been done before, there must be a good reason for not doing it now. Think of all the extra time, effort and money that will have to be mobilized to do something new.

4. **It costs too much.** Watch out, someone will say, "The final results will justify the costs involved." Don't be fooled; you know, deep down, that no one can know whether the results will justify anything. (Also known as Finagle's Principle, after Mrs. Rhoda Finagle, famous anthropologist, who, during her stay with a now-defunct group of Blund Islanders, convinced the natives that they could be more prosperous if they went back to yam farming and stopped making transistors for Japan and the United States.)

5. **It's too radical a change.** Almost self-explanatory. The wording may be unfamiliar, but it's an old concept. "Don't rock the boat." "Take it easy."

6. **We don't have the time.** Face it, if you wanted to work more hours, you would have thought of the idea yourself— or gotten a second job. It takes enough time to merely deal with the old things.

7. **We're too small for it.** Maybe, when we get to be bigger, we can handle it, but not now. Do not let yourself be convinced by the argument that this idea may help you get bigger. You can't be sure of that.

8. **Top management would never go for it.** You know how top management feels about things. You wouldn't be where you

are if you didn't. Maybe, when you are part of top management you will be more receptive to the idea.

9. **We'll be the laughingstock.** Be sure to say this quickly—without pausing. Continue by changing the subject. It is imperative that you do not let anyone continue what you have said with "All the way to the bank." This is not a joke, you know. Be careful of talk of innovation, profits, invention or creativity.

10. **Let's form a committee.** Most-used way to kill an idea. After all else has failed, if an idea continues to survive, use this. You know the classic story: An elephant is a jackass put together by a committee. Set up a committee to study the first committee. Set no deadlines. Outline no procedures. Let the committee go its own way, so that a thorough, proper study can be made.

11. **It's not my job.** This may be the best way. If it is not your job, why should you do it, or even listen to it? Do not be fooled into doing someone else's work.

author unknown

December 15, 1983

The One Minute Manager

Based on *The One Minute Manager*, by Dr. Kenneth Blanchard and Dr. Spencer Johnson, William Morrow & Co., Inc. 1982. From *Modern Material Handling* magazine.

Once there was a bright young man looking for an effective manager. He wanted to work for one. He wanted to become one. Not a "nice" manager whose people seemed to win while their organization lost. Nor a bottom-line-only manager seeking results only. But one who cared about people as well as results. For people who feel good about themselves produce results. After much searching, he found him: the One Minute Manager. And this is what he learned.

"I call myself a One Minute Manager because it takes me very little time to get very big results from people. I set One Minute Goals with people to make sure they know what I hold them accountable for and the performance I expect. Then I try to catch them doing something right so I can give them One Minute Praisings. Finally, when they have all the skills they need to do something right—and they don't do it—then I give a One Minute Reprimand. Otherwise, I leave them alone."

One Minute Goals: Feedback is the key to success. "I insist that my people set one goal for each key area of responsibility—three to six in all. They must record this goal, and its performance standard, in a single page—no more than 250 words. Anyone must be able to read this within a minute. They keep a copy and I keep one so we can both review it every day or so. And they see how well they are progressing toward their goal.

"You really have three choices," the One Minute Manager said. "First, you can hire winners. They are hard to find and cost money. Or, second, you can hire someone with the potential to be a winner. Then you must systematically train him to become one. Otherwise, you have only the third choice left—prayer. Many managers pray daily, 'I hope this person works out!'"

One Minute Praisings: Catch people doing something right—and help them reach their full potential. "When I hire a new person or give someone a new project or responsibility, I always tell them up front that I will give them feedback on performance. First, all praisings are given immediately when I find them doing something right. I don't wait for a performance review. Second, I specify exactly what they did right. Third, I praise them even if things are not going well for me. I tell them how good I feel about their performance, and how it helps the company. Then I stop for a moment of silence to let this sink in. I encourage them to keep it up. Then I shake their hands or put my hand on their shoulder.

"When you start training, praise each improvement, no matter how slight. The key is to catch them doing something nearly right—encouraging them until they do it exactly right. Do not reserve your praise until they do it perfectly—meanwhile focusing on their errors. That's when people will do as little as possible."

One Minute Reprimands: Sometimes you have to care enough to be tough. "If you are first tough on the behavior, and then supportive of the person, it works," the One Minute Manager continued. "First confirm the facts. Then give the reprimand immediately. Every reprimand has two parts. In the first half, I tell them exactly what they did wrong. I tell them how I feel about this mistake, in no uncertain terms. Then I stop for a moment to let this sink in. In the second half, I shake hands or touch them in a way that lets them know I am on their side. I remind them of how much I value them. I again show I think well of them as a person—but not of this specific performance. When the reprimand is over, it's over.

"When I deal with only one mistake at a time, the person can hear what I'm saying. He's not overwhelmed and, therefore, not on the defensive. And I always reprimand the behavior— I never attack the person's value."

February 2, 1984

A number of you have commented on the following article. I am sending it to all officers because I think it has substantive practical information. I call your attention to the first few lines of the article: "Most business failures do not stem from bad times. They come from poor management, and bad times just precipitate the crisis." We intend to do whatever is necessary to be successful in our various businesses, whether it is research and development spending, capital investment, etc. This article astutely calls our attention to certain key fundamentals that we must follow as we do this.

Tom Watson's Timeless Advice

by Thomas P. Murphy
Forbes, January 16, 1984.
Reprint by permission of *Forbes* magazine. ©Forbes Inc., 1984.

Most business failures do not stem from bad times. They come from poor management, and bad times just precipitate the crisis. It is during prosperous times—the kind we are coming into now—when we sow the seeds for the next bumper crop of bankruptcies.

I won't claim credit for the above observation. It came to me from the late Arthur K. (Dick) Watson, younger son of Thomas J. Watson, Sr., who founded IBM. His father, Dick told me, was serene and confident in bad times. While the rest of the world was wringing its hands or sitting on them, Tom Watson was forceful, confident and moving ahead. But prosperity unsettled him. He was uneasy with it. Like a good ship's engineer, he could detect those faint sounds of trouble others found easy to ignore.

As with so many stories I heard from Dick Watson during the years I worked for him, that story about his father puzzled me. I brooded about it: Why this curious fear of good times in business?

It was only after I had been through a whole economic cycle in the venture business that I realized why Tom Watson was unsettled by good times. They really are the times when we sow the seeds of our own later destruction. Recessions are blamed for failures, but in fact they are simply harvest times for the crops of seeds so lightheartedly sown in better days.

What are the signs? What is the difference between taking advantage of prosperity and being beguiled by it?

One sign, I think—it is a broad one—is taking on projects that have to succeed or they will take the company down with them. This is the kind of project some businessmen are tempted to undertake when things are booming and they are feeling especially macho. There is rarely justification for reacting like a poker player turned compulsive gambler and pushing everything into the center of the table. Businesses are just too hard to start to risk them when anything short of survival is at stake. Of course, I am not talking about start-up companies, which are always a gamble, but about drawing to an inside straight with the future of an established business.

Sloppiness, especially with people, is another seed that is sown in good times and reaped in bad. When orders are pouring in, and customers are courting the sales force, it is not hard to convince yourself that now is the time to scoop up everyone you can hire just to fill those orders. Don't do it. Lose orders. Lose share of market. But don't lose control of the business by bringing in weak personnel. Their ineptness, their lack of real loyalty and the inability to train them properly will hurt margins in good times and destroy the business in bad.

Though it shows up later in a business' life, bidding wars to get key personnel are another sign of trouble ahead. For example, this is the second year of boom times on Wall Street, and some wire houses are deep into this kind of thing. I have heard of successful stock salesmen who are demanding—and getting—$75,000 to $150,000 in upfront bonus money, as well as vice presidencies, as a reward for switching loyalties. But loyal for how long?

The millennium delusion is another of prosperity's beguiling traps. In the late 1960s, for instance, a great many otherwise intelligent business people fell into the delusion that prosperity was going to go on forever. With our superior understanding of economics, the reasoning went, the extremes of the business cycle were things of the past. Wise government policy would eliminate them. A sharp little recession in 1971 came as a nasty shock to this belief, but 1974 was the absolute killer. It was a killer because the logic of the millennium delusion leads people to overexpand and to become avid borrowers. And just at the time when they should be cutting back.

Until I had considerable personal experience in running businesses, old Tom Watson's words—as expressed to me by his son—didn't make much sense. How could prosperity be more dangerous than recession? Well it can be and it is. It was for good reason that Tom Watson, Sr., was regarded as one of the great businessmen of all times.

This column may sound fainthearted and old fogyish to ambitious young business people, eager to turn the rising economy to maximum advantage. To paraphrase: **Whom the gods would destroy, they first make overconfident.**

By the way, there is a flip side to Tom Watson's advice: Just as booms are a time for caution so are recessions a time for boldness. Watson knew this well. During the depths of the Depression, Watson, unwilling to lay people off, kept turning out punch-card machines for which there was no visible market. Then came the New Deal and Social Security, and IBM was the only company able to supply the needed equipment. IBM made a great step forward when other companies were pulling in their horns.

The time to be bold is when nearly everyone else is timid. But when nearly everyone else is bold, a little timidity is an excellent thing to have.

October 13, 1987

Work Like Fiends to Smash, Tamper and Fix

Machine and Tool Blue Book, February 1987.
Reprint permission granted.

Mottos and catchy phrases of advice abound in our society. Even automobiles carry bumper stickers that proclaim, "If It Ain't Broke, Don't Fix It" and "Don't Tamper with Success."

These slogans have captured the imagination of all types of people. It is difficult to disagree with their logic when the issue is such work as rolling a stone uphill rather than being smart and using a truck. Also, no one would fumble around or tamper with baby carriages or little red wagons as long as they are serviceable. Yes, the slogans carry a ring of common sense and weighty wisdom, and we do not quarrel with them. In fact, businessmen and politicians intone them with a majesty reserved for the utterances of omniscient oracles.

And yet, when viewed in the light of a nation's industrial capability—if taken at face value—they are utter nonsense, damaging and a block to the country's growth and productivity. **In every country, something needs fixing and tampering, and we need to work hard at it.** We need more positive slogans, more spirited beliefs and more vigorous action.

How do these slogans fail us? "Don't Fix It … " What nonsense! How will anything be improved if it's not fixed? We all used to mow our lawns with a manual lawn mower. It wasn't "broke" when everyone threw the beast on the garbage heap and replaced it with a mechanical mower. We sure "fixed" the manual back-breaker.

Procter & Gamble saved almost $1 billion in 1983 with an effort known as Deliberate Methods Change. The idea was that every process, every job could be improved even though it appeared to be beyond improvement. Nothing was "broke," but P&G's Deliberate Methods fixes packed their vaults with gold.

"Don't Tamper … " If we hadn't tampered with success, we'd still be in an agrarian society. Many countries were successful nations in the early nineteenth century. A bunch of malcontents had to tamper with the lovely farm country and develop steam engines, machine tools, farm machines and railroads—to say nothing of the social and cultural tampering in areas like health, education, social services and work design. Such tampering changed one type of successful country into another type of success. And we continue to tamper.

Given most countries' problems, we need to fix and tamper and work hard at doing so. **Business is in the throes of a transition from the comfortable world of the '50s to the realities of the '80s with dramatically increased global competition.** Nothing is the same, technologically, socially, culturally or financially. Every problem must be addressed with new ideas. Autocratic management must yield to industrial democracy; dictatorship must become leadership; and the human resource must be considered the most important resource.

We must break, smash, revise, fix, tamper and destroy everything that stands in the way of our becoming the most competitive business force in the world. Better products, better service, lower costs. It'll take guts and hard work, not little slogans. Put your faith in your people, continue to believe in the free enterprise system and remember the economist Peter Schumpetar's dictum, "Creative destructiveness is what capitalism is all about."

February 15, 1988

Submitted by Frank Lambrecht, Portable Products Division, Plantation, Florida.

Managing Crises, Chaos and Murphy

Excerpted from *Assembly Engineering*, July 1987.
By permission of the Publisher ©1987. Hitchcock Publishing Co.
All rights reserved.

When you see chaos and confusion on the factory floor, you can bet that Murphy's law is alive and working. Murphy's law asserts that whatever can go wrong will go wrong.

In recent years, managers seem to have become unduly enamored of crises and complexity. **They often find not only their greatest challenges, but also greatest satisfactions amidst turmoil.** In fact, some managers seem to cultivate crises.

Outstanding results are sometimes achieved through complex (though perhaps brilliant) solutions to manufacturing crises. But continued crisis warfare exacts a toll measured in confusion, disruptions, errors, and deteriorating morale. Eventually, these conditions can undermine even the most elegant manufacturing strategies unless some degree of harmony and simplicity are restored.

Management can compound the complexity and confusion inherent in manufacturing by totally disrupting existing systems. In recent years this has been further aggravated by the implementation of a high level of automation. Sophisticated automation increases both system complexity and the number of production variables that can possibly go wrong. Thus, we find management seeking increasingly sophisticated solutions to cover all of the problem variables.

Crises should most times be synonymous with failure. Managers should first seek to simplify the problem and reduce the number of variables. The resulting solution will be simpler, more harmonious, and less costly in terms of money and human disruption. Having simplified the problem as well as the solution, the manager can then plan to automate for improved productivity and efficiency.

It is alleged that many managers seem to be constantly tuning their instruments to combat crises, while the more successful are busy orchestrating harmonious productions.

April 8, 1985

Submitted by Carl Lindholm, executive vice president and general manager, Automotive and Industrial Electronics Group.

Can You Repeat 'Why' Five Times?

by Taiichi Ohno,
Excerpted from *Kaizen*, ©1986, by Masaaki Imai.
Reprinted by permission of the Publisher, McGraw-Hill, Inc.

It's easy to say, but difficult to practice.

1. "Why did the machine stop functioning?"

   "There was an overload, and the fuse blew."

2. "Why was there an overload?"

   "It was because lubrication of the bearing was not sufficient."

3. "Why was the lubrication not sufficient?"

   "Because the lubrication pump was not pumping sufficiently."

4. "Why was it not pumping sufficiently?"

   "The shaft of the pump was worn, and it was rattling."

5. "Why was the shaft worn out?"

   "There was no strainer attached, and this caused a metal scrap to get in."

This quotation jogged me to comment more fully on the tech-nique of continually asking "Why?" when reviewing problems or opportunities. The technique really applies to any kind of evaluative discussion, whether it is an operations review, strat-egy discussion or one-on-one conversation. This means not accepting generalities, but constantly asking questions that require generalities to be broken down into very specific reasons. This technique forces all parties to get to the heart of a partic-ular issue, to the critical path, to what must be done to face a problem or to truly be successful at seizing an opportunity.

This is the type of questioning technique that many of you do use, but that, unfortunately, many of us have not practiced to the degree we used to. It is an established practice of good management; it is not a new invention. The quotation demon-strates well the use of such a technique. Guess what? It's from a Japanese journal and highlights what I personally believe is one of the great strengths of Japanese managers—to understand the reasons why things happen so that they can fix, once and for all, those things that cause problems. They challenge new opportunity proposals in a similar way, which helps ensure that they will succeed. Continually asking "Why?" and "What do we do about it?" does not indicate lack of trust in others, but rather hones the process, and trains new managers and employees to approach problem-solving in a manner that yields substantial results.

BW

December 11, 1985

In my April 8, 1985 philosophy memo I sent out the "Why?" questioning technique, which attacks a problem by asking, in a series of questions, why a particular thing happened. Many times I find that the reason we don't get to the bottom of a problem and solve it is because we haven't asked that question often enough, and taken fundamental action to eliminate the problem. Carlton Braun vice president and director of Motorola Manufacturing Institute sent me the following article, which is about an extension of that technique that helps organizations to use the "Why?" questioning, and to achieve fundamental "fixes". The article is useful because it can be a tool to further reinforce the problem-solving technique of using the multiple "Why-Why" question.

Organize Your Thinking with a Why-Why Diagram

By illustrating chains of symptoms and causes, one can see manageable parts of larger problems
by Howard H. Bailie
Reprinted from *Quality Progress*, December 1985.

Bailie is a project advisor for Westinghouse Electric Corporation, Nuclear Operations Division, Pittsburgh, Penn. He has a B.S. in engineering physics and a B.S. in mechanical engineering, both from the University of Illinois. He is a certified quality engineer and has been approved by the International Atomic Energy Agency (IAEA) for international quality-assurance consulting activities.

Change is the order of the business day. Technology is growing at an accelerating pace. We see a continuing upward trend in the number of new businesses formed and being spun off. But, while entrepreneurship abounds, so do associated problem situations.

New business environments bring new groups of people together. When assembled to solve problems, these people need time to learn how to work together. The learning periods are often filled with stress as the groups struggle to evaluate directions in uncharted territories. There are always time and capital resource constraints—but help is on the way. Why-why diagrams are a good method for organizing the thinking of problem-solving groups.[1]

Our appreciation of the value of why-why diagrams developed in work with quality circles. As in many business situations, circles are made up of people with diverse backgrounds who are assembled to solve problems. We have found that some circles go for months without clearly defining the full scope of their group problem. Others find themselves caught in a web of causes that contribute to their problem, and they struggle week after week to sort them out. Trying to pull all of the pieces together sometimes ends only in pulling the circles apart.

The various names by which problem-solving groups are known—quality circles, task forces, fact-finding committees—make little difference. They usually reflect differences in the structure and terminology used in the work environment, but they all have the common objective of resolving problem situations in a specified time framework.

Difficulties with problem-solving groups often arise when they attempt to deal with matters of broad scope. These occur, for example, when different groups of people and multiple departmental interfaces are involved in the problem. Difficulties also can be found when working on administrative software in larger companies, as this is an area that frequently ties into company policies and management decisions. Other types of difficulties will be present when working with situations that are loosely structured, or poorly defined, or where facts are simply unknown. What can a why-why diagram do to help with these conditions?

A why-why diagram starts with a statement of the problem to be solved. This is followed by statements of the causes believed to contribute to that problem. The causes may be separate or interrelated but, in either case, should be written in the form of a single statement. Here's a simple example:

Problem   **Causes**

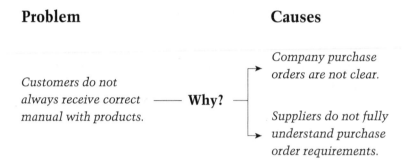

Each of the cause statements on the right side now becomes a new problem statement, and we again ask ourselves why these conditions exist.

This searching leads to a network of reasons why the original condition on the left occurred. Common causes are interconnected, and statements which arrive at logical conclusions are termed end points. An end point represents the root cause of a particular branch to the problem. When the entire diagram is completed, end points identify the areas that need to be addressed to resolve the problem. Solutions to the problem are reached, therefore, by acting on the improvements needed for each end point and then carrying out more detailed improvement steps at the intermediate points on the diagram. The above example is expanded to show a complete network in the diagram featured in Figure 1.

The completed why-why diagram is basically a logic diagram that outlines the elements of a systematic approach to resolving a problem. It flows from left to right or top to bottom.

Generally, statements from the bottom of a horizontal line apply as causes for all statements leading down to them. In Figure 1, for example, "Buyers need additional training" is one cause of the three statements from the top ("Company purchase orders are not clear," "Requirements for manuals are not clear," and "Changes do not highlight impact on manuals.")

Developing a why-why diagram is not always a peaceful process. Different individuals will have strong views on particulars of the contributing problems and causes, as well as of their importance. This is a normal, healthy reflection of the background and experience the group brings to the assessment. It does, however, underscore the importance of gathering sufficient data to support each of the statements on the diagram. This data-gathering activity is the key to the group achieving valid conclusions and should occupy the larger part of their time. A second important point for the evaluation process is the careful selection of a qualified group leader who will keep the group on course.

The facts entered, the problem-solving group will want to thoroughly review the layout of its why-why diagram before going on to solutions. Normally, this review should be a refining process that seeks to eliminate subjective statements that cannot be reasonably supported. These may be views of a problem or cause in the chain that the group believes to be true, but does not have the hard evidence to back up. Also at this time, the group should assure that the meaning of each of the problem/cause statements will be clear to all people who will be involved in reviewing the results. To maintain focus and aid reader understanding, information of a minor nature should be minimized to avoid cluttering the diagram.

Once the layout of the why-why diagram is complete, the problem-solving group will want to examine the end points. A Pareto analysis should be performed to determine the significant contributors to the primary problem. The group may want to

Figure 1. Why–Why Diagram

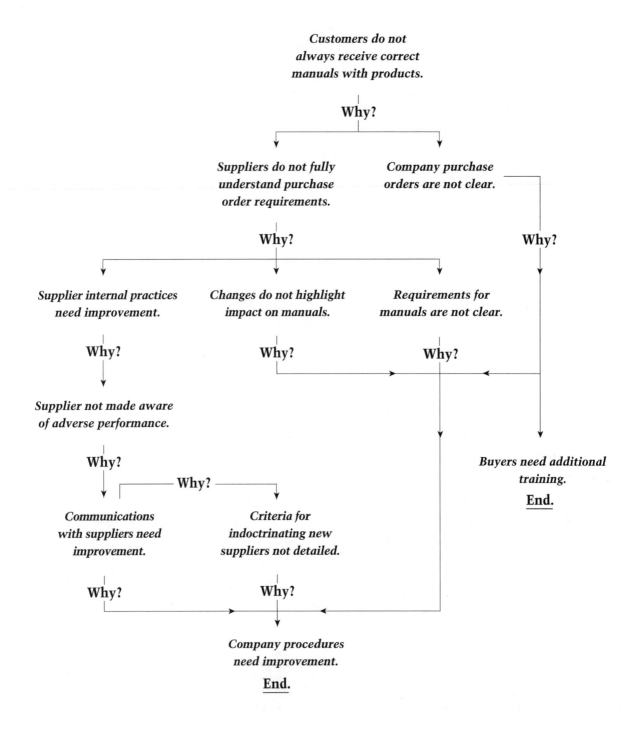

The Philosophy Memos

emphasize immediate action on only the four or five most important contributors. Additional details always can be discussed with those involved, or less important items addressed at a later date.

When considering end points and problem solutions, an additional consideration is worth mentioning. **Problem statements that stretch out toward the bottom to reach an end point are more difficult to resolve than those with short chains.** As can be seen in Figure 1, there are many more aspects that have to be considered when traveling from the root cause of "Company procedures need improvement" to the primary problem on the top, than when traveling from the end point of "Buyers need additional training." Furthermore, the farther to the bottom the root cause falls, the greater the possibility that you are into issues involving management policies and decisions. Such areas can be difficult to handle, as they frequently involve considerations on which the group has limited information. While policy matters can be of prime importance in achieving a permanent solution to problems, they normally take longer to resolve.

The remarks on long end points are not intended to minimize their consideration. They're meant to point out that why-why diagrams help problem-solving groups to recognize the broad network of problem sources, their interrelationship, and the most promising directions to take in pursuing long- and short-range solutions. As a visual aid developed by group consensus, the diagram assists in avoiding the frustrations that can result when, after much work, the problem-solving group gets that uneasy feeling that the size and shape of the trees are obscuring the forest.

In a less specific application, a why-why diagram can be used to sketch out the possible elements to situations that are still under development, such as the start-up of new operations. In addition to laying out those portions of a problem that are understood, the diagram can include best- and worst-case scenarios. This will help to plot directions to take. When new information is gained, it can be added to a revised diagram and refine actions identified.

As a final note, the why-why diagram is an excellent tool for use in management presentations. It pulls together a picture of the primary elements considered in examining a problem and shows the manner in which they relate. With such an aid, group members are in a position to concisely describe the results of their evaluation efforts and to offer recommendations on the most desirable steps to take. Regardless of the outcome, you will bring a new level of understanding to problem situations through good organization of your thinking.

Reference

1. R.J. Barra, *Putting Quality Circles to Work* (New York: McGraw-Hill, 1983).

May 14, 1984

Following along after my March 15 1984 memo to you on "Quality of Performance — High Expectation Levels,"* I have enclosed a copy of a Harvard Business Review article titled Pygmalion in Management *that was sent to me by Bob Bigony of the Communications Sector. This article deals very well with the reaction of organizations to the setting of high expectation levels, and the issue of treating people in a manner that encourages the achievement of those high expectations.*

I know you will be interested in reading it, and will be able to relate to many of the examples used. Note the date of the article — 1969. There is no new, monumental discovery here, just good common-sense management treatment of individuals and our expectations of them.

Pygmalion in Management

A manager's expectations are the key to a subordinate's performance and development

Reprinted by permission of *Harvard Business Review*. Pigmalion in Management by J. Sterling Livingston, July/August 1969. Copyright ©1969 by the President and Fellows of Harvard College; all rights reserved.

FOREWORD

Pygmalion was a sculptor in Greek mythology who carved a statue of a beautiful woman that subsequently was brought to life. George Bernard Shaw's play, *Pygmalion* (the basis for the musical hit, *My Fair Lady*), has a somewhat similar theme; the essence is that one person, by self effort and will, can transform another person. And in the world of management, many executives play Pygmalion-like roles in developing able subordinates and in stimulating their performance. What is the secret of their success? How are they different from managers who fail to develop top-notch subordinates? And what are the implications of all this for the problem of excessive turnover and disillusionment among talented young people in business? Such are the questions discussed here. The title of the article was inspired by *Pygmalion in the Classroom*, a book by Robert Rosenthal and Lenore Jacobson, that describes the effect of expectations on the intellectual development of children.

---

* *See page 333 for this memo.*

Mr. Livingston is professor of business administration at the Harvard Business School, where he is studying the early careers in business of college graduates. In addition to his observation of management in many companies, he draws on extensive personal experience as an executive. He is president of Sterling Institute, which he founded; he was also the founder of Management Systems Corporation and for many years was its president. Other organizations he has served as chief executive are Peat, Marwick, Livingston & Co., Logistics Management Institute, Technology Fund of Puerto Rico, Harbridge House, Inc., and Tamarind Reef Corporation.

In George Bernard Shaw's *Pygmalion*, Eliza Doolittle explains:

"You see, really and truly, apart from the things anyone can pick up (the dressing and the proper way of speaking, and so on), the difference between a lady and a flower girl is not how she behaves, but how she's treated. I shall always be a flower girl to Professor Higgins, because he always treats me as a flower girl, and always will; but I know I can be a lady to you, because you always treat me as a lady, and always will."

Some managers always treat their subordinates in a way that leads to superior performance. But most managers, like Professor Higgins, unintentionally treat their subordinates in a way that leads to lower performance than they are capable of achieving. The way managers treat their subordinates is subtly influenced by what they expect of them. If managers' expectations are high, productivity is likely to be excellent. If their expectations are low, productivity is likely to be poor. It is as though there were a law that caused subordinates' performance to rise or fall to meet managers' expectations.

The powerful influence of one person's expectations on another's behavior has long been recognized by physicians and behavioral scientists and, more recently, by teachers. But heretofore the importance of managerial expectations for individual and group performance has not been widely understood. I have documented this phenomenon in a number of case studies prepared during the past decade for major industrial concerns. These cases and other evidence available from scientific research now reveal:

› What managers expect of their subordinates and the way they treat them largely determine their performance and career progress.

› A unique characteristic of superior managers is their ability to create high performance expectations that subordinates fulfill.

› Less effective managers fail to develop similar expectations, and, as a consequence, the productivity of their subordinates suffers.

› Subordinates, more often than not, appear to do what they believe they are expected to do.

IMPACT ON PRODUCTIVITY

One of the most comprehensive illustrations of the effect of managerial expectations on productivity is recorded in studies of the organizational experiment undertaken in 1961 by Alfred Oberlander, manager of the Rockaway District Office of the Metropolitan Life Insurance Company.[1] He had observed that outstanding insurance agencies grew faster than average or poor agencies and that new insurance agents performed better in outstanding agencies than in average or poor agencies, regardless of their sales aptitude. He decided, therefore, to group his superior agents in one unit to stimulate their performance and to provide a challenging environment in which to introduce new salespeople.

Accordingly, Oberlander assigned his six best agents to work with his best assistant manager, an equal number of average producers to work with an average assistant manager, and the remaining low producers to work with the least able manager. He then asked the superior group to produce two thirds of the premium volume achieved by the entire agency the previous year. He described the results as follows:

"Shortly after this selection had been made, the men in the agency began referring to this select group as a 'super-staff' since, due to the fact that we were operating this group as a unit, their esprit de corps was very high. Their production efforts over the first 12 weeks far surpassed our most optimistic expectations ... proving that groups of men of sound ability can be motivated beyond their apparently normal productive capacities when the problems created by the poor producer are eliminated from the operation.

"Thanks to this fine result, over-all agency performance improved 40 percent and stayed at this figure.

"In the beginning of 1962 when, through expansion, we appointed another assistant manager and assigned him a staff, we again utilized this same concept, arranging the men once more according to their productive capacity.

"The assistant managers were assigned ... according to their ability, with the most capable assistant manager receiving the best group, thus playing strength to strength. Our agency over-all production again improved by about 25-30 percent, and so this staff arrangement was continued until the end of the year.

"Now in this year of 1963, we found upon analysis that there were so many men ... with a potential of half a million dollars or more that only one staff remained of those men in the agency who were not considered to have any chance of reaching the half-million-dollar mark."[2]

Although the productivity of the "super-staff" improved dramatically, it should be pointed out that the productivity of those in the lowest unit, "who were not considered to have any chance of reaching the half-million-dollar mark," actually declined and that attrition among them increased. The performance of the superior agents rose to meet their managers' expectations, while that of the weaker ones declined as predicted.

Self-fulfilling prophesies

However, the "average" unit proved to be an anomaly. Although the district manager expected only average performance from this group, its productivity increased significantly. This was because the assistant manager in charge of the group refused to believe that he was less capable than the manager of the "super-staff" or that the agents in the top group had any greater ability than the agents in this group. He insisted in discussions with his agents that every person in the middle group had greater potential than those in the "super-staff," lacking only their years of experience in selling insurance. He stimulated his agents to accept the challenge of out-performing the "super-staff." As a result, in each year the middle group increased its productivity by a higher percentage than the "super-staff" did (although it never attained the dollar volume of the top group).

It is of special interest that the self-image of the manager of the "average" unit did not permit him to accept others' treatment of him as an "average" manager, just as Eliza Doolittle's image of herself as a lady did not permit her to accept others' treatment of her as a flower girl. The assistant manager transmitted his own strong feelings of efficacy to his agents, created mutual expectancy of high performance, and greatly stimulated productivity.

Comparable results occurred when a similar experiment was made at another office of the company. Further confirmation comes from a study of the early managerial success of 49 college graduates who were management-level employees of an operating company of the American Telephone & Telegraph Co. David E. Berlew and Douglas T. Hall of the Massachusetts Institute of Technology examined the career progress of these managers over a period of five years and discovered that their relative success, as measured by salary increases and the company's estimate of each one's performance and potential, depended largely on the company's expectations of them.[3]

The influence of one person's expectations on another's behavior is by no means a business discovery. More than half a century ago, Albert Moll concluded from his clinical experience that subjects behaved as they believed they were expected to.[4] The phenomenon he observed, in which "the prophecy causes its own fulfillment," has recently become a subject of considerable scientific interest. For example:

In a series of scientific experiments, Robert Rosenthal of Harvard University has demonstrated that a "teacher's expectation for her pupils' intellectual competence can come to serve as an educational self-fulfilling prophecy."[5]

An experiment in a summer Headstart program for 60 preschoolers compared the performance of pupils under (a) teachers who had been led to expect relatively slow learning by their children, and (b) teachers who had been led to believe their children had excellent intellectual ability and learning capacity. Pupils of the second group of teachers learned much faster.[6]

Moreover, the healing professions have long recognized that a physician's or psychiatrist's expectations can have a formidable influence on a patient's physical or mental health. What takes place in the minds of the patients and the healers, particularly when they have congruent expectations, may determine the outcome. For instance, the havoc of a doctor's pessimistic prognosis has often been observed. Again, it is well known that the efficacy of a new drug or a new treatment can be greatly influenced by the physician's expectations—a result referred to by the medical profession as a "placebo effect."

Pattern of failure

When salespersons are treated by their managers as superpeople, as the "super-staff" was at Metropolitan Rockaway District Office, they try to live up to that image and do what they know supersalespersons are expected to do. But when the agents with poor productivity records are treated by their managers as not having "any chance" of success, as the low producers at Rockaway were, this negative expectation also becomes a managerial self-fulfilling prophecy.

Unsuccessful salespersons have great difficulty maintaining their self-image and self-esteem. In response to low managerial expectations, they typically attempt to prevent additional damage to their egos by avoiding situations that might lead to greater failure. They either reduce the number of sales calls they make or avoid trying to "close" sales when that might result in further painful rejection, or both. Low expectations and damaged egos lead them to behave in a manner that increases the probability of failure, thereby fulfilling their managers' expectations. Let me illustrate:

Not long ago I studied the effectiveness of branch bank managers at a West Coast bank with over 500 branches. The managers who had had their lending authority reduced because of high rates of loss became progressively less effective. To prevent further loss of authority, they turned to making only "safe" loans. This action resulted in losses of business to competing banks and a relative decline in both deposits and profits at their branches. Then, to reverse that decline in deposits and earnings, they often "reached" for loans and became almost irrational in their acceptance of questionable credit risks. Their actions were not so much a matter of poor judgment as an expression of their willingness to take desperate risks in the hope of being able to avoid further damage to their egos and to their careers.

Thus in response to the low expectations of their supervisors, who had reduced their lending authority, they behaved in a manner that led to larger credit losses. They appeared to do what they believed they were expected to do, and their supervisors' expectations became self-fulfilling prophecies.

POWER OF EXPECTATIONS

Managers cannot avoid the depressing cycle of events that flow from low expectations merely by hiding their feelings from subordinates. If managers believe subordinates will perform poorly, it is virtually impossible for them to mask their expectations, because the message usually is communicated unintentionally, without conscious action on their part.

Indeed, managers often communicate most when they believe they are communicating least. For instance, when they say nothing—become "cold" and "uncommunicative"—it usually is a sign that they are displeased by a subordinate or believe that he or she is "hopeless." The silent treatment communicates negative feelings even more effectively, at times, than a tongue-lashing does. What seems to be critical in the communication of expectations is not what the boss says, so much as the *way he or she behaves*. Indifferent and non-committal treatment, more often than not, is the kind of treatment that communicates low expectations and leads to poor performance.

Common Illusions

Managers are more effective in communicating low expectations to their subordinates than in communicating high expectations to them, even though most managers believe exactly the opposite. It usually is astonishingly difficult for them to recognize the clarity with which they transmit negative feelings.

To illustrate again:

The Rockaway district manager vigorously denied that he had communicated low expectations to the agents in the poorest group who, he believed, did not have "any chance" of becoming high producers. Yet the message was clearly received by those agents. A typical case was that of an agent who resigned from the low unit. When the district manager told the agent that he was sorry he was leaving, the agent replied, "No, you're not; you're glad." Although the district manager previously had said nothing to the man, he had unintentionally communicated his low expectations to his agents through his indifferent manner. Subsequently, the agents who were assigned to the lowest unit interpreted the assignment as equivalent to a request for their resignation.

One of the company's agency managers established superior, average, and low units, even though he was convinced that he had no superior or outstanding subordinates. "All my assistant managers and agents are either average or incompetent," he explained to the Rockaway district manager. Although he tried to duplicate the Rockaway results, his low opinions of his agents were communicated—not so subtly—to them. As a result, the experiment failed.

Positive feelings, on the other hand, often do not come through clearly enough. For example:

Another insurance agency manager copied the organizational changes made at the Rockaway District Office, grouping the salespeople he rated highly with the best manager, the average salespeople with an average manager, and so on. However, improvement did not result from the move. The Rockaway district manager therefore investigated the situation. He discovered that the assistant manager in charge of the high-performance unit was unaware that his manager considered him to be the best. In fact, he and the other agents doubted that the agency manager really believed there was any difference in their abilities. This agency manager was a stolid, phlegmatic, unemotional man who treated his agents in a rather pedestrian way. Since high expectations had not been communicated to them, they did not understand the reason for the new organization and could not see any point in it. Clearly, the way a manager treats his or her subordinates, not the way he organizes them, is the key to high expectations and high productivity.

Impossible dreams

Managerial expectations must pass the test of reality before they can be translated into performance. To become self-fulfilling prophecies, expectations must be made of sterner stuff than the power of positive thinking or generalized confidence in one's subordinates—helpful as these concepts may be for some other purposes. Subordinates will not be motivated to reach high levels of productivity unless they consider the boss's high expectations realistic and achievable. If they are encouraged to strive for unattainable goals, they eventually give up trying and settle for results that are lower than they are capable of achieving. The experience of a large electrical manufacturing company demonstrates this; the company discovered that production actually declined if production quotas were set too high, because the workers simply stopped trying to meet them. In other words, the practice of "dangling the carrot just beyond the donkey's reach," endorsed by many managers, is not a good motivational device.

Scientific research by David C. McClelland of Harvard University and John W. Atkinson of the University of Michigan[7] has demonstrated that the relationship of motivation to expectancy varies in the form of a bell-shaped curve like this:

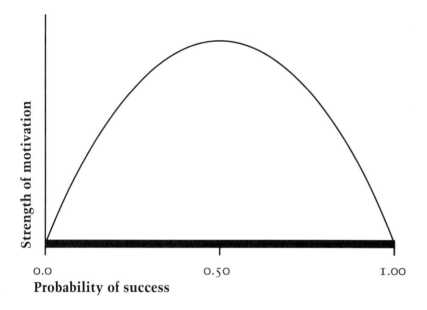

Probability of success

The degree of motivation and effort rises until the expectancy of success reaches 50 percent, then begins to fall even though the expectancy of success continues to increase. No motivation or response is aroused when the goal is perceived as being either virtually certain or virtually impossible to attain.

Moreover, as Berlew and Hall have pointed out, if a subordinate fails to meet performance expectations that are close to his or her own level of aspirations, he or she will lower personal performance goals and standards, performance will tend to drop off, and negative attitudes will develop toward the task activity or job.[8] It is therefore not surprising that failure of subordinates to meet the unrealistically high expectations of their managers leads to high rates of attrition either voluntary or involuntary.

Secret of superiority

Something takes place in the minds of superior managers that does not occur in the minds of those who are less effective. While superior managers are consistently able to create high performance expectations that their subordinates fulfill, weaker managers are not successful in obtaining a similar response. What accounts for the difference?

The answer, in part, seems to be that superior managers have greater confidence than other managers in their own ability to develop the talents of their subordinates. Contrary to what might be assumed, the high expectations of superior managers are based primarily on what they think about themselves — about their own ability to select, train, and motivate their subordinates. What managers believe about themselves subtly influences what they believe about their subordinates, what they expect of them, and how they treat them. If they have confidence in their ability to develop and stimulate them to high levels of performance, they will expect much of them and will treat them with confidence that their expectations will be met. But if they have doubts about their ability to stimulate them, they will expect less of them and will treat them with less confidence.

Stated in another way, the superior managers' record of success and their confidence in their ability give their high expectations credibility. As a consequence, their subordinates accept these expectations as realistic and try hard to achieve them.

The importance of what a manager believes about his or her training and motivational ability is illustrated by "Sweeney's Miracle,"[9] a managerial and educational self-fulfilling prophecy:

James Sweeney taught industrial management and psychiatry at Tulane University, and he also was responsible for the operation of the Biomedical Computer Center there. Sweeney believed that he could teach even a poorly educated man to be a capable computer operator. George Johnson, former hospital porter, became janitor at the computer center; he was chosen by Sweeney to prove his conviction. In the morning, George Johnson performed his janitorial duties, and in the afternoon Sweeney taught him about computers.

Johnson was learning a great deal about computers when someone at the university concluded that, to be a computer operator, one had to have a certain IQ score. Johnson was tested, and his IQ indicated that he would not be able to learn to type, much less operate a computer.

But Sweeney was not convinced. He threatened to quit unless Johnson was permitted to learn to program and operate the computer. Sweeney prevailed, and he is still running the computer center. Johnson is now in charge of the main computer room and is responsible for training new employees to program and operate the computer.

Sweeney's expectations were based on what he believed about his own teaching ability, not on Johnson's learning credentials. What a manager believes about his or her ability to train and motivate subordinates clearly is the foundation on which realistically high managerial expectations are built.

The critical early years

Managerial expectations have their most magical influence on young people. As subordinates mature and gain experience, their self-images gradually harden, and they begin to see themselves as their career records imply. Their own aspirations, and the expectations of their superiors, become increasingly controlled by the "reality" of their past performance. It becomes more and more difficult for them, and for their managers, to generate mutually high expectations unless they have outstanding records.

Incidentally, the same pattern occurs in school. Rosenthal's experiments with educational self-fulfilling prophecies consistently demonstrate that teachers' expectations are more effective at influencing intellectual growth in younger children than in older children. In the lower grade levels, particularly in the first and second grades, the effects of teachers' expectations are dramatic.[10] In the upper grade levels, teachers' prophecies seem to have little effect on children's intellectual growth, although they do affect their motivation and attitude toward school. While the declining influence of teachers' expectations cannot be completely explained, it is reasonable to conclude that younger children are more malleable, have fewer fixed notions about their abilities, and have less well-established reputations in the schools. As they grow, particularly if they are assigned to "tracks" on the basis of their records, as is now often done in public schools, their beliefs about their intellectual ability and their teachers' expectations of them begin to harden and become more resistant to influence by others.

Key to future performance

The early years in a business organization, when young people can be strongly influenced by managerial expectations, are critical in determining their future performance and career progress. This is shown by a study at American Telephone & Telegraph Co.:

> *Berlew and Hall found that what the company initially expected of 49 college graduates who were management-level employees was the most critical factor in their subsequent performance and success. The researchers concluded that the correlation between how much a company expects of an employee in the first year and how much that employee contributes during the next five years was "too compelling to be ignored."[11]*

Subsequently, the two men studied the career records of 18 college graduates who were hired as management trainees in another of the American Telephone & Telegraph Co.'s operating companies. Again they found that both expectations and performance in the first year correlated consistently with later performance and success.[12]

Berlew and Hall summarized their research by stating:

"Something important is happening in the first year ... Meeting high company expectations in the critical first year leads to the internalization of positive job attitudes and high standards; these attitudes and standards, in turn, would first lead to and be reinforced by strong performance and success in later years. It should also follow that a new manager who meets the challenge of one highly demanding job will be given subsequently a more demanding job, and his level of contribution will rise as he responds to the company's growing expectations of him. The key ... is the concept of the first year as a critical period for learning, a time when the trainee is uniquely ready to develop or change in the direction of the company's expectations."[13]

Most influential boss

A young person's first manager is likely to be the most influential person in his or her career. If this manager is unable or unwilling to develop the skills the young employee needs to perform effectively, the latter will set lower personal standards than he or she is capable of achieving, that person's self-image will be impaired, and he or she will develop negative attitudes toward the job, the employer, and—in all probability—his or her career in business. Since the chances of building a successful career with the employer will decline rapidly, he or she will leave, if that person has high aspirations, in hope of finding a better opportunity. If, on the other hand, the manager helps the employee to achieve maximum potential, he or she will build the foundation of a successful career. To illustrate:

With few exceptions, the most effective branch managers at a large West Coast bank were mature people in their forties and fifties. The bank's executive explained that it took considerable time for a person to gain the knowledge, experience, and judgment required to handle properly credit risks, customer relations, and employee relations.

However, one branch manager, ranked in the top 10 percent of the managers in terms of effectiveness (which included branch profit growth, deposit growth, scores on administrative audits, and subjective rankings by superiors), was only 27 years old. This young person had been made a branch manager at 25, and in two years had improved not only the performance of the branch substantially but also developed a younger assistant manager so that the assistant, in turn, was made a branch manager at 25.

The assistant had had only average grades in college, but in just four years at the bank had been assigned to work with two branch managers who were remarkably effective teachers. The first boss, who was recognized throughout the bank for unusual skill in developing young people, did not believe that it took years to gain the knowledge and skill needed to become an effective banker. After two years, the young person was made assistant manager at a branch headed by another executive, who also was an effective developer of subordinates. Thus it was that the young person, when promoted to head a branch, confidently followed the model of two previous superiors in operating the branch, quickly established a record of outstanding performance, and trained an assistant to assume responsibility early.

For confirming evidence of the crucial role played by a person's first bosses, let us turn to selling, since performance in this area is more easily measured than in most managerial areas. Consider the following investigations:

In a study of the careers of 100 insurance salesmen who began work with either highly competent or less-than-competent agency managers, the Life Insurance Agency Management Association found that men with average sales aptitude test scores were nearly five times as likely to succeed under managers with good performance records as under managers with poor records; and men with superior sales aptitude scores were found to be twice as likely to succeed under high-performing managers as under low-performing managers.[14]

The Metropolitan Life Insurance Company determined in 1960 that differences in the productivity of new insurance agents who had equal sales aptitudes could be accounted for only by differences in the ability of managers in the offices to which they were assigned. Men whose productivity was high in relation to their aptitude test scores invariably were employed in offices that had production records among the top third in the company. Conversely, men whose productivity was low in relation to their test scores typically were in the least successful offices. After analyzing all the factors that might have accounted for these variations, the company concluded that differences in the performance of new men were due primarily to differences in the "proficiency in sales training and direction" of the local managers.[15]

A study I conducted of the performance of automobile salesmen in Ford dealerships in New England revealed that superior salesmen were concentrated in a few outstanding dealerships. For instance, 10 of the top 15 salesmen in New England were in 3 (out of approximately 200) of the dealerships in this region; and 5 of the top 15 men were in one highly successful dealership; yet 4 of these men previously had worked for other dealers without achieving outstanding sales records. There seemed to be little doubt that the training and motivational skills of managers in the outstanding dealerships were the critical factor.

Astute selection

While success in business sometimes appears to depend on the "luck of the draw," more than luck is involved when a young person is selected by a superior manager. Successful managers do not pick their subordinates at random or by the toss of a coin. They are careful to select only those who they "know" will succeed. As Metropolitan's Rockaway district manager, Alfred Oberlander, insisted: "Every man who starts with us is going to be a top-notch life insurance man, or he would not have received an invitation to join the team."[16]

When pressed to explain how they "know" whether a person will be successful, superior managers usually end up by saying something like, "The qualities are intangible, but I know them when I see them." They have difficulty being explicit because their selection process is intuitive and is based on interpersonal intelligence that is difficult to describe. The key seems to be that they are able to identify subordinates with whom they can probably work effectively—people with whom they are compatible and whose body chemistry agrees with their own. They make mistakes, of course. But they "give up" on a subordinate slowly because that means "giving up" on themselves—on their judgment and ability in selecting, training, and motivating people. Less effective managers select subordinates more quickly and give up on them more easily, believing that the inadequacy is that of the subordinate, not of themselves.

Developing young people

Observing that his company's research indicates that "initial corporate expectations for performance (with real responsibility) mold subsequent expectations and behavior," R.W. Walters, Jr., director of college employment at the American Telephone & Telegraph Co., contends that: "Initial bosses of new college hires must be the best in the organization."[17] Unfortunately, however, most companies practice exactly the opposite.

Rarely do new graduates work closely with experienced middle managers or upper-level executives. Normally, they are bossed by first-line managers who tend to be the least experienced and least effective in the organization. While there are exceptions, first-line managers generally are either "old pros" who have been judged as lacking competence for higher levels of responsibility, or they are younger people who are making the transition from "doing" to "managing." Often, these managers lack the knowledge and skills required to develop the productive capabilities of their subordinates. As a consequence, many college graduates begin their careers in business under the worst possible circumstances. Since they know their abilities are not being developed or used, they quite naturally soon become negative toward their jobs, employers, and business careers.

Although most top executives have not yet diagnosed the problem, industry's greatest challenge by far is the underdevelopment, underutilization, and ineffective management and use of its most valuable resource—its young managerial and professional talent.

Disillusion & turnover

The problem posed to corporate management is underscored by the sharply rising rates of attrition among young managerial and professional personnel. Turnover among managers one to five years out of college is almost twice as high now as it was a decade ago, and five times as high as two decades ago. Three out of five companies surveyed by *Fortune* magazine in the fall of 1968 reported that turnover rates among young managers and professionals were higher than five years ago.[18] While the high level of economic activity and the shortage of skilled personnel have made job-hopping easier, the underlying causes of high attrition, I am convinced, are underdevelopment and underutilization of a work force that has high career aspirations.

The problem can be seen in its extreme form in the excessive attrition rates of college and university graduates who begin their careers in sales positions. Whereas the average company loses about 50 percent of its new college and university graduates within three to five years, attrition rates as high as 40 percent in the *first* year are common among college graduates who accept sales positions in the average company. This attrition stems primarily, in my opinion, from the failure of first-line managers to teach new college recruits what they need to know to be effective sales representatives.

As we have seen, young people who begin their careers working for less-than-competent sales managers are likely to have records of low productivity. When rebuffed by their customers and considered by their managers to have little potential for success, the young people naturally have great difficulty in maintaining their self-esteem. Soon they find little personal satisfaction in their jobs and, to avoid further loss of self-respect, leave their employers for jobs that look more promising. Moreover, as reports about the high turnover and disillusionment of those who embarked on sales careers filter back to college campuses, new graduates become increasingly reluctant to take jobs in sales.

Thus ineffective first-line sales management sets off a sequence of events that ends with college and university graduates avoiding careers in selling. To a lesser extent, the same pattern is duplicated in other functions of business, as evidenced by the growing trend of college graduates to pursue careers in "more meaningful" occupations, such as teaching and government service.

A serious "generation gap" between bosses and subordinates is another significant cause of breakdown. Many managers resent the abstract, academic language and narrow rationalization typically used by recent graduates. As one manager expressed it to me: "For God's sake, you need a lexicon even to talk with these kids." Noncollege managers often are particularly resentful, perhaps because they feel threatened by the bright young people with book-learned knowledge that they do not understand.

For whatever reason, the "generation gap" in many companies is eroding managerial expectations of new college graduates. For instance, I know of a survey of management attitudes in one of the nation's largest companies which revealed that 54 percent of its first-line and second-line managers believed that new college recruits were "not as good as they were five years ago." Since what managers expect of subordinates influences the way they treat them, it is understandable that new graduates often develop negative attitudes toward their jobs and their employers. Clearly, low managerial expectations and hostile attitudes are not the basis for effective management of new people entering business.

Conclusion

Industry has not developed effective first-line managers fast enough to meet its needs. As a consequence, many companies are underdeveloping their most valuable resource—talented young men and women. They are incurring heavy attrition costs and contributing to the negative attitudes young people often have about careers in business.

For top executives in industry who are concerned with the productivity of their organizations and the careers of young employees, the challenge is clear: it is to speed the development of managers who will treat their subordinates in ways that lead to high performance and career satisfaction. Managers shape not only the expectations and productivity of their subordinates, but also influence their attitudes toward their jobs and themselves. If managers are unskilled, they leave scars on the careers of the young people, cut deeply into their self-esteem, and distort their image of themselves as human beings. But if they are skillful and have high expectations of their subordinates, their self-confidence will grow, their capabilities will develop, and their productivity will be high. More often than one realizes, the manager is Pygmalion.

References

1. "Jamesville Branch Office (A)," METOO3A, and "Jamesville Branch Office (B)," METOO3B (Boston, Sterling Institute, 1969).
2. "Jamesville Branch Office (B)," p. 2.
3. "Some Determinants of Early Managerial Success," Alfred P. Sloan School of Management, Organization Research Program #81-64 (Cambridge, Massachusetts Institute of Technology, 1964), pp. 13-14.
4. Robert Rosenthal and Lenore Jacobson, *Pygmalion in the Classroom* (New York, Holt, Rinehart, and Winston, Inc., 1968), p. 11.
5. Ibid., Preface, p. vii.
6. Ibid., p. 38.
7. John W. Atkinson, "Motivational Determinants of Risk-Taking Behavior," *Psychological Review*, Vol. 64, No. 6, 1957, p. 365.
8. David F. Berlew and Douglas T. Hall, "The Socialization of Managers: Effects of Expectations on Performance," *Administrative Science Quarterly*, September 1966, p. 208.
9. Rosenthal and Jacobson, op. cit., pp. 3-4.

10. Ibid., pp. 74-81.

11. "Some Determinants of Early Managerial Success,"
    pp. 13-14.

12. Berlew and Hall, op. cit., p. "The Socialization of
    Managers: Effects of Expectations on Performance," p. 219.

13. Ibid., pp. 221-222.

14. Robert T. Davis, "Sales Management in the Field," HBR
    January-February 1958, p. 91.

15. Alfred A. Oberlander, "The Collective Conscience in
    Recruiting," address to Life Insurance Agency Management
    Association Annual Meeting Chicago, Illinois, 1963, p. 5.

16. Ibid., p. 9.

17. "How to Keep the Go-getters," *Nation's Business*,
    June 1966, p. 74.

18. Robert C. Albrook, "Why It's Harder to Keep Good
    Executives," *Fortune*, November 1968, p. 137.

July 16, 1984

Demand Better Results—and Get Them

Managers can break through the barriers that keep their performance expectations too low

Reprinted by permission of *Harvard Business Review*. Demand Better Results–and Get Them by Robert H. Schaffer, November/December 1974. Copyright ©1974 by the President and Fellows of Harvard College; all rights reserved.

"Teamwork does not just happen; it is the planned result of imaginative, perceptive and competent executive supervision."
M. A. Harvey

FOREWORD

Why do so few organizations reach their productivity potential? Because, the author maintains, managers fail "to establish high performance improvement expectations in ways that elicit results." They fail because imposing heavy demands entails risks and threatens subordinates. So it is safer to ask for less. To avoid facing facts, a manager may rationalize that his subordinates are doing the best that can be expected or that better performance requires more authority or greater resources. He may place his chips on "incentive plans" or a variety of other managerial programs and technologies, hoping they will produce improvement without his intervention. He may actually establish high goals—but permit his subordinates to escape accountability for results. Top management, the author advises, needs a few tangible successes in asking for more and getting it, and he outlines a strategy for accomplishing this.

Mr. Schaffer heads a management consulting company bearing his name and located in Stamford, Connecticut. He has served a wide variety of industries as well as public and voluntary organizations. For HBR he has previously written "Putting Action into Planning" (November-December 1967) and co-authored "Making Staff Consulting More Effective" (January-February 1969).

One of the most dramatic, large-scale productivity improvements with which I am familiar occurred in a regulated public utility—an industry category not noted for such performance breakthroughs. In the early 1960s this company's productivity was about average among 20 similar companies in North America, as both workload and work force were rapidly rising. In 1966 the company's productivity ranked about the best in its industry. The difference between average performance and best was worth savings of more than $40 million a year—well over one-third of its net income at that time.

What produced this gain? Neither new technology nor labor-saving machinery was a significant factor. No major change of management took place. The company was not reorganized. Nor were programs incorporating management by objectives, organization development, mathematical modeling, or management information systems responsible for the shift. The key to the turnaround was a decision by the principal operating officer (with backing from the chief executive) that the company must and could make substantial productivity gains. Naturally, many supportive programs and activities were necessary to translate this determination into results. These activities, however, would have produced little in the absence of a clear demand for improved performance that was placed on the company's management team.

Most organizations have the potential for as great—or greater—gains. Very few, however, ever realize them. Why? Because few managers possess the capacity—or feel compelled—to establish high performance improvement expectations in ways that elicit results. Indeed, the capacity for such demand-making could be the most universally underdeveloped management skill.

Why demands aren't made

Pushing for major gains can appear very risky to managers, and these perceived risks exert a tremendous inhibition on performance expectations. If the newly installed manager asserts that major gains are possible, he may threaten his predecessor and his current boss—and thus arouse their antagonism—by implying that they were content with less than what is possible. Even if he has been in the job for a while, he subjects himself to the same criticism.

Great demands increase the risk of resistance from subordinates, and the possible embarrassment of setting ambitious goals and failing to reach them. The manager who sets unusually high demands may be challenged by others. He must therefore be sure of his facts and clear about directions. The struggle to upgrade performance may expose his uncertainties, weaknesses and inadequate knowledge. More modest expectations reduce all these risks.

In addition, establishing well-defined and unequivocal expectations for superior performance creates the worry that failure of subordinates to produce will call for drastic action. The vice president of the manufacturing operation recently mused out loud about a long-needed productivity improvement effort. "What would happen," he asked, "if we set specific targets and my people didn't meet them? I'd have to do some-thing—maybe let some of them go. Then I'd have to bring in people I trusted even less." Before determining whether he could create an effective strategy, this man was already para-lyzed by the anticipated consequences of failure.

The fear of rejection is also a powerful motivator. Asking subordinates to do much more than they assert they can do runs the risk, at least in a manager's mind, of earning their resentment, if not their dislike. Many managers have been only too eager to adopt the model of the manager portrayed by the human relations movements of the 1950s and 1960s—the loving, understanding and supportive father figure. The stern, demanding father model was portrayed as a villain.

Although many exponents of "human relations" did emphasize the importance of high expectations and tough goals, managers frequently overlooked those parts of the mes-sage. Instead, they saw that high expectations for performance could lead to psychological rejection by subordinates. Prevail-ing opinions seemed to suggest that by adopting the right tech-niques, managers could avoid confronting subordinates on performance expectations and asking them to produce much more than the managers estimated they would be likely to obtain from these subordinates anyhow.

Psychological camouflage

Are managers conscious of the discrepancy between the perfor-mance they are requiring and what might be possible? To an extent, they are. Most sense that their organizations could achieve more, but their vision is obstructed. To avoid the uneasiness and feelings of guilt produced by too clear a vision of the performance gaps, managers unconsciously employ a variety of psychological mechanisms for obstructing the truth.

Avoidance through rationalization

A manager may escape having to demand better performance by convincing himself that he has done all he can to establish expectations. For instance, he may assert that everyone already knows what must be accomplished. When asked whether he has made the goals clear to his people, he responds with a variation of: "If they don't know what the goals of this outfit are by now, they don't belong in their jobs."

Sincere in their belief that their subordinates are doing better, managers frequently look for sub-par performance elsewhere. Do the following statements sound familiar?

> "We can reduce back orders, but you're going to have to pay for plenty of overtime."
> "If you want us to cut inventories any further, be prepared for delayed shipments."
> "Ever since they trimmed our maintenance budget, we haven't been able to keep this plant operating properly."

Performance improvements always seem to call for an expansion of resources or an increase in authority. Overlooking the possibility of obtaining greater yields from available resources, managers often fail to impose greater demands and expectations on their employees. And when a manager does try to demand more, his subordinates are quick to point out that they are doing all that can be done. Thus all levels of management may share the illusion of operating at the outer limit when, in fact, they are far from it.

To avoid having to impose new requirements on subordinates, the manager may decide to take on the job himself. He reassures himself that his people are already overloaded or that they lack some qualification that he possesses.

At the other extreme is the manager who covers up his reluctance to make demands with toughness, gruffness or arbitrariness. He may threaten or "needle" subordinates without actually specifying requirements and deadlines for results.

In the folklore of management, such toughness of manner is equated with a preoccupation with achievement.

Reliance on mechanisms and procedures

A manager may avoid the necessity of demand-making by putting his chips on a variety of management programs, procedures, mechanisms and innovations that he hopes will produce better results. They may help an organization respond to demands, but they are no substitute for good management.

For example, a manager may try an incentive system aimed at seducing subordinates into better performance through the promise of "goodies." Many top officers are perpetually preoccupied with new kinds of salary, profit-sharing and stock-option plans and other so-called incentives like promotions, titles and other perquisites. The management assumes that if the right carrots are held out, managers and employees will run like rabbits.

Or infusions of new management technology may appear to be the key to performance improvements. Management will install information systems, mathematical planning models, industrial engineering studies, training programs or any of dozens of other "programs" offered by technical staff or outside consultants. Top management may even reorganize the company—or parts of it. Even the best-trained staff technicians and management consultants—perhaps convinced of the magic in their medicines—become the unwitting co-conspirators of managers who fail to establish higher performance requirements for subordinates. In one well-known international company, an internal consulting group put together a mathematical planning model to maximize corporate profits in interdivisional negotiations. But the president used a flimsy excuse to escape from the struggle of requiring his division heads to operate within the framework of the models.

Attacks that skirt the target

A manager may set tough goals and insist they be achieved—and yet fail to produce a sense of accountability in subordinates. For example, managers often define goals—even significant ones—in vague or general terms that make accountability impossible. The R&D director is told that he "must get more new products out this year;" the personnel director hears that "turnover must be reduced;" the executives of a transportation company insist that "safety is our number-one objective." When reporting time comes, who can say whether these objectives have been met?

Or the manager may establish goals, but insist that he cannot hold a subordinate accountable for producing a result, because the subordinate lacks the authority to get the job done. The case of a petro-chemical plant whose product quality was well below par illustrates this point. Quality depended on how well a number of interdependent departments processed components. Top management charged department heads to improve operations and monitored these activities, but it failed to hold any individuals responsible for the quality of the end product on the grounds that none of them was in sufficient control of all the factors. The quality improvements failed to meet expectations.

Sometimes, when pressed by superiors, a manager will establish "expectations" in a way that communicates to subordinates that he is merely following instructions from above. In fact, he unconsciously hopes that his subordinates will fall short, "proving," as he has asserted all along, that the new stretch goals cannot be attained.

Ironically, management by objectives programs often create heavy paper snowstorms in which managers can escape from demand-making. In many MBO programs, as the lists of goals get longer and the documents get thicker, the focus becomes diffused, bulk is confused with quality, and energy is spent on the mechanics rather than on results. A manager challenged on the performance of his group can safely point to the packet of papers and assert, "Every one of my managers has spent many hours developing his goals for the year."

Strategy for action

The avoidance mechanisms just described act as powerful deterrents to major performance improvement—but they do not have to. There are ways to accelerate progress.

If you are convinced that you must achieve better results in your organization and you are willing to invest time and energy, you can learn to expect more and get more. I have seen the process work in a refinery that expanded its output while reducing its force by half, in a large urban teaching hospital that had to shift its mission and direction radically, in a poorly maintained detergent and foodstuffs plant that had to become more competitive without more investment, and in school systems where determined leaders generated innovation despite the inertia of tradition.

The key to the strategy is to make an initial successful attempt at upgrading expectations and obtaining a response—and then use this achievement as the foundation for a succession of increasingly ambitious steps. A series of demands, initially limited, then more ambitious—each supported by careful plans, controls and persistence—makes success more likely than does a big plunge involving demands for sweeping changes.

Step 1

Select the goal. You should start with an urgent problem, such as: Are the costs of one department too high? Is a budget being seriously overrun? Is a quality spec being consistently missed?

Is there a shortfall in meeting a sales quota? You should begin with problems like these because it is essential to generate the feeling that achievement of the goal is imperative, not merely desirable.

As you are selecting the goal, you should assemble the information needed to frame the performance demand. You must have this information not only to define the need and specify the target, but possibly also to convince subordinates why improvement of performance is essential.

It is wise to sound out your subordinates on the opportunities for improvement. Their responses will give you a sense of their readiness as you shape your demand. By way of illustration, the management at a newspaper publishing plant tried to launch a comprehensive improvement effort. The needs were so great and resistance by managers at lower levels was so strong that very little was accomplished. Interviews with the composing room supervisors revealed that they shared higher management's distress over the number of typographical errors in news and advertising matter. This information provided the clue that made it possible to design an initial project mobilizing supporters of change.

The more participation by subordinates in determining goals, the better. Managers should not, however, permit their dedication to the participatory process to mean abdication of their own responsibilities in this determination.

Step 2
Specify the minimum expectation for results. Broad, far-reaching or amorphous goals must be narrowed to one or two specific, measurable ones. A manager may protest with "I have too many things that have to get done to concentrate on only one or two of them," but the fragmentation of a manager's attention in trying to push them all ahead can keep him perpetually trapped in

the same defense mechanisms from which he is trying to escape. Whether the first-step goal is a modest advance or a bold one, it must focus the energy of the organization on one or two sharply defined targets.

For example, one company, in treading a path between mass production and tailored engineering, was losing money because it could not clarify its proper place in the market and develop the appropriate products. Top management spent hundreds of hours in conferences and in making studies to define the business, the product line and the pricing strategy. These produced more frustration than progress.

The undertaking was transformed, however, when the president asked the group to select, from a dozen being considered, the one new product the executives agreed would most likely be profitable and conform to their vision of the business. He directed them to sketch out a market plan and pricing policy for this product. They were to draw some generalizations from the effort which could be applied to policy determination. The president was convinced that the group could produce the results in a short time. And he was confident that the initial step would provide insights into the nature of the next steps in clarifying company directions.

Step 3

Communicate your expectations clearly. You should share with the responsible persons, orally and in writing, the determination of the goal, the locus of responsibility, the timetable and the constraints. It is important to make clear that you are not asking for permission to set the goal, not securing their advice on whether the goal is attainable, and not implying that if they do not meet the target you will nevertheless appreciate their efforts. It should be clear that this is not a goal that should be achieved; it is one that must be achieved.

Step 4

Monitor the project, but delegate responsibility. The use of work-planning disciplines is essential in these projects to keep them from fading into the ether. Trying, for instance, to keep the goals, commitments and plans only in your mind is sure to undermine the project; rather, the manager responsible for each goal or subgoal should provide you with a written work plan of steps to be taken to reach the goal. This work plan should also specify how progress will be measured and how it will be reported to you.

Moreover, the responsibility for achieving each goal must be assigned to one person, although the contributions of many may be essential for success. Consider the case of a company whose technically complex new product was failing to perform as promised. The president talked about the problem with his marketing, engineering and manufacturing vice presidents; each claimed that his function was doing its job and that the problems originated elsewhere. Even spending much more time than warranted with his subordinates, the president was able to effect only a slight improvement.

The turnaround came when he called together the department heads concerned and told them it was unwise for him to get involved in trying to solve the problem. That was their job. He was therefore giving full responsibility to them, he said, to come up with a plan to reduce the frequency of unacceptable products to a target level within three months. He assigned to one executive the responsibility for shaping an integrated plan and for making certain it was adequate to achieve the result. In addition, the president said that each of the other managers would have to produce a plan specifying his own functions, contributions and timetable. After many months of struggling for a solution, these moves for the first time 1) pinpointed a goal to be achieved, 2) established responsibilities for achievement, and 3) introduced work-planning disciplines to manage the process in an orderly way.

The frustrations experienced by this president demonstrate that as long as responsibility for results is not explicitly assigned, subordinates tend to "delegate" it to the boss, especially if he tries to play a helpful role in the project. The boss must make certain that his subordinates clearly understand their full responsibility for results. He must not permit them to seize his offers of help and support as an opportunity to pass the buck.

Step 5

Expand and extend the process. Once some success has been achieved on a first set of demands, it should be possible to repeat the process on new goals or on an extension of the first. This will lead to further expansion.

As an example, consider the efforts of a large railway express terminal that handled tens of thousands of shipments daily. It was performing very poorly on many counts: Costs were high, productivity was low, and delivery deadlines were often missed. Studies had identified the potential for hundreds of thousands of dollars' saving, but little had been achieved. Then the head of the terminal and his boss ceased talking about what was going wrong and all the improvements that were needed. Instead, they identified the most crucial short-term goals.

From these few they selected one: getting all of one category of shipments out on time each day. It was not an easy goal, but it was clear and understandable; it could be defined sharply and measured, and action steps could be quickly identified. Meeting that target was the all-important first success that launched the terminal on a major improvement program. Once the first traffic category was under control, top management planned a series of slightly more ambitious improvement programs. Gradually, the terminal's managers gained confidence in asking for more and their subordinates gained confidence that they could respond. Eventually, many of the sizable savings promised in the earlier studies were realized.

Psychodynamics of action

While moving ahead through successive sets of demands, top management has some essential work to do on the psychological front as well. The methods and procedures for negotiating goals with subordinates are well known; almost overlooked, but more significant, are the often unconscious negotiations that the manager carries on with himself. A manager frequently bargains himself down to comfortable expectation levels long before he confronts his subordinates. He must learn to share the risk-taking that he wants his subordinates to assume. He may have to live with the "testing" to which subordinates may subject him, and he may need to engage in "consciousness-raising" to make sure he does not slip into rationalizations for failing to see that his directives are carried out.

Without intending to, the manager often ensures that he will share in the glories of his subordinates' successes, but that they will take the blame for failures. For example, a plant manager had been pressuring the head of maintenance to realign the responsibilities of supervisors and workers in order to increase efficiency. The step would make a number of persons redundant. Low-level managers and supervisors resisted the move, warning of various disasters that would befall the plant. The deadlock was broken only when the plant manager—through transfers, early retirements and a very modest layoff—reduced the maintenance force to the level needed after the proposed reorganization. Now that the most painful step had been taken, maintenance management quickly installed the new structure. Instead of insisting self-righteously that the key to action was overcoming the resistance of maintenance management, the plant manager assumed the risk and broke the logjam by reducing the staff.

When the manager lets his subordinates know that he expects better results, they may express their own lack of self-confidence in the form of "tests." They may still do exactly what they have been doing, as if to say they heard his words but disbelieve the message. Or they may imply that "It can't be done." Some subordinates may advise him, dropping their voices confidentially, that for his own good—considering the high risks involved—he should lower his sights. They may even withdraw their affection and approbation from him.

Such testing is usually the expression of their anxiety over whether they can actually achieve the goal; it is a way to seek reassurance from the boss. If the boss is as anxious as they are, he will be upset by the testing and he may react against what he perceives as defiance. If he has confidence in himself, he will accept the testing for what it is and try to help his subordinates deal with the problem—without, however, eroding his expectation levels.

In breaking out of productiveness-limiting traps, "consciousness-raising" may be needed to help managers assess more objectively their approach to establishing demands. Consultants—inside or outside—can help managers gain the necessary perspective. Or several managers who are working through the same process may join forces, since each can be more detached about the others' behavior than about his own. They may meet periodically to probe such questions as: Have you adequately assessed the potential for progress? Have you made the performance requirements clear to your associates?

Are these goals ambitious enough? Are you providing your subordinates with enough help? Are you sharing the risks with them? How well are you standing up to "testing"? Have you defined goals that at least some of your subordinates can see as exciting and achievable?

Perhaps the most important function of consciousness-raising has to do with getting started in the first place. It is very difficult to alter the pattern of relationships involving superior and subordinate, especially if they have been working together for a long time. You cannot take the very first step without worrying that your people may say (or think), "Oh, come off it, Bob. We know who you are!"

The rewards are there
The strategy for demanding better performance—and getting it—begins with a focus on one or two vital goals. Management assesses readiness and then sharply defines the goals. The organization receives clearly stated demands and unequivocally stated expectations. Management assigns the responsibility for results to individuals, and work-planning discipline provides the means for self-control and assessment of progress. Management keeps wired in, tenaciously, making sure the project moves. Early successes provide the reinforcement to shoot for more ambitious targets, which may be extensions of the first goal or additional goals.

There is no limit to the pace or scope of expansions. As this process expands, a shift in management style and organizational dynamics gradually takes place. Sophisticated planning techniques, job redesign, closer line/staff collaboration and other advances result as natural developments of the process.

With clearly conveyed "nonnegotiable" expectations and a step-by-step expansion strategy, you may find that the anticipated difficulties and dangers fail to materialize. Instead, if your subordinates are like most, they will respond to the higher

demands. They will be able to accomplish what is expected—
or most of it. And, despite a bit of "testing" or hazing, most of
them will enjoy working in a more results-oriented environment. Thus you will be creating an environment in which there
is more job satisfaction, greater mutual respect and better relationships among levels—as well as a multiplied return on the
organization's human and material resources.

"There is nothing more difficult to take in hand, more perilous to conduct, or more uncertain in its success, than to take
the lead in the introduction of a new order of things."
Machiavelli, *The Prince*

Note to the reader: *After finishing this article, please read my
memo, Immediately following, which discusses it.* **BW**

July 16, 1984

I was sent a note from one of the people who received the last article titled, "Demand Better Results—And Get Them." The note reads: "This article does not reflect the managers of the '80s. It reflects the managers of the '50s, '60s and early '70s. Suggest you read articles on human resources."

My thanks to the writer—it gives me the opportunity to expand further on my views of the article. I assume that you all believe that I do read articles on human resources, notwithstanding the comment made to me in the note. I think the article I sent you has very substantive meaning. While I don't agree with every comment, I do agree with what I think the author, whom I happen to know, is saying. I also happen to believe that I am a reasonably participative manager, though some may think otherwise.

Now to the article. I suspect that the use of the word "demand" is what has bothered the author of the note. The word "demand" seems to indicate an autocratic, dictatorial approach to setting goals, making it out of line with our participative thrust. I frankly do not read it that way, and I would like to give you a few reasons why.

Let's use Motorola's top 10 corporate goals as an example. These goals were developed by the policy committee of the corporation after six months of discussion, for many hours, in a participative fashion. When the goals were agreed upon, they were literally placed "top down" on the Motorola organization.

As I am sure each of you will agree, there are certain times when the total picture can only be seen from high levels of management, and this refers to many of the top 10 goals, which affect the corporation in its entirety. In effect, the policy committee "demanded" that the corporation achieve the results outlined by these goals. I don't believe that this is a contravention of the participative philosophy.

As you read the article carefully, you find the following quotes, which shed some light on the emphasis given to participation:

"The more participation by subordinates in determining goals, the better. Managers should not, however, permit their dedication to the participatory process to mean abdication of their own responsibilities in their determination.

"The turnaround came when he called together the department heads concerned and told them it was unwise for him to get involved in trying to solve the problem. That was their job. He was therefore giving full responsibility to them, he said, to come up with a plan to reduce the frequency of unacceptable products to a target level within three months. He assigned to one executive the responsibility for shaping an integrated plan and for making certain it was adequate to achieve the result. In addition, the president said that each of the other managers would have to produce a plan specifying his own functions, contributions and timetable. After many

months of struggling for a solution, these moves for the first time 1) pinpointed a goal to be achieved, 2) established responsibilities for achievement and 3) introduced work-planning disciplines to manage the process in an orderly way.

"The frustrations experienced by this president demonstrate that as long as responsibility for results is not explicitly assigned, subordinates tend to 'delegate' it to the boss, especially if he tries to play a helpful role in the project. The boss must make certain that his subordinates clearly understand their full responsibility for results. He must not permit them to seize his offer of help and support as an opportunity to pass the buck."

The article goes on to describe the methodology for setting goals, which includes selecting the goal, specifying the minimum expectation for results, communicating expectations clearly and monitoring the project, but with delegated responsibility. I do not believe that the author intended to eliminate participative discussion, but participative management does not mean abdication of responsibility for decision-making by the manager in the final analysis.

We at Motorola must find out how to set higher expectations, discipline our achievement to those expectations and hold ourselves accountable for those results. Setting high expectations indeed can be equated to "demanding" better results. In the words of that great sage and philosopher Vince Lombardi of the Green Bay Packers, "If you ask for perfection, you will be surprised how often you achieve it. If you never ask for it, you can be sure you will never achieve it."

I hope all of you can retain your participative management skills while "demanding" better results. If you do, you can be sure that we will be an unbeatable corporation with the appropriate management technique for the '80s and beyond.

BW

June 27, 1986

This article impressed me because it points out dangers of a too-rigid strategy-planning process. As we look at corporate strategy and direction in our policy committee meetings, we should bear in mind the key points covered in the article. Particularly, there is a caution about getting into a mode of thinking based on forecasts (what do we think is going to happen?), rather than visions (what do we want to happen?). We want to set directions and communicate them well, and not develop "cast in concrete" strategies based on rigid forecasts of the future.

Strategic planning—forward in reverse?

_____

FOREWORD

With all the time and resources that American manufacturing companies spend on strategic planning, why has their competitive position been deteriorating? Certainly not because the idea of doing such planning is itself misguided. Nor because the managers involved are not up to the task. Drawing on his long experience with the nuts and bolts of operations deep inside American and foreign companies, the author proposes a different answer. Perhaps the problem lies in how managers typically approach the work of planning: first by selecting objectives or ends, then by defining the strategies or ways of accomplishing them, and lastly by developing the necessary resources or means. A hard look at what the new industrial competition requires might suggest, instead, an approach to planning based on a means-ways-ends sequence.

Mr. Hayes is the William Barclay Harding Professor of Management of Technology at the Harvard Business School. He is the author or co-author of three McKinsey Award-winning articles in *HBR* and, with Steven C. Wheelwright, of *Restoring Our Competitive Edge* (Wiley, 1984), which was selected by the Association of American Publishers as the best book on business, management, and economics published in 1984.

———————

Since I began to study American industry almost 30 years ago, there has been a revolution in the science and practice of management and, especially, in the attraction of bright, professionally trained managers to the work of strategic planning. **Yet as corporate staffs have flourished and as the notion of strategy has come to dominate business education and practice, our factories have steadily lost ground to those in other countries where strategy receives far less emphasis and the "professionalization" of management is far less advanced.**

Over the years, I have prowled through hundreds of American factories and talked at length with innumerable line managers. Of late, I have been increasingly troubled by a recurring theme in the explanations they give for their companies' competitive difficulties. Again and again they argue that many of those difficulties—particularly in their manufacturing organizations—stem from their companies' strategic planning processes. Their complaint, however, is not about the *mis*functioning of strategic planning but about the harmful aspects of its *proper* functioning.

In explaining why they continue to use old, often obsolete equipment and systems in their factories, some of these managers assert that their corporate strategic plans call for major investments elsewhere: in acquisitions, new lines of business, new plants in new locations, or simply the subsidization of other parts of their organizations. Their job, they say, is to "manage for cash," not to upgrade the capabilities of their existing plants. Others complain that their companies' strategic plans force on them new products and equipment that require capabilities their organizations do not have (or, worse, no longer have). Still others report that they must assimilate acquired companies that "do not fit" or must grow faster than is prudent or even possible. With money being thrown at them faster than they can absorb it, much of it is poorly spent.

These comments do not come from ineffective managers who are looking for excuses. Nor are their companies unsophisticated in the art of strategic planning. Most of them have been at it for a long time and are widely regarded as experts. How, then, are we to make sense of the fact that, although the United States has poured more resources—both in total and on a per company basis—into strategic planning over the past 20 years than has any other country in the world, a growing number of our industries and companies today find themselves more vulnerable strategically than when they started? Not only do they fall short of goals, but they also lag behind competitors, largely of foreign origin, that place much less emphasis on strategic planning.[1]

Consider, for example, the experience of one company that, for a dozen years, emphasized the expansion of its market and the achievement of "low-cost-producer" status while allowing its R&D budget to fall to just over half its previous level (in constant dollars). The company has now come to realize that the high-volume, low-cost end of its business has moved irretrievably offshore and that its only hope for survival lies in rapid product innovation. There is, however, little innovative spark left in the organization, and neither increases in the R&D budget nor additions of new people appear to have had much impact. In desperation, the company is contemplating a merger with another company that has a better record of product innovation, but it is finding stiff resistance to its advances because of its reputation as a "researcher's graveyard."

Or consider the experience of another company that has a reputation for having modern production facilities and for being in the forefront of product technology in its fast-changing industry. As soon as it tests out the process for making a new product, management builds a new factory dedicated to that product. Unfortunately, once in place, this new facility tends to ossify because management also believes that the product life cycle in its industry is so short that continual investment in process improvement is uneconomic. As a result, the company has recently found itself losing market position to competitors that have pushed ahead in process technology. Although loath to cede business to those who came later, it has so far been unable to muster the ability (or, some say, the commitment) to keep up with its challengers' processing capabilities. Worse, management is realizing that the next generation of new products will require many of the manufacturing skills that it has neglected and its competitors have forced themselves to master.

How can these well-run companies that impose on themselves the rigorous discipline—and employ the sophisticated techniques—of modern strategic planning end up worse off than when they started? Is this a statistical accident or is there something about the process itself that is bad for corporate health? In this article, I will argue that, under certain circumstances, the methodology of normal strategic planning and, even worse, the organizational attitudes and relationships that it often cultivates can impair a company's ability to compete. Moreover, the circumstances under which this occurs is true for much of U.S. industry today.

To understand the damaging effect of that methodology, we must take a hard look at the logic that shapes it. The traditional strategic planning process rests on an "ends-ways-means" model: establish corporate objectives (ends), given those objectives, develop a strategy (ways) for attaining them, then marshal the resources (means) necessary to implement this strategy.

There are two familiar lines of argument for keeping these three elements of the planning process (ends, ways, means) in their current order. First, ends should precede ways because managers must know what their objectives are before deciding how to go about attaining them. A generation of MBA students has had pounded into their heads the story of Lewis Carroll's logician, the Cheshire Cat in *Alice in Wonderland.* When Alice comes upon the Cat and asks, "Would you tell me, please, which way I ought to go from here?" the Cat responds, "That depends ... on where you want to get to." Alice answers, "I really don't much care where," and the Cat tells her, "Then it doesn't matter which way you go!"

The second argument has a different basis: to maximize efficiency, the choice of strategy should precede the assembling of the resources for carrying it out. Because each strategy is likely to require a different mix of resources, developing resources before choosing one of them exposes a company to the risk that it will be short of some resources and have too much of others.

What is wrong with this model? Let me raise questions about four of its aspects: (1) the ends that companies usually select, (2) the ways they try to attain those ends, (3) the means through which they carry out those ways, and (4) the logic that strings these elements together in the ends-ways-means order.

Choosing Ends

Most companies select goals that are too short-term. It is almost impossible for a company to create a truly sustainable competitive advantage—one that is highly difficult for its competitors to copy — in just five to ten years (the time frame that most companies use). Goals that can be achieved within five years are usually either too easy or based on buying and selling something. Anything that a company can buy or sell, however, is probably available for purchase or sale by its competitors as well.

A series of short-term goals also encourages episodic thinking. When attention focuses on meeting immediate objectives, organizations often find the successive hurdles they have set for themselves increasingly difficult to surmount. Finally, the accumulated weight of deferred changes and seemingly innocuous compromises becomes too great, and managers trip badly on a hurdle that seemed no higher than the rest.

In most of the companies that I have observed, the goals are not only short-term but also highly quantitative, focusing on rates of growth in profitability, return on investment, and market share. Unfortunately, quantitative goals follow Gresham's Law: they tend to drive out nonquantitative goals. It is easy for an organization tied to quantitative goals to believe (or to act as if it believes) that anything that is not quantitative is not important.

In practice, the danger is that hard numbers will encourage managers to forget that different kinds of goals have different values at different levels in an organization. Goals like return on investment have great meaning and value for senior managers, who understand the need to allocate capital efficiently and who are themselves evaluated on their ability to do so. ROI has almost no meaning for production workers, however, whose only contact with investment decisions is indirect: roofs that leak, old equipment that does not hold tolerances, new equipment that creates more problems than it solves. What does have meaning for these workers is quality (getting the work done correctly), timing (meeting delivery schedules), the working environment, and the satisfaction that comes from doing a good job as part of an appreciative organization.

Objectives that have little meaning for large segments of an organization cannot be shared and cannot weld it together. Nor, for that matter, can episodic goals ("last year's emphasis was on quality, but this year's emphasis is on productivity"), which succeed only in diffusing commitment.

Developing ways

Short-term goals also work to back companies into a mode of thinking that is based on forecasts (What do we think is going to happen?) rather than on visions (What do we want to happen?). Unfortunately, even though the usual five- to ten-year time periods are too short to achieve truly strategic objectives, they are much too long to obtain accurate forecasts.

Consider, for example, the forecasts made more than a decade ago of a stable, slow-moving enterprise: the U.S. economy. In 1970, when a number of eminent economists tried to predict how the economy would fare during the sizzling seventies, their consensus was that inflation would continue at about 2.5%, productivity growth would average about 3%, and real growth in GNP would approach 4.5%. Instead, inflation averaged 8%, productivity growth only 1.3%, and real GNP a bit over 3%. As a result, the average American in 1980 enjoyed an income nearly 15% less than that predicted ten years before.

In the early 1970s, many U.S. corporations based their strategies on comparable forecasts of economic growth, as well as on their own forecasts of the much less predictable behavior of particular markets and competitors. Should we be surprised that most of their forecasts were totally off the mark, as were the elaborate strategies to which they gave rise? I suspect that the surge in domestic merger and acquisition activity in the late 1970s reflected in part the growing frustration of American managers who realized they could not reach the forecast-driven goals they had set for their companies and themselves through internal activities alone.

Inevitably, quantitative goals and reliance on long-term forecasts, combined with too-short planning horizons, lead corporate strategists to spend most of their time worrying about structural, rather than behavioral, means for achieving their objectives. After all, they reason, specific, measurable results come through "hard," measurable efforts: investments in new plants and equipment, the introduction of new products, the redesign of organization charts, and so on. This leads them to neglect less easily measured factors like performance evaluation and reward systems, work-force policies, information systems, and management selection and development policies. As the recent interest in "corporate culture" suggests, however, real strategic advantage comes from changing the way a company behaves, a task far more difficult and time-consuming than simply making a few structural decisions.

Another problem with today's strategic planning processes is that they reduce a company's flexibility. Like all organizational processes, strategic planning is subject to the first law of bureaucracy: If you give a smart, ambitious person a job to do, no matter how meaningless, he or she will try to make it bigger and more important. Jack Welch learned this lesson soon after he became chairman and CEO at General Electric. According to Welch, "Once written, the strategic document can take on a life of its own, and it may not lend itself to flexibility ... An organization can begin to focus on form rather than substance."[2] He also described to a group of Harvard MBA students how GE's strategic plans had become less and less useful as they got bigger and bigger, as more and more hours went into preparing them, and as planners embellished them with increasingly sophisticated graphics and fancy covers.

William Bricker, chairman and CEO of Diamond Shamrock, has much the same reaction: "Why has our vision been narrowed? Why has our flexibility been constricted? To my mind there is one central reason our strategies have become too rigid ... A detailed strategy [is] like a road map ... [telling] us every turn we must take to get to our goal ... The entrepreneur, on the other hand, views strategic planning not as a road map but as a compass ... and is always looking for the new road."[3] This is a provocative analogy: When you are lost on a highway, a road map is very useful; but when you are lost in a swamp whose topography is constantly changing, a road map is of little help. A simple compass—which indicates the general direction to be taken and allows you to use your own ingenuity in overcoming various difficulties—is much more valuable.

Strategies: leaps or small steps?
The difficulties that highly visible U.S. industries are now experiencing surprise and puzzle many Americans. Why is the nation that put a man on the moon and invented genetic engineering unable to produce a consumer videocassette recorder (all those sold by U.S. companies are imported, even though a U.S. company produced the first commercial video-tape machine 30 years ago) or even a better small car than Toyota? One possible reason, of course, is that we *can* put a man on the moon. **The very skills and psychology that enable us to conceive and carry out something like the Apollo project may hamper us when we are in a competitive environment that bases success more on a series of small steps than on a few dramatic breakthroughs.**

Consider the graph in *Exhibit I,* where the horizontal axis measures the passage of time and the vertical, competitive effectiveness (lower cost, better quality, more features, faster delivery). In a free market, a company's competitive effectiveness should improve over time—that is, it will move from a position in the lower left of the graph to a position in the upper right. Now, how does a company accomplish this movement?

One approach, shown in *Exhibit II*, is through a series of strategic leaps, a few giant upward steps at critical moments. These leaps may take a variety of forms: a product redesign, a large-scale factory modernization or expansion, a move to another location that promises great improvement in wage rates or labor relations, an acquisition of a supplier of a critical material or component, or adoption of a new manufacturing technology. **Between taking these giant steps, managers seek only incidental improvements in competitiveness, as the company digests the last step and contemplates the next.**

At the opposite extreme, as shown in *Exhibit III*, a company may try to progress through a series of small steps whose cumulative impact will be just as great. Rather than rely on a series of discontinuities, such a company continuously strives to bolster its competitive position through a variety of incremental improvements.

Which approach is best? Both can get you to the same point, but each places different demands on an organization and exposes it to very different risks.

Strategic leaps. Each step in *Exhibit II* is highly visible and usually requires a major expenditure of funds. Thus the timing of the change becomes important. A decline in profits, a potential acquisition, a sudden surge of orders that pushes the organization to the limit of its resources—any such development can delay the project or put it on hold. Further, managers at all levels in an organization must get involved in analyzing and approving the decision to take the step. Extensive staff involvement is also essential, as is the expertise of many specialists—financial analysts, strategic planners, legal experts, scientists, outside consultants, and public relations personnel—who often have more allegiance to their own "professions" than to the company itself.

Because each step is so big and so visible, whoever proposes the change takes on an enormous risk in return for the

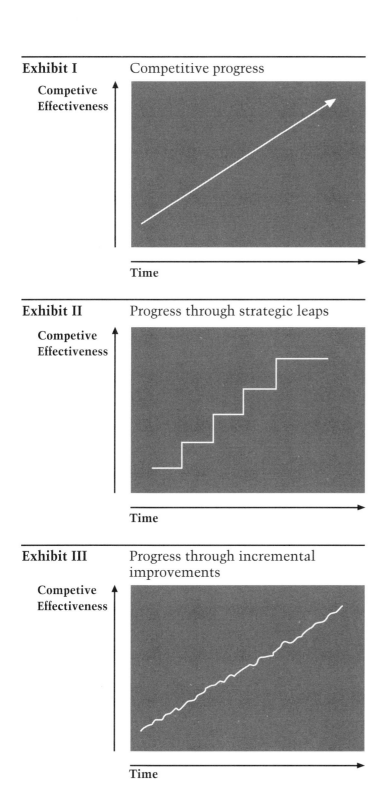

Exhibit I   Competitive progress

Competive
Effectiveness

Time

Exhibit II   Progress through strategic leaps

Competive
Effectiveness

Time

Exhibit III   Progress through incremental improvements

Competive
Effectiveness

Time

chance to reap huge rewards. Success creates heroes; failure brings severe consequences. **The people who rise to the top in such organizations usually fall into one of two camps: they are either "lucky gamblers," who were involved in two or three successful leaps, or "corporate kibitzers," who managed to avoid entanglement in any disasters.**

Such companies regard the corporate staff as an elite group and treat assignments of line managers to staff positions as promotions. At lower levels in the organization, however, there is little need for outstanding, highly trained people. The task of people at these levels is simply to operate the structure that top management and its staff of experts have created. It does not seem necessary in such companies to put much time and effort into training and upgrading factory workers or managers because the next strategic leap may make their newly developed skills obsolete. Nor do personnel policies that reward employee longevity seem particularly desirable because they reduce the company's flexibility—its ability, say, to pull up stakes and move to a new location, to sell the business, or to implement a significant reduction in employment as part of an automation program.

In similar fashion, a reliance on strategic leaps makes it unnecessary for workers or lower-level managers to have a detailed understanding of how their own operations affect— and are affected by—other parts of the organization. The same logic robs employee suggestion programs of their usefulness, for workers cannot possibly understand how the changes they may propose fit into the company's overall strategy, much less the leap it is contemplating next.

Small steps. If, however, a company follows an incremental approach to improvement, few of the steps it takes are highly visible or risky. Because major capital authorization requests are seldom necessary, there is little need for much staff assistance or outside advice. Rather than put massive resources into the development of elaborate plans in the rarefied atmosphere of a remote headquarters, such a company expects the bulk of its improvements to bubble up, in an entrepreneurial fashion, from lower levels in the organization. Its corporate staff is much smaller and less powerful than that of a strategic leap organization. Its main role is to offer support services. In effect, the organization charts of these companies look more like tables than pyramids.

This incremental approach requires immense low-level expertise—not expertise *of* a low level, but expertise *at* low levels. Developing this kind of expertise takes a long time. Executives need to expend great effort on recruiting people who are both loyal and trainable, and on continuously improving their capabilities once hired—through both formal education programs and job assignments that provide a broad understanding of the company's products, processes, and competitive environment. In turn, top management needs to augment this understanding and keep it up-to-date by disseminating information about current financial results, market behavior, and competitors' activities.

Having made so extensive an investment in low-level expertise, a company will do its best to retain the people who have it. Long-time employees have another advantage: Over time, through their multiple job assignments, they develop relationships with people in different parts of the organization. These relationships make it easier to implement the small changes that require communication and cooperation among several different groups.

Incremental projects generally require so little capital that managers can often fund them out of a plant's annual operating budget. It stands to reason that plant managers will support such efforts if they are intimately familiar with the production systems and people involved and are committed to the plant's long-term success because they expect to stay in their jobs for a long time. Such projects are also more likely to thrive if workers, plant engineers, and lower-level managers participate in developing them—through suggestion programs, quality circles, and the like—and if they identify the company's long-term success with their own.

This kind of company does not believe that many of its problems can be solved by top management. **The information and expertise needed for dealing with them reside lower down in the organization, and the problems themselves are continuously evolving.** Therefore, top management's role is less to spot and solve problems than to create an organization that can spot and solve its own problems.

The tortoise & the hare

Up to this point, I have been describing, rather abstractly, two contrasting "pure" strategies. In practice, of course, few companies choose approaches so extreme; most strategies fall somewhere along the spectrum between them. U.S. companies do, however, tend to adopt approaches toward the strategic leap end; those of our two most powerful international competitors, Germany and Japan, tend to seek incremental improvements within an existing structure and technology. They are the tortoise; we are the hare.

In the fable, as we may recall with some apprehension, the tortoise won the race. Are we to share the hare's fate? To answer that question, let us examine the risks and rewards of each approach.

The central risk of following the incremental approach is that a company will be "leap-frogged" and left behind by a competitor that abandons its traditional technology, location, or corporate strategy and adopts a new and more successful one. The folklore of American business is full of such examples: the replacement of piston engines by jet engines, of vacuum tubes transistors, of ditto machines by xerography, of New England textile companies by those that moved south. The list goes on and on.

Conversely, the central risk of following the strategic leap approach is that a breakthrough may not always be available exactly when it is needed. After seizing a major competitive advantage, a company may see its lead nibbled away by competitors that gradually adapt themselves to the new technology or strategy and then push it beyond its initial limits. This is the time to make another leap, but what if the company's technicians and strategists reach into their hats and find nothing there?

One obvious response to this predicament is to use an incremental approach, like that of the competition, until a breakthrough does become available. Doing so, however, is not easy for a company that has organized itself around the expectation of repeat breakthroughs. As I have argued, the kind of organization adept at making strategic leaps bears little resemblance to one that takes the incremental approach. **Entrepreneurship from below cannot be "ordered" by managers from above—particularly when, as is usually the case, top-down, staff-dominated planning and control systems have caused most of the entrepreneurs to leave.**

Unfortunately, the reverse is not true. As our Japanese and German competitors are demonstrating all too well, companies that adopt an incremental approach *can* eventually accommodate themselves to a new technology. As a rule, they're not as fast but, if given the time, they can do it. In other words, the ability to progress through incremental change does not preclude, although it may slow down, a company's ability to master discontinuous change. In fact, an organization that is used to continuous small changes, that has balanced strategic expertise at the top with operating expertise and entrepreneurship at the bottom, is probably better prepared for a big leap than is an organization that has gone for several years without any change at all.

Assembling means

The third element (after ends and ways) in the strategic planning paradigm is the selection and assembling of the resources necessary to implement the chosen strategy. Although a strategy will usually require many different types of resources, strategic planning in most corporations devotes most of its attention to just one: financial wherewithal. There are two reasons for this.

First, since managers usually state their ultimate objectives in financial terms, it is natural for them to state required resources in financial terms as well. Second, resources get used most efficiently when management provides only those that are absolutely necessary. **Understandably, companies try to maintain their resources in as liquid (that is, financial) a form as possible for as long as possible, for doing so gives them maximum flexibility to convert liquid resources into the desired form at just the moment they are needed.**

Such a practice works well if reasonably efficient markets exist for important assets like market position, worker or manager skills, and technological capabilities. Many companies have come to realize, however, that technology, market position, and organizational skills are not as transferable as they had expected. As a result, those that try to buy them often run into the infrastructure problems I described earlier.

Informed businesspeople, who understand well the danger of trying to place a modern steel mill in a less developed country like Bangladesh, have sometimes been willing to try to implant advanced new technologies in organizations that are unprepared to receive them. In most cases, these organizations respond by starving the new technology of understanding and resources — just as the human body tries to reject a heart transplant that is essential to its survival. No matter how brilliant its technological underpinnings, a new product will fail if the company's manufacturing organization is unable to make that product efficiently or if the company's sales force is unable to sell it effectively. Such capabilities cannot be bought from the outside. They must be grown from within, and growing them takes time.

The logic of ends-ways-means

When managers in strategic planning demand that ends should precede ways and both should precede means, they make certain assumptions about the environment and the nature of competition. First, they assume that the world of competition is predictable and that clear paths can be charted across it much like a highway system across a road map. Equally important, they assume that reasonable objectives, arrived at by thoughtful people, can be achieved through purposeful activity and that progress toward those objectives is both measurable and controllable.

The managerial logic of ends-ways-means also attributes a certain stability to the company itself. There is an expectation that the company's values and needs will not change over the planning horizon and that the objectives it sets will seem as desirable up close as they do from afar. Managers can, therefore, concern themselves with "static optimization"—that is, with making a few key decisions and then holding to them. There is a further expectation that, once these objectives and the strategies for achieving them are in place, managers can assemble the necessary resources in the required time frame and convert them into the appropriate form.

Underlying all these assumptions is the belief that responsibility for organizational success rests primarily on the shoulders of top management. This "command and control" mentality allocates all major decisions to top management, which imposes them on the organization and monitors them through elaborate planning, budgeting, and control systems.

In many ways this logic is similar to that which underlies modern conventional warfare: Generals set the strategy, provide the resources, establish the detailed plan of action, and continuously monitor the progress of engagements as they occur.

Does this logic make sense? Earlier I questioned the notion that means should follow ways on the ground that important resources—technology, skills, and effective working relationships—cannot always be purchased when needed. Now I also question whether managers should decide on ends before selecting ways.

Taken to an extreme, these questions could turn into a general attack on logic as applied to business planning. Such attacks are more and more common these days, from *In Search of Excellence's* claim that "detached, analytical justification for all decisions … has arguably led us seriously astray" to *The Washington Post's* insistence that "preoccupation with logic has helped to improve and reform the world, but it has also put professionals dangerously out of touch with the gritty everyday world." **My point is not to disparage the relevance of all logic to planning but to suggest that there may be alternative logics worth exploring. One of them, in fact, is to turn the ends-ways-means paradigm on its head: means-ways-ends.**

How might such a logic work? First, it suggests that a company should begin by investing in the development of its capabilities along a broad front (means). It should train workers and managers in a variety of jobs; educate them about the general competitive situation and the actions of specific competitors; teach them how to identify problems, how to develop solutions for them, and how to persuade others to follow their recommendations. It should acquire and experiment with new technologies and techniques so that workers and managers gain experience with them and come to understand their capabilities and constraints. It should focus R&D activity on fewer lines but spread it more widely throughout the organization. Managers should have cross-functional assignments so that they develop a broad understanding of the company's markets, technologies, and factories.

Second, as these capabilities develop and as technological and market opportunities appear, the company should encourage managers well down in the organization to exploit matches wherever they occur (ways). Top management's job, then, is to facilitate this kind of entrepreneurial activity, provide it with resources from other parts of the company, and, where feasible, encourage cooperative activities. **In short, the logic here is, Do not develop plans and then seek capabilities; instead, build capabilities and then encourage the development of plans for exploiting them. Do not try to develop optimal strategies on the assumption of a static environment; instead, seek continuous improvement in a dynamic environment.**

The guiding force throughout such disparate activities will not come from a set of directions or controls. To the contrary, it will come from a balance between integration, which arises out of a sense of organizational unity and camaraderie, an instinctive banding together in the face of common enemies, and direction, which arises out of a set of shared values rooted in a long-term vision of the kind of company that its people want it to become—in short, group cohesion and a compass. **A compass, remember, is not an end; it only provides a sense of direction, a means to a variety of possible ends.**

Under what circumstances might such a means-ways-ends logic be effective? When the competitive world is like a swamp that is shifting in unpredictable ways, particular objectives are likely to lose their attractiveness over time. Even so, a common vision can keep people moving ahead, moving around unforeseen obstacles and beyond immediate (largely because they are visible) objectives.

Is guerrilla warfare always better?

An organization that takes a means-ways-ends approach to strategic planning assumes everybody is responsible for its prosperity. Its success rests on its ability to exploit opportunities as they arise, on its ingenuity, on its capacity to learn, on its determination and persistence.

There is an obvious analogy here with guerrilla warfare. It would, of course, be wrong to suggest that strategic planning based on a strategic leap approach is always less effective than that based on an incremental approach. Even in guerrilla warfare, someone must decide where to fight and which goals to seek. Someone must select and train leaders and rally soldiers to the cause. On occasion, conventional pitched battles are perfectly appropriate.

Sometimes companies must change their objectives; they may decide to enter a new business or abandon an old one. These decisions seldom bubble up from the bottom. Instead, they flow down from the top. The trick, of course, to managing such discontinuities without alienating the organization or undermining its capabilities is to employ a patient, consensus-seeking decision process in which all parties have an opportunity to be heard. More important, everyone must regard a necessary leap as the exception, not the rule. Once a guerrilla army decides that the only person with any real authority is the supreme leader, its field commanders lose their credibility.

Therefore, I suspect that the Japanese and German companies that are currently studying the American approach to strategic planning do not intend to make it a way of life. They intend simply to graft it onto their existing systems so they can be better prepared for dealing with the discontinuities that sometimes confront them. What they may not appreciate is how seductive such an approach can be for top management.

When the balance of power begins to shift, when the "counters" gain ascendancy over the "doers," the best doers may seek to become counters. Or they go elsewhere, where they can do it *their* way.

Further, in most mature industries, the development of markets and technology is not discontinuous but moves forward in a steady, almost predictable manner. Even in high-technology industries like semiconductors and computers, for example, progress during the past decade has taken place within technological frameworks that were essentially in place more than 15 years ago. The opportunities for dramatic breakthroughs and strategic "end runs" have diminished as sophisticated multinational companies have identified most of the untapped markets and have uncovered most of the unexploited pools of low-cost labor in the world. They are running out of islands to move to.

Seen in this light, the present struggle between U.S. companies and their foreign competitors can be likened to a battle between a bunch of hares, trained in conventional warfare and equipped with road maps, and an unknown number of tortoises, equipped with compasses and an expertise in guerrilla warfare. Unfortunately, the battle is taking place in a swamp and not on a well-defined highway system.

The logic of ends-ways-means that got the hares into this situation is unlikely to get them out. They will need to explore a new logic, possibly a reverse logic, and be willing to question the basis of formal strategic planning as it is practiced today. Perhaps they should return to the approaches they used to follow—when they spent less time developing strategies but their industrial capabilities were the envy of the world.

References

1. A number of studies suggest there is either no relationship between planning and various measures of organizational performance or a negative one. See, for example:
   P.H. Grinyer and D. Norbura, "Planning for Existing Markets: Perceptions of Executives and Financial Performance," *Journal of the Royal Statistical Society* (A) 138, pt. 1
   (1975), p. 70.
   Ernest A. Kallman and H. Jack Shapiro, "The Motor Freight Industry—A Case Against Planning," *Long Range Planning*, February 1978, p. 81.
   Ronald J. Kudla, "The Effect of Strategic Planning on Common Stock Returns," *Academy of Management Journal*, March 1980, p. 5.
   Milton Leontiades and Ahmet Tezel, "Planning Perceptions and Planning Results," *Strategic Management Journal*, January-March 1980, p. 65.
   Leslie W. Rue and Robert M. Fulmer, "Is Long-Range Planning Profitable?" *Academy of Management Proceedings* (1973), p. 66.

2. "Managing Change," keynote address, Dedication Convocation, Fuqua School of Business, Duke University, April 21, 1983.

3. "Entrepreneurs Needed," *Oil and Gas Digest*, November 15, 1982.

Product Management Philosophies

Communications Division Product Managers Conference.

Management Speeches

Welcome to our first Product Managers Conference.

This may be the first of many similar meetings, and it may be the first and last. We'll see how this one turns out.

Unlike Homer Marrs and his managers, we see each other every day. The need for regular meetings is not as great. However, we're all running very hard and fighting fires daily, so we don't always have time to think of the long-term goals; the solutions to basic problems rather than specific situations.

Some of you will remember that some years back we used to meet once a month or bi-monthly for dinner and an evening of discussion with no prepared agenda—sort of a bull session on our business and its problems. I thought these were good. They presented a tremendous opportunity for passing on philosophy, for getting people to let their hair down, and for getting to know and respect others in our organization. I sometimes feel sorry that we've gotten away from this. I feel that we must have a better, possibly more formalized program of communicating the Motorola philosophy of doing business to all our people. I think we have a fine, tightly knit, "Galvinized" group, right down to our department heads, but we've grown so rapidly that I wonder if we've successfully passed down our way of life below that level. If we don't, we will be losing one of the major things that makes us a successful company.

I've thought of approaching this a number of ways 1) renew old meetings, 2) have a section managers' or group leaders' meeting with me on a regular basis or 3) simple philosophy meetings with entire departments. This meeting today is a first attempt to solve that problem.

Later, as we listen to John Mitchell talk about improving our people by giving them training in the technical mechanics of their jobs, think about how you can train your key people in the philosophies and attitudes with which they do their jobs. Think about this whole meeting and the things we say and do here. How do we get this across to our people? How do we get them to think about basics that, once mastered, apply to all tasks? That is the purpose of this meeting. **Today, away from the daily hustle and bustle of the plant, we'll be training ourselves.** We'll be looking at the basic problems, determining long-term objectives so that once we all understand them, everything we do can be done in a way that points toward the long-term goal. To that end, I've asked almost all of you to appear on the program— to prepare a topic that will get you thinking on some of the basics. I've asked each of you to allow ample time for group discussion, because these topics need substantial discussion. I hope nobody is worried about who will get credit or blame for specific situations, and that our discussions will not be inhibited because of this. I know we are all objective and that we are interested in only one thing—successfully solving our mutual problems. So be frank! Ask embarrassing questions. Let's get to the root of each of these topics, and I know the meeting will be successful.

Now to my topic—the product manager and his operating philosophy. As you know, I couldn't resist taking this as my topic. While I'm no Socrates, I am one of Motorola's oldest remaining product managers, dating back to the early fifties, and you are among Motorola's newest. I think I can safely say that in the last 12 or 13 years I have probably made most of the mistakes that a product manager can make. I remember one of our ex-employees telling me on the day that I was made two-way product manager (and, incidentally, his new boss) that he couldn't understand how I got promoted, considering all the mistakes I had made. He was right, of course, about the mistake part—I did make some beauties and so will you—or should I say, so are you. But mistakes come from trying, and success and longevity come from learning from past mistakes and not making them again, but continually improving your batting average. **The integrated result of mistakes and learning is called experience, and nobody will do a good job without it.** I gave a great deal of thought to what to cover in this session. I decided against discussing the mechanics of a product manager's job. I figure that learning about procedures and processes is something that you'll all master. You know that you're responsible for everything about your product line, and your success will depend greatly on the response you get from all kinds of people.

So from now on, let me just discuss the problems of the product manager, and some of the philosophies I've learned in the past years that help get the most from people. Being a product manager in our division is a tough job. Let's forget the glamorous talk about tremendous responsibility that rests upon you, etc., and get down to basics. In the Communications Division, a product manager has complete responsibility for all factors that contribute to profitable operation of his products, even though he doesn't have direct authority over many. I've heard the statement many times that "It's hard enough to get a job done when all the people concerned report directly to you, but it can be practically impossible when many of them report elsewhere." In fact, I think I made that statement many times. Therein lies the toughness—therein lies the secret of success. I remember how I complained regularly that I couldn't possibly be held responsible for profit when I didn't have control of all the things that affected profit. I only had line authority over engineering and in-plant marketing. I didn't control sales, production, purchasing or many other service functions. The easiest solution for the fledgling product manager is to get control over all these operations, and then, by God, he'll really do a job. But I don't think this is the best way to do the job. The best arrangement of direct reporting and supplied services differs from product to product. We do it differently from product line to product line. Our organization works, not because of organization lines but because of people—objective people who act together to get a job done, regardless of who is the boss. **Your success as a product manager will depend on how well you get people who don't report to you to do the best possible job for your products.** This is really no different from the way you should be getting results from your own people.

I know that one of the biggest complaints of product managers is that they have to spend too much time spoon-feeding or cajoling or persuading some other major department head that he should do something. The length of time it takes for such "non-productive" activity is inversely proportional to the other people understanding the problem, and the respect he has for you. Many times we lose patience with the other person because he doesn't immediately agree to our suggestion, because he doesn't attach the same importance to our problems

that we do. This is a good place to interject philosophy No. 1—
"Everyone is trying to do the best possible job he can in an
objective manner." If you believe this, and I do, then the only
thing preventing agreement is a lack of common understanding
about the problem. People in different positions view situations
from different viewpoints and under different conditions. And
it's just possible that because of his specialization in his particular activity, someone who's fouling up the works just may be
right instead of you. Of course, the final decision rests with the
product manager. As in all situations, however, if the other
department head feels strongly, he can always appeal to the
next highest authority who may be me or Art Reese. The same
situation occurs at lower levels in your own organization, and
the same rules prevail. How we who make the final decisions
in these cases act is a major factor in whether or not success
will be achieved.

If you're a good product manager, you'll learn how to handle these situations. You'll learn to work around the negatives
in people and take advantage of the positives. You'll learn to
respect the opinions of the people who don't report to you.
You'll learn to listen to them, even when they expound on
something you think they know nothing about or isn't their
responsibility. You'll learn that there is a time for rule by edict
and a time for agreement through diplomacy; a time for compromise and a time for exercising prerogatives. The most successful organizations are those whose managers have authority
but don't have to assert it; who have responsibility but don't
have to continually remind everyone of it. **Someone once said
that there's no limit to how much good you can do if you don't
care who gets the credit.**

Now let me briefly outline operating philosophy No. 2. "It
is better to receive than to give." For the product manager, this
means that it is better to get whatever help you can from someone else, than to always attempt to do it yourself. If the support

groups to your activity aren't giving you proper service, don't take the easy way out by doing it yourself. Work for the improvement of the service groups. Don't duplicate activities on the premise that you must do it yourself in order to get the job done right. **Remember that while someone else may not do the job exactly as you or your people would, their approach and their results may be just as good as yours.** Doing it yourself many times results in the build-up of new organizations, systems or paperwork that are nothing more than duplications of existing operations. Analyze all your activities, your systems and your projects. Are you doing something that you can eliminate and buy the service elsewhere? Must you set up that new system because the existing one that everyone is using isn't quite what you need? The same is true of product. Are you designing new kits that are just a little different than existing ones? Listen to Bob Peth later today and you'll get a feel for the magnitude of this problem.

Not only should you accept help and suggestions when offered, but a good manager also knows when to ask for help when he's in trouble and before his ship sinks. In the last few months we've had some specific situations that could have been saved if the manager on the job had assessed the situation and asked for help, instead of getting to the point where there was no latitude for assistance. Personal pride and lack of understanding of the freedom of action and resources that his superiors possess keep many individuals from asking for that little bit of help that makes a failure into a success. Adequate periodic checking by superiors, and proper insertion of themselves into problems at the right time, in the right way, not only eliminates catastrophes but trains the people involved.

The next philosophy is: "Pay attention to details." The big problems always get solved, but the difference between success and failure many times can get measured by the attention paid to details. Your customers make major decisions based on details. Tighten up on the details in your own organizations. Sloppiness in the details on the little things soon leads to sloppiness in details on the big things. Whether it's getting to work on time, keeping adequate records or meeting a technical specification 100 percent with full integrity, let's run a tight ship. Let's be sure that all across the line we treat the details of our procedures and products with importance. As a corollary to this, a product manager should personally field-test every new product in his line, and have full knowledge of its strengths and weaknesses. He should periodically check the old products. Challenge your people on everything. I think I sent a philosophy memo to you recently that said, "If you insist on the best, you'll be surprised how many times you get it."

My last philosophical uttering is: "Have a feel for the situation." A "feel" of the situation is one of the most subjective, but important, requirements for proper decision-making and planning. You can't get that feel by sitting in your office reading reports or doing paperwork. So, get out of your offices. Get into the lab or the marketing offices. Go down on the production floor, talk to the testers and the builders. Get out in the field. Talk to the salespeople, visit the customers. Spend your time with your people. Train them by having them participate with you in the solution of a problem, but do it so as not to take the initiative away from them. In the past, I have adopted temporary rules governing my own behavior to ensure that I get out of the office. For periods of time I never scheduled meetings in the mornings. I did paperwork at home, so I had the necessary time to spend with people at the plant. I used to allot a certain amount of my time each day to visit all my key managers. Ask key questions—even make up reasons for seeing them. Follow them through something in which they're engaged. Participate in tests and discussions, always trying to see that your people follow the proper paths of logic and investigation without them knowing that you're leading. Let your managers make the decisions where possible, but help them by exploring alternatives, possible results and problems.

As you have found out, the product manager is responsible for everything, and I mean everything. One of the ways to be sure everything is done right is to do it yourself—be every place, do everything, know everything that's going on and make all the decisions. Of course this is impossible, but if you train your managers right, if they understand and believe in the Motorola philosophies, if they put these philosophies into practice all the way down the line to the last person doing the work, then you don't have to worry about the results.

I hope I haven't sounded too much like a lecturer, but I feel very strongly on this subject of management training in attitude and philosophy. With all the specialized courses in management that can be taken at various schools, the most important training is that which is given on the job. Here is where the manager is made. Here is where we must put our effort, because training our people properly is the surest way to ensure excellent results for our product lines.

1964 will probably be a good year, at least for most of you. During good times it is always easy to loosen up a little on expenses, efficiency and discipline. **But it is the company that concentrates even further on its costs and maintains good disciplines during the good years that weathers the storm of the bad years.** We are going to be just such a company. 1964 is our year for improved performance and cost control coupled with dynamic new product thrust.

BW

June 17, 1971

Management for a New Decade

Presented to the Industrial Management Institute graduation, Lake Forest College, Lake Forest, Illinois.

Today, more than ever before, the importance of well-trained managers cannot be overemphasized. We are living and working in an era when business is being berated from all sides for cheating the public, exploiting the masses, polluting the atmosphere and God knows what else. A recent survey indicates that the public's attitude toward business has been steadily and seriously declining since 1965.

Frankly, it is my opinion that there are no more crooked businesspeople than there are crooked doctors, lawyers, clerks, factory workers or teachers. Forgotten is the fantastic increased standard of living that did not come by accident. It was the result of technological achievement made practical, and delivered to the public in an affordable manner by business, down through the ages. Each of you will play a major role, not only in the continued growth of the free enterprise business system, but possibly in its very survival. History has shown that things tend to swing from one end of the spectrum to the other, passing the center with ever-increasing speed. If you and I and others like us don't persuade the general public that they ought to take a more balanced view of things, there may be a stampede to see how fast the baby can be thrown out with the bath water.

There have been some basic changes in the American economy, and in people's attitudes as well. We simply cannot laugh these off and return to the old way of doing things. **Standing on the record of past success must not lull us into complacency.** It is mandatory that all managers never let themselves think that our business is immortal or that it can't happen here. The fact is, many good businesses degenerate because their managements don't recognize the signs. Let me illustrate this with some purely business examples:

The railroads lost out to trucks, airlines, buses, autos and pipelines.

Everybody once knew that the Sears type of department store wouldn't work.

Established publishers knew that paperback books would never make the grade.

The great A&P company believed that the supermarket was ill-adapted to the American homemaker's shopping interest.

Careful determination of the changes in your business, and in the public's attitude toward it, must be made. Astute decisions that recognize these changes may call for substantial "do differentlies" to be implemented.

You are on the threshold of many crucial strategic changes as you face the challenge of the '70s.

An advertising executive named Tom Dillon pointedly noted that:

"Business has generally evolved along Darwinian lines. Like all living things, a business sought to adapt itself to its environment, and when it failed to adapt itself to changes in that environment, it died.

The business that died out was much like the dinosaur. The dinosaur presumably made good day-to-day adaptations to its environment. It probably made a pretty good choice of what leaves to eat off what trees, and selected the most desirable swamps in which to slosh. At a tactical level of decision, we have no reason to believe that these giant beasts were not reasonably competent.

But when faced with major changes in Earth's climate and the competitive behavior of other animal and plant life, the dinosaur was unable to make a strategic adaptation to its new environment.

For centuries, business organizations have lived and died much as the dinosaur, unable to adapt themselves strategically to their environment with the speed necessary to maintain survival.

The environment of a business is the market, the technology, the competition, the customer's attitude toward business in general and a company in particular. If it chooses to do so, a business can continually make strategic adaptations to these changing environments. It can change its organization, its products and services to maximum adaptation, thereby avoiding the necessary fatalities of the Darwinian system of natural selection."

If we are to survive the fate of the dinosaur, we must have dynamic, strategic market, product and business plans adapted to the changes that will take place, both in the competitive marketplace and in public attitude.

To fail to master your environment is a sure route to failure. Change where change is proper must be accomplished, but change is not always the right answer. Sometimes, rededication to basic points is proper. Each of you must play an important part in this process. You must change and successfully implement new techniques and programs where that is the answer, but you must revitalize customer service or product integrity where that is necessary. Each of you must succeed for all of us to succeed.

There is only one way to do that, and that is to manage your organization, whatever it may be, in the best possible way. Only performance can win the battle—no amount of words will.

I'd like to give you my opinion of the way to do this. It revolves around the question of why a company exists, its relationship to the people associated with it and your responsibility as managers in the enterprise.

Our chairman, Bob Galvin, defines the purpose of a business, "to honorably serve the needs of the community at a profit." In my company's case, our products not only provide entertainment, they help fight crime, work for industry, support national defense and lead scientific breakthroughs. We think we are good corporate citizens in all the communities in which we live, all around the world. Our people work hard in community affairs. We educate our employees, support the local schools, work for social welfare and contribute financially to many areas of the community. We do almost everything that any good private citizen can be expected to do. I'm sure that even though your products or services may be different, each of your organizations can relate a similar story. The very fact that we do all these things, create jobs and turn out useful products at real value, is in itself a major contribution to society that far too few people understand.

Now, what about the words "at a profit"? **Profit is probably one of the most misunderstood and maligned words in our vocabulary.** To some foes of the American system it has become a dirty word. To those who really understand why the United States has achieved a standard of living superior to all others, it is a very important concept.

Let me read you a quote. "The worst crime an employer can commit against the worker is to fail to make a profit." That statement was not made by a big businessman. It was made by Samuel Gompers, founder of the labor union movement in the United States. What did he mean? Well, let's spend a moment talking about profit.

Profit is important not simply because a company greedily wants to make money. Profit is important in a well-managed company because of what it does for people. Profit gives a company—a conglomeration of people—the ability, through the distribution of that profit, to raise the standard of living of the people associated with the company. Whether it is in salaries or profit-sharing to the employees, in dividends to the stockholders, the increasing price of your stock on the market, educational assistance, suggestion payouts or patent awards, the source is always profits. Without the earning of profit, we could have none of these.

Equally important, we must use that profit to invest in new plants, tools, materials and receivables in order to maintain our share of the business, and to grow. If a company starts losing its share of the business and doesn't make these investments, it starts losing position ever more rapidly. The companies that do increase their share, at the losing company's expense, can now make lower-cost products because of their volume. They can invest more in engineering or in improved services to make their company step out in front. It is a snowballing situation when the company that does not make a fair profit and re-invest some of it in the business will have to shut its doors and put *all* of its people out of work. Obviously, a company that sustains a loss may substantially hasten this final result. Business history is replete with these situations. Samuel Gompers knew that in our competitive society, to protect the jobs of the working people, companies must operate efficiently and be profitable.

Simply said, for people to share in a company's profits and thus achieve a better personal life, the company must make a profit. To make a profit, it must be successful in competition with other companies that are in similar businesses. The success of a company is in the hands of the customers, despite the horror stories of many who believe that businesses dominate and exploit the customer. The customer must be served with good product or service at a fair value, or he or she will simply take their business elsewhere, or stop buying. To be successful, a company must have people who do the best possible job, so that it will be number one in every field in which it participates. The success of the individual and of the company, which is really a vehicle for its people, are completely intertwined. We cannot have success for one without success for the other.

The question then becomes, how do we achieve leadership in all our fields of endeavor? I am convinced that, as in the past, people will continue to make the difference, not machines or technology. The right people in the right places will create the technology and design and operate the machines.

Clarence Randall, in his forward to the book *Managers for Tomorrow*, writes:

"We hear much these days about the technological revolution which has transformed American industry in this generation, but altogether too little is being said about the human revolution, which has made this possible. The second is as significant as the first...

The challenge to the manager of tomorrow is to find ways by which each individual can be given opportunity for self-realization and will be valued for himself. Every person within an organization should have the opportunity to grow; the purpose of management is neither to tend nor to tame men, its purpose is to realize the power of men."

If we are to be excellent managers, I suggest that we stop now—all of us, without exception—to review and evaluate our performance in this regard. You've spent four years studying about the mechanics, the technical aspects and the techniques of management. But your studies will be worthless if you can't implement all you've learned in the right way.

One of the ways of measuring the extent to which you are succeeding, to measure the excellence of an organization, and to check if it is truly people-oriented, is to look at its spirit and enthusiasm. In every one of your companies and departments, people should be real fireballs about the importance of their jobs, the company and their opportunity to grow with it. If people aren't so enthusiastic that they can't wait to get to work each day, then you haven't got the kind of spirit and morale that will ensure a leadership position. Given such spirit, average people can do fantastic things. Without it, excellent people turn in second-rate performances.

My question for your critical self-evaluation is: Do you have it everywhere? If not, you've got a lot of homework to do.

Today, many managers blame poor performance and lackadaisical attitude on our present state of economic affluence. They say that people don't want to work hard anymore, and that people aren't interested in giving that little bit of extra effort for perfection. I don't believe any of that.

I believe that 99 $^{44}/_{100}$ percent of the people want to do a good job. More accurately, they want to do the best possible job. The problem is not poor people, it is poor management. Obviously, there is an occasional bad apple, but that is the exception, not the rule. People want to be proud of their company's activities, and proud of their personal contributions to the success of those activities. The challenge to us as managers is to find ways to ensure that all of our people can feel that pride in whatever they do, and in the achievements of their organization, regardless of who did it. Every one of Motorola's 40,000 employees should be proud of the role our company played in the success of the Apollo moonshots, whether they work in the Government Electronics Division, or anywhere else in the corporation.

How do you get pride and enthusiasm? Well, it starts with a deep and abiding concern about people. **Each individual must feel that he or she is important to the success of the business.** In our company, a woman on the production line in our semiconductor products division has got to believe that she fights crime every time she makes a perfect transistor that eventually goes into a Motorola Handie-Talkie® unit; that the quality of her work may save a police officer's life some day when he or she calls for help over that radio. A janitor in our consumer products division has got to know that he or she contributed to the quality of the Quasar TV set in a meaningful way and helped make it the set that both the Holiday Inn and the Marriott chain selected because of its fine performance and reliability.

There is no big razzle-dazzle program that you can put on to get pride. Good people-oriented management is the most significant builder of pride. We as managers must do the major part. The most important job of management is to create the environment and the atmosphere in which each and every person can contribute to the maximum of his or her own capability.

Every individual must feel that the organization truly does offer all the opportunities for his or her own self-fulfillment. As managers, we must ensure that personal challenge and opportunity for growth exist for all who are capable. The individual has a responsibility, too. He or she must put forth their very best effort. They must seek and work to grow. They must also realize that such growth is tied intimately to the success of the enterprise as a whole.

Participative management techniques; continuous, fair, objective people evaluation; and development programs that help a person become more proficient at work and inspire them to take on more and varied responsibility are mandatory. By the way, I'm not just talking about clerks or lower-level supervisors. Department heads and key managers are people, too, and they should get the same concern and treatment.

Proper reward tied to personal contribution is mandatory. Promotions, patent awards and suggestion systems payouts are all ways in which our people can share in the fruits of their own labor and in the success of our company as a whole. Many tools are available. Others tailored to your specific situation must be created by each of you. The challenge and opportunities are there. View it as your responsibility—not anyone else's. You only build pride and spirit by your everyday personal leadership, which must set the example for your people. We can only turn the tide back in favor of business by ensuring that our businesses are concerned about people. Such a business will operate with integrity and honesty, will develop high-quality products and will be properly concerned about its role in contributing to every phase of the public welfare. Because the whole is merely the sum of its parts, we can only achieve the very lofty ideals if people at the grass-roots level practice them in every little way, every day. It is our job to see that we give people the opportunity to do so.

The expert manager of people has to constantly work at developing a proficiency of this talent, until he or she lives and breathes the philosophy of the importance of people. Even then, you must challenge yourself regularly to be sure that in the crush of the moment, you are still taking the time to pay proper attention to people motivation and management, because only by taking the time to do this can you fulfill the requirements for excellence in leadership.

Yes, it takes time and effort to build team spirit, morale and enthusiasm. We must work at it. To those who say they haven't got the time it takes to do this, there is only one reply: You can't afford not to take the time.

You managers will help determine whether or not our system will survive.

I ask of you a continuous concern at all levels for a superb performance in the motivation and management of people.

I commend to you the building and maintaining of unbeatable teams bursting with enthusiasm and pride in all parts of your organization.

I challenge you to: develop new, improved, creative and innovative techniques to turn out more and better product or service at lower cost; operate your organizations at higher efficiency; master the art of flexible planning; and be better than your competitors.

I place upon you the requirement that you must achieve excellence in management, the mandatory results of which must be the success of your organization in fulfilling its business role. For only in this way can we as managers meet our commitment to a better life for our people, and in doing so, revitalize the free enterprise system.

Nothing less is acceptable!

BW

Management Quotations, Poems & Lists

Management

Looking for ideas to improve your area of operation? Pinpoint the need first, and then fill the need. To find the need, answer these questions in terms of your own job:

What made me mad today?
What took too long?
What was the cause of a complaint?
What was misunderstood?
What cost too much?
What did we waste?
What was too complicated?
What was just plain silly?
What job took too many people?
What job took too many motions?
author unknown

"A ship in harbor is safe, but that is not what ships are built for."
John Shedd

"Every successful man I have heard of has done the best he could with conditions as he found them, and not waited until next year for better."
E. W. Howe

"Before it can be solved, a problem must be clearly stated and defined."
William Feather

"A man would do nothing, if he waited until he could do it so well that no one would find fault with what he has done."
author unknown

"To fail to prepare is to prepare to fail."
author unknown

"Failure to make a decision will quickly brand a man as unfit for a position of responsibility. Not all of your decisions will be correct … but it is better to be right 51% of the time and get something done, than it is to get nothing done because you fear to reach a decision."
H.W. Andrews

"Decision is a sharp knife that cuts clean and straight; indecision a dull one that hacks and tears and leaves ragged edges behind it."
author unknown

"One can resist the invasion of armies, but not the invasion of ideas."
Victor Hugo

"The only things that evolve by themselves in an organization are disorder, friction, and malperformance."
Peter Drucker

"It is a fine thing to have ability, but the ability to discover ability in others is the true test."
Elbert Hubbard

Ten Commandments for Handling Ideas

1. *I will never vote no to any idea because "It's impossible ... "*

2. *I will never block a helpful thought because it entails problems, or wait to begin until I find solutions.*

3. *I will never oppose possibility because I've never done it and can't imagine how it could be done.*

4. *I will never obstruct a plan because it runs a risk of failure.*

5. *I will never cooperate in defeating a potentially good idea because I can see something wrong with it.*

6. *I will never squelch a creative idea because no one else has ever succeeded in perfecting it.*

7. *I will never declare any constructive concept to be impossible because I lack the time, money, brains, energy, talent, or skill to exploit it.*

8. *I will never discard a plan or project just because it's imperfect.*

9. *I will never resist a proposal because I didn't think of it, won't get credit for it, won't personally benefit from it, or may not live to see and enjoy it.*

10. *I will never quit because I've reached the end of the rope. I will tie a knot and hang on!*

reprinted from **Daily Power Thoughts** by **Robert H. Schuller,** minister and founder of the Crystal Cathedral

"Good supervision is the art of getting average people to do superior work."
author unknown

"Be realistic—demand the impossible."
author unknown

"No psychology of handling people really works unless we are genuinely and truly interested in other people. All else is mere trickery and will sooner or later fail."
author unknown

"A good manager gets out of his chair and finds out first hand what his people are thinking and doing."
author unknown

"My greatest strength as a consultant is to be ignorant and ask a few questions."
Peter Drucker

"Good managers are people who aren't worried about their own careers, but rather the careers of those who work for them. My advice: Don't worry about yourself. Take care of those who work for you and you'll float to greatness on their achievements."
H.S.M. Burns

"They rise highest who lift as they go."
Gary Price, Sculptor

"The quality of coordination in an organization is the most essential determinant of its survival."
Chester Barnard

"A nation must have doers as well as dreamers if it is to attain greatness. All national greatness has been founded on national prosperity. And it is men and women of deeds rather than unapplied airy theory that bring forth prosperity. The modern business Napoleon is no less of a dreamer than the long-haired visionary; but such a person toils effectively to transform dreams into realities. Many a business leader in this democracy today is as ardent an idealist as the most impractical daydreamer whose only forte is cynicism."
B.C. Forbes

"When we treat man as he is, we make him worse than he is. When we treat him as if he already were what he potentially could be, we make him what he should be."
Herbert E. Klein

"People want to be appreciated, not impressed. They want to be regarded as human beings, not as mere sounding boards for other people's egos. They want to be treated as ends in themselves, not as means toward the gratification of another's vanity."
Sydney J. Harris

"The greatest problem in communication is the illusion that it has been accomplished."
George Bernard Shaw

Teamwork

"Be considerate of others; be a good teamworker; commend more and condemn less; be a propelling force, not a brake."
B. C. Forbes

"Coming together is a beginning; keeping together is progress; working together is success."
Henry Ford

"Large-scale success today is spelled 'Teamwork.' The successful teamworker doesn't wear a chip on his shoulder; he doesn't look for slights; he is not constantly on the alert lest his 'dignity' be insulted. He puts the good of the house, the firm, the institution, the company first. And if the whole prospers, he, as an active, effective, progressive part of it, will prosper with it."
B. C. Forbes

Teamwork
They may sound your praise and
    call you great,
They may single you out
    for fame,
But you must work with your
    running mate
Or you'll never win the game;
Oh, never the work of life
    is done

By the man with a selfish dream,
For the battle is lost or the battle
    is won
By the spirit of the team.

It's all very well to have courage
    and skill
And it's fine to be counted
    a star,
But the single deed with its touch
    of thrill
Doesn't tell the man you are;
For there's no lone hand in the
    game we play,
We must work to a bigger
    scheme,
And the thing that counts in the
    world today
Is, how do you pull with
    the team?

You may think it fine to be
    praised for skill,
But a greater thing to do
Is to set your mind and set
    your will
On the goal that's just in view;
It's helping your fellowman
    to score
When his chances hopeless seem;
It's forgetting self 'til the
    game is o'er
And fighting for the team.
Edgar A. Guest

"Cooperation is doing with a smile what you have to do anyway."
taken from ***Bits & Pieces***

The Parable of the Spoons

A holy man was having a conversation with the Lord one day and he said, "Lord, I would like to know what Heaven and Hell are like."

The Lord led the holy man to two doors. He opened one of the doors and the holy man looked in. In the middle of the room was a very large, round table. In the middle of the table was a large pot of stew, which smelled delicious and made the holy man's mouth water.

The people sitting around the table were thin and sickly. They appeared to be famished. They were holding spoons with very long handles and each person found that it was possible to reach the pot of stew to take a spoonful, but because the handle of the spoon was longer than the person's arm, one could not get the food back into one's mouth.

The holy man shuddered at the sight of their misery and suffering.

The Lord said, "You have seen Hell."

They went to the next room and opened the door. It was exactly the same as the first one. There was a big round table and the same pot of delicious stew, which again made the holy man's mouth water. The people, as be- fore, were equipped with the same long-handled spoons—but here the people were well nourished and plump, laughing and talking.

The holy man said, "I don't understand."

"It is simple," said the Lord.

"It requires but one skill. You see, they have learned to feed each other."

author unknown

What makes the grass grow

"Attempts at despotism ... represent, as it were, the drunkenness of responsibility. It is when men .... are overwhelmed with the difficulties and blunders of humanity, that they fall back upon a wild desire to manage everything themselves ...

This belief that all would go right if we could only get the strings into our own hands, is a fallacy almost without exception ... The sin and sorrow of despotism is not that it does not love men, but that it loves them too much and trusts them too little ...

When a man begins to think that the grass will not grow at night unless he lies awake to watch it, he generally ends either in an asylum or on the throne of an emperor."

G.K. Chesterton,
Robert Browning (1903)

Attitude

August 7, 1967

Attitude Memos

"The greatest stimulus to the
success of the worker is the
attitude of the boss."
David J. Cox

Just Do It!

I attended a division managers meeting the other day. During the meeting, Ray Zack, general manager of the Control Systems Division, told us about an interesting device he has started using in his organization and, in his opinion, has been effective beyond his anticipation. I think the mechanism is equally applicable to any organization because the situation is not unique to the Control Systems Division. Let me explain it to you.

Ray found as time went on that more and more people were coming into his office to talk about what ought to be done, and were making some really fine plans for the future. But sometimes, the plans were good while the implementation was not. Whether it was the feeling that after planning was done the results would follow automatically; or whether it was because the people were waiting for someone to make a decision; or whether it was because too much time was spent in planning and not enough time left for action, is not really known. But the results weren't being achieved. Ray finally got to the point one day of putting a big sign on his office door that said "**Do It**." As Ray put it, it is an adjunct to the philosophy "**Think**."

Of course, thinking and planning are important, but are of no use if thoughts and plans aren't put into operation. Doing is what counts! The good manager uses proper judgment, does his planning and then really goes. It's really a complementary philosophy of the old Communications Division "**Can Do**" attitude.

The program in the Control Systems Division grew to the point that they actually had cards made up, which began to appear in various places around the plant and now appear in large sizes on bulletin boards and walls. I've got one of the "**Do It**" cards on my desk, and seeing it constantly has (I'm ashamed to admit) gotten me off my rear end to do some things I have been putting off and off!

The "**Can Do—Do It**" philosophy is terrific. I plan to discuss it in my next **Comm-Talk** editorial.

Let's pep up our organization. The Communications Division "**Can Do**" attitude creates pride in our performance.

Can Do? You bet!

Do It!

BW

The "Can Do" Attitude

I'm sure you've all heard the expression, "The difficult we do immediately, the impossible takes a little longer." That truly could have been our slogan. Years ago, we shortened it to "**Can Do**!" The people of Motorola have always been proud of the "**Can Do**" attitude and spirit that we've enjoyed since the company was formed. This determination to do anything and everything necessary to do the job, serve the customer and beat the competition, properly restricted by the bounds of ethics and integrity, has built the leadership position we now enjoy.

Whether it's in your personal life or your business career, the successful people are those with the "**Can Do**" attitude. Life in general has become more complicated, both at home and at work. We all make great plans, which, if carried out successfully, would mean something to us, our families or our job. However, while our plans may be wonderful, the implementation many times is not. It is difficult to determine whether it is because we feel that after the planning is done, the results will naturally follow; because we waited for someone to make a decision; because we felt it was someone else's responsibility; or too much time was spent in planning and not enough in doing. But when the results were in, we didn't accomplish the goal. Thinking and planning are important, but doing is what counts. My recent series of memos on Quality of Perfor-

"Don't cry; try!"
author unknown

"Too many of us wait to do the perfect things with the results that we do nothing. The way to get ahead is to start now."
author unknown

mance—High Expectation Levels was designed to set the proper tone, and help all of us have the proper objectives.

Many years ago, one of our division managers had large cards printed that simply said, "**Do It**." They were posted all over the division. Some years later, I added a "**Can Do**" card and did the same thing in the division I managed. It was a good general motivation technique and worked well.

BW

Doing the right thing

Back in 1967, the general manager of one of our divisions implemented the idea of using "**Do It**" signs around his organization to emphasize the necessity of getting things done and not just talking about or studying them. At that time, I took that idea and widely circulated the cards in the Communications Division, where I was the general manager.

Some years later, we added the "**Can Do**" card to indicate that if we really make up our minds to do something, and it is physically possible, we at Motorola can do almost anything. Over the years, we have reinforced the "**Can Do—Do It**" attitude and I see wall cards with both of these sayings in almost every Motorola facility I visit around the world.

I think it is appropriate that we modify the "**Do It**" card in light of our continuing emphasis on **6 Sigma**™ quality as it applies to everything we do—whether it be in marketing programs, management decisions, product development or manufacturing. In a recent conversation with Bob Galvin, he voiced the thought that what is important is not just doing something, but doing the right thing. We don't want to do the expedient thing or the simplest thing that gets the job done if it doesn't get the job done the right way for the long term, the best result of the situation. What's really important is understanding, believing and, in fact, acting—doing whatever is the

"The power of man's virtue should not be measured by his special efforts, but by his ordinary doing."
Blaise Pascal

"right thing now." No short cuts, no improper rationalization. In that regard, and in the hope that we will have the same successful proliferation of wall cards stating this philosophy, I have had printed a substantial number of cards that incorporate the **6 Sigma**™ attitude, and the result that we wish to ensure is our byword. It says simply "**Do the Right Thing Now**." One card is attached to this memo; others are available upon request. **BW**

These are examples of the attitude cards which were distributed with the original memos, reduced for reproduction in this book.

Smile and Say Hello

The importance of being pleasant and friendly was driven home to me the other day by one of my longtime friends: A serious and foreboding look on my face in the cafeteria may make 500 people worried. You may have the same effect in your plant or office. While it is true that everybody can't constantly be happy, I think it is important for us to be pleasant whenever possible.

Another interesting comment that was made to me was the fact that many of our managers just seem to forget to say hello to people as they pass them in the halls or on the plant floors. Certainly this is an affront to anyone you know personally, and a friendly hello or smile is always welcomed. The absence of any greeting has been interpreted by many as an "I'm too good for that sort of thing" attitude. You and I both know that nothing is further from the truth. Maybe sometimes we are concentrating on a particular problem, but I think saying hello would have a positive effect in dealing with our people, since we are a people-oriented company. So, just remember to smile and say hello when you pass somebody in the building.

BW

"Inward sincerity will of course influence the outward deportment; where the one is wanting, there is great reason to suspect the absence of the other."
Laurence Sterne

October 1, 1986

Smiling Means More Than You Might Think

In 1968, I sent out a philosophy memo that was titled "Smile and Say Hello." The other day I received a memo from Bob Killackey of GEG, which commented on just how important being pleasant and friendly really is. He wrote:

> *"I have wondered if top managers realize how much a greeting or even an offhand 'hi' means to a subordinate. To some employees, the top manager is a celebrity.*
>
> *"We all know that top managers are usually completely preoccupied with multifarious business problems and situations as they traverse the halls. That often accounts for them not realizing that someone just walked by. That is understandable. It is also understandable that the person who was seemingly ignored might go home and say something like, 'That guy believes that his position excuses him from the human race.'"*

"For success, attitude is equally as important as ability."
Harry F. Banks

Unfortunately, it is true that many people just seem to forget to say hello to others as they pass them in the hall or on the plant floor. As Bob Killackey points out, the absence of any greeting has been interpreted by many as an "I'm too good for that sort of thing" attitude. You and I both know that nothing is further from the truth. Maybe sometimes we are concentrating on some particular problem, but friendly greetings have a real positive effect. So, just remember to smile and say hello when you pass somebody in the building.

BW

March 15, 1980

Submitted by Barney O'Connor, international sales manager, Telephone and Paging Systems Communications International Division, and Jim Wright, market planning manager, Subscriber Paging Producers Portable Products Division

Who Killed George Dey?

The enthusiasm that George Dey brought to the job the day he came to work for the telephone company was a sight to behold. He listened carefully, absorbed everything he could, did his work the best way he knew how and really tried to learn. George looked at things with a fresh viewpoint and the ideas started coming.

"Why don't we..." "Have they ever tried...?" "I bet we could save if we..." The suggestions poured out. Someone in exasperation finally said, "George, why don't you keep quiet and learn to do things the way they're supposed to be done before you start trying to change the world?" George was crestfallen. He only wanted to help. OK, if that's the way they wanted it, he would keep quiet.

But he wasn't going to be discouraged. He was going to make the people in his department proud of him. He was going to have everyone in the outfit glad to have him on the team. He was going to earn a name for himself as a fellow who really knew his job and wasn't afraid of hard work. That's what he was going to do, and he did. Then one day someone said to him, "Aw, come on, George, what are you trying to kill it for? What are you doing, trying to make the rest of us look bad? Who are you trying to impress?"

George was confused. "Maybe I was wrong," he thought. Maybe he was working too hard. He didn't want others to dislike him. So he shrugged his shoulders and said to himself, "I guess you can't fight city hall."

But if George was discouraged, he didn't show it when he talked about the company with friends and relatives. Selling was the most natural thing in the world as far as he was concerned, and whenever the conversation turned to the telephone (as it often did when people heard he was with the company), he made it a point to let people know about the new equipment and new services that were available.

And when people had a question or an unfavorable opinion about the company he tried to talk it over and see if he could straighten it out for them. At least he did for a while. That ended one night at a party attended by two other telephone people. George was explaining the free calling area in answer to a misunderstanding, when one of the other telephone people (it may have been his girlfriend, who also worked for the company) said, "Oh, for heaven's sake, George, why don't you put your soapbox away? All you ever talk about is the telephone company. Who cares what the free calling area is anyway?"

Well, that's when George Dey began to die. It took a few more incidents, but not many. Oh, he's still walking around, all right. You'll find him dragging through the day, doing the best he can, but it's not much fun anymore. At meetings he'll say things like, "Well, we've always done it this way," or "I don't think it can be done," or "I don't have an opinion." Sometimes you'll see him talking to a new employee, saying something like, "Why don't you keep quiet and learn to do things the way they're supposed to be done before you start trying to change the world?"

There are some who say George died of unknown causes. There are others who suspect he was murdered. What do you think? Who killed George Dey?

author unknown

The Pyramid of Success

John R. Wooden
Head Basketball Coach, UCLA
Reprint permission granted.

Success

Success is peace of mind which is a direct result of self-satisfaction in knowing you did your best to become the best that you are capable of becoming.

Faith
through prayer

Patience
good things take time

Fight
effort and hustle

Competitive Greatness
"When the going gets tough, the tough get going." Be at your best when your best is needed. Real love of a hard battle.

Reliability
others depend upon you

Resourcefulness
proper judgment

Poise
Just being yourself. Being at ease in any situation. Never fighting yourself.

Confidence
Respect without fear. Confident, not cocky. May come from faith in yourself in knowing that you are prepared.

Integrity
speaks for itself

Adaptability
to any situation

Condition
Mental-Moral-Physical. Rest, exercise and diet must be considered. Moderation must be practiced. Dissipation must be eliminated.

Skill
A knowledge of and the ability to properly execute the fundamentals. Be prepared. Cover every detail.

Team Spirit
An eagerness to sacrifice personal interests or glory for the welfare of all. The team comes first.

Honesty
in all ways

Ambition
properly focused

Self-control
Emotions under control. Delicate adjustment between mind and body. Keep judgment and common sense.

Alertness
Be observing constantly. Be quick to spot a weakness and correct it or use it as the case may warrant.

Initiative
Cultivate the ability to make decisions and think alone. Desire to excel.

Intentness
Ability to resist temptation and stay with your course. Concentrate on your objective and be determined to reach your goal.

Sincerity
makes friends

Industriousness
There is no substitute for work. Worthwhile things come from hard work and careful planning.

Friendship
Comes from mutual esteem, respect and devotion. A sincere liking for all.

Loyalty
To yourself and to all those dependent upon you. Keep your self-respect.

Cooperation
With all levels of your co-workers. Help others and see the other side.

Enthusiasm
Your heart must be in your work. Stimulate others.

March 28, 1984

The advertisement by TRW attached to this memo was sent to me by Jerry Orloff, director, Public Relations–Communications Sector. It has a very important message. I hope we don't have too many dimming light bulbs in Motorola. Encouragement of creative, innovative ideas is the lifeblood of a company like ours, whether it is in a new business area or in our major core businesses. Reprint permission granted.

It was just an idea.

An idea is a fragile thing. Turning it off is much easier than keeping it lit.

A company called TRW lives on ideas. So we look for people who have them and for people who won't snuff them out. In recent years TRW has been issued hundreds of patents in such diverse fields as fiber optics, space, lasers and transportation electronics.

Those ideas shone because somebody had them and somebody helped them. And nobody turned them off.

Tomorrow is taking shape at a company called TRW.

A Company Called TRW

February 16, 1970; May 1, 1981 and August 1, 1982

The National Car Rental Company ran an ad recently. You may have seen it. The philosophy, of course, applies to any operation or organization, and it is summed up in the last paragraph. If we want to be the champs, there is only one way to do it. Submitted by Steve Morgan, Semiconductor Group. Reprint permission granted for the use of the copy.

What it takes to be No. 1

"There is no doubt that man is a competitive animal. And there is no place where this fact is more obvious than in the ring. There is no second place. Either you win, or you lose. When they call you champ, it is because you don't lose.

A professional prize fight can last forty-five minutes. That's a long time to keep going. You have to be physically prepared. That means you have to understand pain. There is pain in training. In running that extra mile, when your legs feel like logs. In the dull, monotonous grind, at the light bag and the heavy bag. But there's a reason for it. The moment you step into the ring, you know it was all worth it. If you've pushed your body into its best shape, there's one thing less to worry about. Maybe it will give you one minute's more stamina. That minute can win you the fight.

Then there's the fear. That's always there. You're not in the ring to demonstrate courage. You're in there to win the fight. So you handle the fear, maybe even use it. It's out of sight, somewhere behind you, but if you're not completely prepared, it pops up in front of you and then you're finished.

To win takes a complete commitment of mind and body. When you can't make that commitment, they don't call you champ anymore."

by Rocky Marciano

Why Not the Best

I had applied for the nuclear submarine program, and Admiral Rickover was interviewing me for the job. It was the first time I met Admiral Rickover, and we sat in a large room by ourselves for more than two hours, and he let me choose any subject I wished to discuss. Very carefully, I chose those about which I knew most at the time—current events, seamanship, music, literature, naval tactics, electronics, gunnery—and he began to ask me a series of questions of increasing difficulty. In each instance, he soon proved that I knew relatively little about the subject I had chosen.

He always looked right into my eyes, and he never smiled. I was saturated with cold sweat.

Finally, he asked me a question and I thought I could redeem myself. He said, "How did you stand in your class at the Naval Academy?" Since I had completed my Sophomore year at Georgia Tech before entering Annapolis as a Plebe, I had done very well, and I swelled my chest with pride and answered, "Sir, I stood fifty-ninth in a class of 820!" I sat back to wait for the congratulations—which never came. Instead, the question, "Did you do your best?" I started to say, "Yes, sir," but I remembered who this was, and recalled several of the many times at the Academy when I could have learned more about our allies, our enemies, weapons, strategy, and so forth. I was just human. I finally gulped and said, "No, sir, I didn't always do my best."

He looked at me for a long time, and then turned his chair around to end the interview. He asked one final question, which I have never been able to forget—or to answer. He said, "Why not?" I sat there for a while, shaken, and then slowly left the room.

Jimmy Carter

June 24, 1987

This cartoon was created by Jeff Danziger and appeared in
The Christian Science Monitor ©1987 TCSPS.

March 30, 1970

Submitted by Bill Mahoney, Consumer Products Division.

Keep the Faith, Baby!

by Charles A. Hill
Reprinted from the November issue of
Modern Office Procedures, and copyrighted ©1969 by
Penton Publishing, subsidiary of Pittway Corporation.

*Attitude
Articles*

Top executives are looking closely at an important motivation element to see if incoming business leaders can be selected more precisely. What makes one man succeed when another fails, even when both seem equally intelligent, equally logical and equally hard-working? What makes one idea work and another fail when both seem to have equal merit?

Obvious and terribly important characteristics are: knowledge, dedication, ability to get along with people, willingness to put in many more hours than the average, articulateness, health, fast decision ability and a constant drive to learn. Many top executives now believe a very old-fashioned term, *faith*, has more to do with success than any other factor. The absolute and complete belief, or faith, that a company, a policy, a program, or a rule is probably right, and if not right, that it can be changed and made right, is common to all successful top executives. **This faith should not be confused with resistance to change or as an excuse to hold onto the past.** On the contrary, it encourages change. It creates the acceptance of change to make the company better in all ways.

You get the greatest benefit when this faith is applied to people, whether your subordinates or superiors. Successful top executives believe in the abilities of their people. You find greater delegation of responsibility when an executive has faith in his subordinates.

Doubting Thomases say this permits too many mistakes, allows inept men to remain in responsible positions. Not true. Failure is failure under any system, but in those companies where everyone believes that he and others can do the job, there is less questioning, explaining and dickering for position, and more time to work on the tasks to be done.

The same faith seems to make ideas succeed. Although machine technology has advanced further than our ability to use it, procedures are available which make it possible for most companies to greatly improve their white collar production levels. **Too often these procedures don't work in a company's best interest because the people involved in making them work don't believe the procedure will succeed.**

The faith principle is not new. We have known for a long time that the salesman who believes in his product will sell more than the salesman who does not. However, it is new to apply the faith principle to executive motivation and idea implementation. It takes a great amount of sophistication and introspection to admit that faith helps you do a better job. Perhaps a new term is needed or perhaps business leaders aren't ready to accept such simple characteristics as a management tool, but more frequently, you hear successful men say, "I believed we could do it, so we did it!"

If this management concept is to be implemented, it must start with the individual. Check yourself. Do you have faith in your ability? Do you have complete faith in your company and your company's ability to correct its imperfections? **If you don't believe in your company, and you don't believe in the people around you, then it's time you found a company in which you can have faith.**

September 9, 1970

*The attached article was sent to me by Fred Hamm of the
Communications Division.*

Nobody Gives a Damn

Something has gone wrong with our country. We live with a
constant, sickening frustration which goes beyond racial problems, pot and pollution, yippies and hippies.

More and more, nobody gives a damn.

The sickness is national in scope. Like cancer, it feeds on
itself. Each of us feels more and more abandoned by his fellow-
men. We are at the mercy of machines. We become just numbers in the lottery of life. We begin to live only for ourselves.

We look to our own ease and profit. We don't care about
anyone else's river, lake or forest—or even the air they breathe.
We'll sell anybody anything so long as it makes money. We
seem to feel the world owes us—and we owe it nothing. Give
us the eternal coffee break.

The results of such attitudes are all around us now.
Services are deteriorating. It's hard to find repairmen who
will do a good job the first time—or even the second or third.
Expensive new products lose knobs and buttons like cheap
toys. Waiters act as if they're doing you a favor to serve you.
Sales people gossip while you wait. Doctors' offices schedule
appointments in thoughtless clusters—as if your time is worth
nothing. Cleaners not only fail to get the spot out but end up
losing the whole suit.

With far fewer trains running than a decade ago, there
are nearly twice as many derailments. Airlines misdirect thousands of bags. Department stores can't straighten out your
billings. People who handle complaints don't bother to call you

back. And, yes, magazines foul up on subscriptions, and you get letters demanding payment for copies you never received.

Granted, good services and products can still be found—but it's something to talk about when it happens. We are over-joyed when a mechanic fixes our car the first time around, or when a clerk thanks us after taking our money.

Now foul-ups happen even in smaller communities. No longer do the big cities have an exclusive on don't-give-a-damn-ism. Taken alone, each failure is a mere annoyance. But when you add them all up, they are destructive to the individual and to our nation.

No man can live without caring. He loses his drive to be responsible, his competence declines, he ends up without pride or purpose. Mutual concern and cooperation are the adhe-sives of society. Without them, no society can solve its prob-lems, build a healthy future, gain the respect of its young—indeed, survive.

Our sorry state of affairs is usually blamed on the pressures of overpopulation, on mass production, planned obsolescence, computerization. All these excuses have one thing in common. They pass the buck to intangibles. People seldom seem to be personally at fault.

The apologies are feeble. True, the population explosion results in a crush of consumers. But wouldn't you expect that more consumers would mean more producers? As for mass production, who wrote the rule that it must be sloppy? And planned obsolescence is not, as so many people seem to think, inherent in the products they buy. Instead, it results more often from the emergence of new and different designs. It's a fact that major consumer items are more expertly engineered than ever before, but the best design can't overcome careless workmanship.

Computers? They can't do anything by themselves. Computers are fast—not dumb. Man can't come close to computers in speed, but he has intelligence. Whatever computers do, right or wrong, starts with the human input. That's what everything comes down to: people. And people isn't the other guy, it's all of us. It's you.

This is why there's still hope. When people really want to do something, it gets done. Take pollution. For years we've accepted the damage we were doing to our environment as the price we had to pay for progress. But because enough of us became concerned, things suddenly are beginning to happen. It remains to be seen if we have the guts to follow through on this enormous chore.

Admittedly it's easier to rally to a cause when danger threatens from outside. The really tough problem: when we ourselves are the problem.

So what can we do? To start with, we must strive to get back our sense of personal worth—that wonderful feeling that our job counts for something and that our life counts for something. It's a matter of self-respect.

Look at your work not only as a means to produce a paycheck but as a contribution. Even if your job bores you, you'll enjoy it more if you set yourself the challenge of doing it better every time.

Stop blaming the other guy. This doesn't mean we should be willing to accept low standards. Just don't expect more from others than you expect from yourself.

Let's encourage responsibility where we find it, praise the efforts and good work of others, show them that they are appreciated. On the other hand, when you are hit by a foul-up, really raise hell. Don't hesitate to carry your beef all the way to the top. If this fails, take your business away. It's better to do without than to live with second-rate products or services. It's a fact that people who run businesses today are more concerned about consumer complaints than ever before. You may find that hard to believe, but it's true. Above all, let's cut out the rotten excuse that we are "only human," that we're entitled to some daily quota of error or indifference. Only human? What an incredible denial of the human potential. Only human? This is the ultimate insult.

Remember that man's greatness does not lie in perfection but in striving for it. Once we don't give a damn, we have lost everything.

Success and the Uncommon Denominators

by Cheryl Kilbourn
Reprint permission granted by *Room Mate* magazine,
Red Lion Hotels and Inns.

Often as I travel about speaking to businesses and organizations I am asked the question, "What does it take to make it ... what do I need to do in order to be successful?" Or, "What are the special principles, the secret of achievement, the unique guidelines to the hidden path?"

Men and women alike propose these questions as though they really expect a magical success formula! **The one sure thing about success is simply this ... there is no formula.**

Today the word success has become well-worn and used in almost every imaginable way. Yet, few people find it easy to define. Working with business executives, business owners and corporate employees, I find people who pass the test of success by all outward appearances (substantial income, beautiful home, nice cars) but on the inside something is missing ... they really don't feel successful.

What then, is success? My definition is this: Success is being who you really are and striving to become all that you are capable of becoming ... the very best you. Although there is no magical formula, there are a few common denominators, or perhaps "uncommon denominators," of the successful person, as follows:

1. **Believe in yourself.** You do have unlimited potential, but to tap it you must begin by believing in yourself. What most of us really want more than anything else is the awareness that we are worthy persons. All our other drives for pleasure, power, love, search for meaning and

creativity are attempts to fulfill that primal need for personal dignity. Believing in yourself is essential to personal happiness and effective functioning because it affects every aspect of your life. Most people don't know what a success they could be if they would only believe in themselves. Simply put, it is a positive self-image, which gives rise to self-confidence. As someone once said, "There is no defeat in life except from within, unless you are beaten there, you are bound to win."

2. **Set Goals.** Without goals we wander and drift like a ship without a rudder. Likewise, even a well-equipped ship without a course is likely to end up in the wrong place. **Too often we proceed through life without ever asking the question, "Where am I headed … what is it I want to accomplish?"** There are several important areas to consider as you set goals: personal relationships, vocational, recreational and financial. All are important and need to be in balance for you to experience the fullness in life that is meant for you. As you establish goals, give some thought to each area. Don't plan only vocational goals, as you may find yourself lopsided—and down the road, burned out.

    Unless you have definite, precise, clearly set goals it is difficult to tap the unlimited potential that lies within. The decisions you make today will affect the rest of your life … and many of those decisions are based on your goals.

3. **Develop self-discipline.** There is a price for success in any area of life, and that price is discipline. Without discipline it is difficult to believe in yourself, to try to persist. Successful people are those who have learned to do things failures don't want to do. And that requires discipline.

4. **Believe in hard work … not a life of idleness.** People who are idle often are those who have tried and failed, or those who have never set goals or become excited about working towards their goals. Just as a successful career requires

work, so do successful relationships, spiritual growth ... and every other area of life. They all take desire, determination and work. **Those who want to be the best they can must be willing to work ... or expect a life of mediocrity.**

5. **Learn to be patient.** Accomplishment is the result of both patient waiting and working. The road to any goal will not be too long if you take it one step at a time. You cannot hurry success any more than a flower can bloom before its season. Just as walls are built one brick at a time and races are won one step at a time, so success is a journey made one step at a time. To persevere without patience is difficult and to be ambitious without patience can destroy the most hopeful career.

6. **Eliminate the word impossible.** What does impossible mean to you? Does it describe a task you cannot perform, a goal you cannot attain? Or does impossible describe a task you *believe* you cannot perform, a goal you *believe* you cannot attain? What you believe are impossible goals today, can be tomorrow's achievements. Look at it again, this time in a new, positive way. Separate the first two letters from the rest of the word and what does it say? I'm possible. Never think of the impossible. It is dangerous because your mind always tries to complete what it pictures. Instead, stamp on your mind the word "possible." Develop and build on the possibility principle knowing you can do anything your mind can conceive if you truly believe. Live by it, live with it ... and you can accomplish outstanding possibilities.

7. **Learn to smile at adversity.** Remember that adversity need never be a permanent condition. Difficult obstacles, reverses or other setbacks are a part of life, but it is how you choose to look at them that makes the difference. It is true, of course, that we cannot always control conditions and circumstances, but we can choose the attitude and

thoughts we will have about them. **Though your heart is broken and you feel bruised and torn, know that conditions will change, just as the sun will rise and the calm will follow the storm.** In the darkness, remember that failure and adversity are our stepping stones to success … and two of our greatest teachers.

8. **Give yourself away.** Live life with a sense of service. Charles Dickens said, "No one is useless in this world who lightens the burden of it to anyone else." "Being" means being in relationship to others. Lift yourself by lifting others and remember—we make a living by what we get … but we make a life by what we give. The reality is that we are rich only through what we give and poor only through what we keep.

9. **Act.** Procrastinate and you will struggle in vain. The journey of a thousand miles begins with the first step. Goals will remain dreams unless you work towards them. Once your goals are established, the time for action has come. The finest goals, the most well-thought-out plans will be useless unless you take action. Don't wait for the moment of absolute certainty because that moment almost never comes. Everything between birth and death is checkered with uncertainty. Your efforts must not be diluted because setbacks occur or some other barrier interferes. Keep yourself sold on the idea that for every problem there is a solution, and you will find it. The trouble with most people is they imagine problems and obstacles and quit before they start.

10. **Be yourself.** You are one of a kind and gifted with special skills, abilities and talents no one but you can use. Use them, whatever they may be, and forget about being someone else. A talented salesperson can win awards and a sub-

stantial income with his skills, but let him build houses and he will starve. Many people spend countless hours, days, weeks ... even years trying to be like someone else and wishing they were someone else. Remember, when you try to be someone else the best you can be is second best. Admit your limitations (we all have them) and then go beyond them. Be committed to building on all the good within. No one can take your place! Realize this and be yourself.

You need not be a loser in life. You can enjoy the fruits of victory. **The greatest enemy any of us have is the enemy within that holds us back needlessly.** Remind yourself regularly that you are better than you think ... and you will find you can accomplish whatever you want to accomplish if you have the desire and believe. Successful people are not supermen or superwomen and success does not require a super intellect. Neither is there anything mythical about success. And, it isn't based on luck. Successful people are people just like you who have developed a belief in themselves and what they can do.

Erich Fromm says, "Their greatest tragedy in life is that most human beings die before they are fully born." Life is a journey, success is a journey, and it is how you make the journey that counts. Do the very best you can, in the things you do best. **You have no obligation to succeed — but you do have an obligation to be who you really are and strive to become all that you are capable of becoming.** Do this, and you will find, deep down, that you have found true success.

Attitude Quotations, Poems & Lists

Winners vs. Losers

The Winner—is always a part of
the answer;

The Loser—is always a part of the
problem;

The Winner—always has
a program;

The Loser—always has an excuse.

The Winner—says, "Let me do
it for you;"

The Loser—says, "That's not
my job."

The Winner—sees an answer for
every problem;

The Loser—sees a problem in
every answer.

The Winner—sees a green near
every sand trap;

The Loser—sees two or three sand
traps near every green.

The Winner—says, "It may be
difficult, but it's possible;"

The Loser—says, "It may be possible, but it's too difficult."

author unknown
Reprint permission granted by
Great Lakes Chemical Corp.

The Art of Getting Along

Sooner or later, a man, if he is
wise, discovers that life is a mix-
ture of good days and bad, victory and defeat, give and take.

He learns that it doesn't pay to
be a sensitive soul; that he should
let some things go over his head
like water off a duck's back.

He learns that he who loses
his temper usually loses out.

He learns that all men have
burnt toast for breakfast now and
then, and that he shouldn't take
the other fellow's grouch
too seriously.

He learns that carrying a chip
on his shoulder is the easiest way
to get into a fight.

He learns that the quickest way
to become unpopular is to carry
tales and gossip about others.

He learns that buck-passing
always turns out to be a boo-
merang, and that it never pays.

He comes to realize that the
business could run along perfectly well without him.

He learns that it doesn't
matter so much who gets the
credit so long as the business
shows a profit.

He learns that even the janitor
is human and that it doesn't do
any harm to smile and say
"Good Morning," even if it is
raining.

He learns that most of the
other fellows are as ambitious as
he is, that they have brains that
are as good or better, and that
hard work and not cleverness is
the secret of success.

He learns to sympathize with
the youngster coming into the

business, because he remembers how bewildered he was when he first started out.

He learns not to worry when he loses an order, because experience has shown that if he always gives his best, his average will break pretty well.

He learns that no man ever got to first base alone, and that it is only through cooperative effort that we move on to better things.

He learns that bosses are no monsters, trying to get the last ounce of work out of him for the least amount of pay, but that they are usually fine men who have succeeded through hard work and who want to do the right thing.

He learns that folks are not any harder to get along with in one place than another, and that the "getting along" depends about 98 percent on his own behavior.
Wilfred Peterson

Enthusiasm is the ingredient that transforms a philosophy into a reality, or a principle into action. For example, at 211 degrees water is merely hot water—inert and powerless; at 212 degrees water is live steam with more inherent power than man has ever been able to harness at full efficiency, notwithstanding all his engineering knowledge and skill. At 211

degrees the water in a locomotive boiler exerts not one ounce of pressure, and the locomotive is as powerless as if the firebox were cold and empty; but at 212 degrees that same water provides awesome power to haul a mile-long train of cars over a mountain.

Many of us are, figuratively speaking, walking around at 211 degrees; and for want of but one additional degree of temperature, we are relatively inert, powerless and much less effective than we could be. If, however, we would throw only one more log on the fire, we could raise our temperature to 212 degrees, thus increasing our power to infinity.

Just one degree added to 211 may seem insignificant by itself, yet it is of incomparable and immeasurable importance. The man who cannot or will not elevate his temperature to the boiling point may never achieve anything worthwhile in this world; but the man who can and will maintain his temperature at or above 212 degrees, who can and will operate his boiler at full steam, who can and will stoke his fire of enthusiasm at white heat, can achieve anything in this world to which he may reasonably aspire.
author unknown

"Whether our work be pleasant or unpleasant depends less upon the work itself—provided it be honest—than upon our attitude towards it. Let us strive to regard our work as our best friend in the whole wide world, and the chances are that our work will become friendly to us. The worker whose heart is in his pay envelope is little likely ever to become a filler of pay envelopes for others. It isn't our position, but our disposition towards our position that counts."
B.C. Forbes

"He only is exempt from failures who makes no efforts."
Richard Whately

"We can do anything we want to do if we stick to it long enough."
Helen Keller

"More trouble is caused by doing nothing than by doing too much."
Italian proverb

"Nine times out of ten the best thing that can happen to a young man is to be tossed overboard and compelled to sink or swim for himself."
James Garfield

"If you are doing nothing worth doing, then life is not worth much to you. There is infinitely more joy in honest endeavor than in any surfeit of ease. The bumps and the knocks and the hammer blows broaden us. The disappointments and failures enrich our characters. Even our disillusionments should not stop us from trying to 'see good in everything.'"
B.C. Forbes

"The wise and active conquer difficulties by daring to attempt them. Sloth and folly shiver and shrink at sight of toil and hazard, and make the impossibility they fear."
Nicholas Rowe

"Life gives nothing to man without labor."
Horace

"There is no impossibility to him who stands prepared to conquer every hazard."
Sarah J. Hale

"Have patience, remembering that everything worth building costs much expenditure of zeal and effort and sweat. Also have faith, and never for a moment doubt your ability to do the thing you really want to do."
B.C. Forbes

"He who desires but acts not breeds pestilence."
William Blake

"Man is a reasonable animal who always loses his temper when he is called upon to act in accordance with the dictates of reason."
Oscar Wilde

"He that is patient will persevere; and he that perseveres will often have occasion for as well as trial of patience."
Tryon Edwards

"Many people fail to recognize opportunity because its favorite disguise is hard work."
Two Minutes

"What danger can ever come from ingenious reasoning and inquiry? The worst speculative skeptic ever I knew was a much better man than the best superstitious devotee and bigot."
David Hume

"Who never doubted, never half believed. Where doubt is, there truth is—it is her shadow."
Gamaliel Bailey

"No one knows what he can do 'til he tries."
Publilius Syrus

"How much better off all of us would be if we would tackle our present work in the spirit that the gold prospector seeks his precious metal! Look for your gold mine in the job you are doing now."
author unknown

"Ambition is the last refuge of the failure."
Oscar Wilde

"Not his job makes a man little or big, it is himself, his spirit, his character. If these be right, then his job will sooner or later reflect the fact. He will not forever be kept down when his merits entitle him to be raised up. The wait may be long. But it will not be heartbreaking. His inner consciousness of faithful effort will buoy him up. Life's 'failures' do not all wear rags; some of the most pitiable of them can write their names to seven-figure checks. The 'successes' are not all recognizable on sight."
B.C. Forbes

"Every production of genius must be the production of enthusiasm."
Disraeli

"Too many young people are so busy getting ready for the next job they don't do a good job where they are."
Greenman

"Wrinkles should merely indicate where smiles have been."
Mark Twain

"The individual who knows the score about life sees difficulties as opportunities."
Norman Vincent Peale

"Success is better when it's harder to achieve."
Aristotle

"Things may come to those who wait, but only the things left by those who hustle."
Abraham Lincoln

"All through the ages the most worthy characters have been those who were dynamically enthusiastic over some definite aim and end. The young man who is afraid to manifest enthusiasm lest his dignity suffer is not likely to have much dignity to lose by and by. Enthusiasm is the propelling force that is necessary for climbing the ladder of success."
B.C. Forbes

"Our own opinion of ourselves should be lower than that formed by others, for we have a better chance at our imperfections."
Thomas À. Kempis

"Initiative is to success, what a lighted match is to a candle."
O.A. Battista

"It doesn't take great men to do things, but it is doing things that makes men great."
Arnold Glasow

"Some men see things as they are and ask, 'Why?' I dream of things that never were and ask, 'Why not?'"
Robert F. Kennedy

"Don't find fault, find a remedy. Anybody can complain."
Henry Ford

Enthusiasm
That certain something that makes us great—that pulls us out of the mediocre and commonplace—that builds into us Power. It glows and shines—it lights up our faces—Enthusiasm, the keynote that makes us sing and makes men sing with us.

Enthusiasm—The maker of friends—the maker of smiles—the producer of confidence. It cries to the world, "I've got what it takes." It tells all men that our job is a swell job—that the house we work for just suits us—the goods we have are the best.

Enthusiasm—The inspiration that makes us "Wake Up and Live." It puts spring in our step—spring in our hearts—a twinkle in our eyes and gives us confidence in ourselves and our fellow men.

Enthusiasm—It changes a deadpan salesman to a producer—a pessimist to an optimist—a loafer to a go-getter.

Enthusiasm—If we have it, we should thank God for it. If we don't have it, then we should get down on our knees and pray for it.

Upon the plains of hesitation, bleached the bones of countless millions who, on the threshold of victory, sat down to wait, and waiting they died.
author unknown

"Refuse to become discouraged ... If at first you don't succeed—you're running about average! No one knew this better than Thomas Edison, who, to find a substitute for lead in the manufacture of storage batteries, conducted 20,000 unsuccessful experiments."
author unknown

"No one ever finds life worth living. One always has to make it worth living."
Richard H. McFeely

"Nearly every important achievement in this world has been done by people who refused to give up."
author unknown

"American institutions—which are here taken for granted, like oxygen—are the subject of our wildest dreams in Eastern Europe. I have a certain pity for the Americans, because they do not know how to cherish what they have, and what others know they have."
Leopold Tyrmand

"There is no comparison between that which is lost by not succeeding and that lost by never trying."
author unknown

"Our days are like identical suitcases; all the same size, but some people can pack more into them than others."
Advance

"Failure is not falling down; it is failing to get back up ... quickly!"
author unknown

"The reason why most men do not achieve more is because they do not attempt more."
author unknown

"Weak men wait for opportunities, strong men take them."
Orison Swett Marden

"Ninety percent of the work done in this country is done by people who don't feel well."
Teddy Roosevelt

"Discipline is the refining fire by which talent becomes ability."
Roy L. Smith

"It is the unquestioning acceptance of the already existing that keeps people from being creative; it is an attitude of mind, rather than the lack of innate ability to create."
Kaiser Aluminum News

"Our greatest glory is not in never falling, but in raising every time we fall."
Confucius

"Every man takes the limits of his own field of vision for the limits of the world."
Arthur Schopenhauer

"I have simply tried to do what seemed best each day, as each day came."
Abraham Lincoln

"The strong man, the positive, decisive man who has a program and is determined to carry it out, cuts his way to his goal regardless of difficulties. It is the discouraged man who turns aside and takes a crooked path."
Orison Swett Marden

"A man with ability and the desire to accomplish something can do anything."
Donald Kircher

"If you have a great ambition, take as big a step as possible in the direction of fulfilling it, but if the step is only a tiny one, don't worry if it is the largest one now possible."
Mildred McAfee

"Incompetence springs from indifference."
Arnold Glasow

"Lack of will power and drive cause more failures than lack of ability and intelligence."
Harry F. Banks

"You win not by chance, but by preparation."
Roger Maris

"There is no fun equal to the satisfaction of doing one's best. No amount of money got by questionable expedients can win success or bring happiness. The things that are most worthwhile in life are really those within the reach of almost every normal human being who cares to seek them out."
B.C. Forbes

"Life is like a game of poker: If you don't put any in the pot, there won't be any to take out."
Moms Mabley

"A man rarely succeeds at anything unless he has fun doing it."
author unknown

"A man in earnest finds means, or, if he cannot find, creates them."
William Ellery Channing

"Nothing is impossible; there are ways that lead to everything, and if we had sufficient will, we should always have sufficient means."
La Rochefoucauld

"People are always blaming their circumstances for what they are. I don't believe in circumstances. The people who get on in this world are the people who get up and look for the circumstances they want and, if they can't find them, make them."
George Bernard Shaw

If you think you are beaten, you are;

If you think that you dare not, you don't;

If you'd like to win, but you think you can't,

It's almost certain you won't.

If you think you'll lose, you've lost;

For out in the world you'll find

Success begins with a fellow's will—

It's all in the state of mind.

If you think you are outclassed, you are;

You've got to think high to rise;

You've got to be sure of yourself before

You can ever win a prize.
Life's battles don't always go

To the stronger or faster man;

But sooner or later the man who wins

Is the man who thinks he can.
author unknown

The attitude that "the only way I can get things done is to do it myself" is a dangerous one if the tasks referred to can and should be accomplished by a subordinate. Being busy is no virtue in itself—not if you're doing other people's work.

How are you fixed for time?
Spiegel, Inc.

"The struggle for success is so keen in every line of business that responsible positions are awarded to men of solid merit, of indefatigable energy, of unbounded enthusiasm, of unflinching courage and possessing infinite faith in the worthiness of their life's work. In return, these men must be thoroughly organized, must give each executive assistant responsibilities and allow him scope to discharge them. And, above all, non-swell-headedness!"
B.C. Forbes

"Genius is one percent inspiration and 99 percent perspiration."
Thomas Edison

"The chief ingredients for success are imagination plus ambition and the will to work."
Thomas Edison

"It's amazing what ordinary people can do if they set out without preconceived notions."
Charles F. Kettering

"A closed mind, like a closed room, can become awfully stuffy."
author unknown

"What the mind can conceive and believe, the mind can achieve."
W.C. Stone

"Minds are like parachutes. They only function when open."
James Dewar

Don't Quit

"When things go wrong, as they
sometimes will,

When the road you're trudging
seems all uphill,

When the funds are low and the
debts are high,

And you want to smile, but you
have to sigh,

When care is pressing you down
a bit—

Rest if you must, but don't
you quit.

Success is failure turned inside out—

The silver tint of the clouds of
doubt,

And you never can tell how close
you are,

It may be near when it seems
afar;

So stick to the fight when you're
hardest hit—

It's when things seem worse that
you mustn't quit."
author unknown

___

They Tell of Adam

"How frightened he must have
been when, for the first time, he
saw the sun disappear, ending the
light of day.

It was Adam's first darkness.

How could he accept the night,
when he had never seen a dawn.

After the splendor of the sun,
how dark the darkness was for
him, how desperate the long ter-
ror of the first fall of night—until
Adam learned that day would
come again; could see that there
is light and order in the universe.

And then Adam began to see
how much light remains in the
sky at night; the stars, and their
enduring promise of the sun, the
returning star of day.

Adam learned that the night is
never wholly dark, and that no
night is endless.

Even as each of us must learn
it; in our own times of trouble
and of darkness.

The light is never far."
author unknown

___

"The great problem with some
people is that the key to success
doesn't fit their ignition."
author unknown

___

"Failure is success ... if we learn
from it."
Malcolm S. Forbes

___

"The worst bankrupt in the
world is the man who has lost
his enthusiasm. Let a man lose
everything else in the world but
his enthusiasm and he will come
through again to success."
H.W. Arnold

___

"Men must try and try again.
They must suffer the consequences of their own mistakes,
and learn by their own failures
and their own successes."
Lawson Purdy

___

"How much you do is important.
How well you do it is decisive."
author unknown

___

"In all things, do your best. The
man who has done less than his
best has done nothing."
**Charles W. Schwab,
Bethlehem Steel Company**

___

"We all find time to do what we
really want to do."
William Feather

___

"The reason why so few people
are agreeable in conversation is
that each is thinking more about
what he intends to say than
about what others are saying,
and we never listen when we
are eager to speak."
La Rochefoucauld

"While the right to talk may be the beginning of freedom, the necessity of listening is what makes the right important."
Walter Lippmann

"Nine-tenths of the serious controversies which arise in life result from misunderstandings; result from one man not knowing the facts which to the other man seem important, or otherwise failing to appreciate his point of view."
Louis D. Brandeis

"Men are never so likely to settle a question rightly as when they discuss it freely."
Thomas Macaulay

"Conversation means being able to disagree and still continue the conversation."
Dwight MacDonald

"Better to remain silent and be thought a fool, than to speak and remove all doubt."
Abraham Lincoln

"How it is said is as important is what is said ... so listen with both eyes and ears."
author unknown

"Everytime you talk, your mind is on parade."
author unknown

Four Kinds of Bones
1. There are the **Wishbones,** who spend all their time wishing somebody else would do all the work.
2. There are the **Jawbones,** who do all the talking, but they do very little else.
3. There are the **Knuckle-bones,** who knock everything that everybody else tries to do.
4. Finally, there are the **Back-bones,** who get under the load and do all the work.

author unknown

"It is better to become bent from hard work than to become crooked from avoiding it."
author unknown

"Human beings can alter their lives by altering their attitudes of mind. As you think so shall you be."
William James

Look For the Good and Praise It!
In everything the good is there; our goal is to find it.

In every person the best is there; our job is to recognize it.

In every situation the positive is there; our opportunity is to see it.

In every problem the answer is there; our responsibility is to provide it.

In every setback the victory is there; our task is to claim it.

In every adversity the blessing is there; our adventure is to discover it.

In every crisis the reason is there; our challenge is to understand it.

Be different, be original, be unique ... Look for the good and praise it!
William Arthur Ward

Winners and Losers
When a loser makes a mistake, he says, "It wasn't my fault;" when a winner makes a mistake, he says, "I was wrong."

A loser blames his "bad luck" for losing—even though it isn't bad luck; a winner credits his "good luck" for winning—even though it isn't good luck. A loser is always "too busy" to do what is necessary; a winner works harder than a loser, and has more time. A loser makes promises; a winner makes commitments.

A loser says, "I'm sorry," but does the same thing next time; a winner shows he's sorry by making up for it. A loser says, "I'm not as bad as a lot of other people;" a winner says "I'm good, but not as good as I ought to be."

A loser would rather be liked than admired, and is even willing to pay the price of mild contempt for it; a winner would rather be admired than liked, although he would prefer both.

A loser says, "I only work here;" a winner feels responsible for more than his job.

A loser says, "That's the way it's always been done here;" a winner says, "There ought to be a better way to do it."
author unknown

"O, do not pray for easy lives; pray to be strong personally. Do not pray for tasks equal to your powers; pray for powers equal to your tasks. Then the doing of your work will be no miracle."
Phillips Brooks

"Any fool can criticize, condemn and complain— and most fools do."
Dale Carnegie

"Rare is the job in which ability alone is sufficient. Needed also are loyalty, sincerity, enthusiasm and cooperation."
author unknown

"Enthusiasm is self-generated pressure in the tank. Little is accomplished without it."
Arnold Glasow

"No one is really beaten until he is discouraged."
John Lubbock

"A man without mirth is like a wagon without springs. He is jolted disagreeably by every pebble in the road."
Henry Ward Beecher

"Only those who have the patience to do simple things perfectly will acquire the skill to do difficult things easily."
Friedrich von Schiller

"The more I want to get something done, the less I call it work."
Richard Bach

"Whatever you do, you need courage. Whatever course you decide upon, there is always someone to tell you you are wrong."
Ralph Waldo Emerson

"The world is crying for men who know what should be done and who have the courage to do it."
Arnold Glasow

"You won't learn to hold your own in the world by standing on guard, but by attacking and getting well hammered yourself."
George Bernard Shaw

"Experience shows that sometimes success is due less to ability than to zeal. The winner is he who gives himself to his work, body and soul."
Charles Buxton

"Most men fail, not through lack of education, but, from lack of dogged determination, from lack of dauntless will."
Orison Swett Marden

Man who says, "It cannot be done," should not interrupt man who is doing it.
Chinese proverb

"Your success is not predicated on the failure of others. When you help others succeed, they help you succeed."
Robert Half

"Faith that the thing can be done is essential to any great achievement."
Thomas N. Carruthers

"Nothing is achieved before it be thoroughly attempted."
Philip Sidney

Most Important Words
The 6 most important words: "I admit I made a mistake."
The 5 most important words: "You did a good job."
The 4 most important words: "What is your opinion?"
The 3 most important words: "If you please."
The 2 most important words: "Thank you."
The least important word: "I."

John H. Harland

Aim So High You'll Never be Bored

The greatest waste of our natural resources is the number of people who never achieve their potential. Get out of that slow lane. Shift into that fast lane. If you think you can't, you won't. If you think you can, there's a good chance you will. Even making the effort will make you feel like a new person. Reputations are made by searching for things that can't be done and doing them. Aim low: boring.
Aim high: soaring.
©United Technologies Corporation, 1989

"Ninety percent of life is just showing up. The other 10 percent—what you do after that—is the important part."
George Bush

"History is full of instances where victory instead of defeat would have resulted by battling only a little longer. Many need to be reminded of this. Any weakling can surrender; any coward can give up. To succeed, we must have the will to succeed, we must have stamina, determination, backbone, perseverance, self-reliance, faith. Let us grit our teeth and heroically resolve to keep on keeping on. Triumph often is nearest when defeat seems inescapable."
B.C. Forbes

"Whether we find pleasure in our work or whether we find it a bore, depends entirely upon our mental attitude toward it, not upon the task itself. Almost every conspicuously successful American owes his rise to having thrown himself heartily into his work and to having done it better than ordinary. Promotion comes to those who demonstrate that they can do more and better work than others. Look upon your work as the lever by which you can rise in the world. To get the best and most out of life, put the best and most of yourself into it. Eventually each of us gets the reward we merit."
B.C. Forbes

Youth

Youth is not a time of life; it is a state of mind; it is not a matter of rosy cheeks, red lips and supple knees; it is a matter of the will, a quality of the imagination, a vigor of the emotions; it is the freshness of the deep springs of life.

Youth means a temperamental predominance of courage over timidity, of the appetite for adventure over the love of ease. This often exists in a man of sixty more than a boy of twenty. Nobody grows old merely by living a number of years. We grow old by deserting our ideals.

Years may wrinkle the skin, but to give up enthusiasm wrinkles the soul. Worry, fear, self-doubt bows the heart and turns the spirit back to dust.

Whether 60 or 16, there is in every human being's heart the lure of wonder, the unfailing child-like curiosity of what's next, and the joy of the game of living. In the center of your heart and mine there is a wireless station; so long as it receives messages of beauty, hope, cheer and courage, you are young.

When the aerials are down, and your spirit is covered with the snows of cynicism and the ice of pessimism, then you have grown old, even at 20. But so long as your aerials are up, to catch the optimism, there is hope you may die young at 80.
Samuel Ullman

"Authority without wisdom is like a heavy ax without an edge, fitter to bruise than polish."
Anne Bradstreet

"Great Spirit: Grant that I may not criticize my neighbor until I have walked a mile in his moccasins."
Indian prayer

"If you look for fault in man, you'll surely find it."
Abraham Lincoln

Attitude

"I could not help recalling a story that seems to be quite applicable to the present situation of the foreign businessman in Japan. It is a story about two salesmen from Europe who visited a less developed country some time ago. One of the salesmen sent a cable back home, **'PLS Forward five million shoes because nobody wears any shoes,'** *whereas the other salesman sent a telegram to his office saying,* **'Impossible to sell any shoes here.'"**
Professor Kobayashi, Tokyo's SANNO Institute of Business Administration and Management

"Before you can discipline others successfully, you must discipline yourself."
William Feather

"Gentleness is a divine trait: Nothing is so strong as gentleness, and nothing is so gentle as real strength."
Ralph W. Scokman

"Praise makes good men better and bad men worse."
Thomas Fuller

"Responsibility is a detachable burden easily shifted to the shoulders of God, fate, fortune, luck or one's neighbor."
Ambrose Bierce

"How oft the highest talent lurks in obscurity!"
Plautus

"Trust men and they will be true to you; treat them greatly and they will show themselves great."
Ralph Waldo Emerson

"It often happens that I wake at night and begin to think about a serious problem and decide I must tell the Pope about it. Then I wake up completely and remember that I am the Pope."
John XXIII

"There is no such thing as a born hard-worker, a born salesman or a born genius. We are all born ignorant, with innate underdeveloped abilities. What we do with these underdeveloped abilities is up to us. You can't afford to merely let things happen. If you want to be successful, you have to make things happen."
Mark Brinkerhoff

"There is a thing called knowledge of the world which people do not have until they are middle-aged. It is something which cannot be taught to younger people because it is not logical and does not obey laws which are constant. It has no rules."
T.H. White

"He conquers who conquers himself."
Latin proverb

"If a man can have only one kind of sense, let him have common sense. If he has that and uncommon sense, too, he is not far from genius."
Henry Ward Beecher

"What counts in any system is the intelligence, self-control, conscience and energy of the individual."
Cyrus Eaton

"In helping others to succeed we ensure our own success."
William Feather

This is a story about four men named Everybody, Somebody, Anybody and Nobody.
There was an important job to be done and Everybody was asked to do it. Everybody was sure Somebody would do it. Anybody could have done it and Nobody was prepared to do it. Somebody got angry about that because it was Everybody's job. Everybody thought that Anybody could do it but Nobody realized that Somebody would not do it.
It ended up that Everybody blamed Somebody but in actual fact Nobody blamed Anybody.
author unknown

Decisions, Decisions

"Sometimes the decision to do nothing is wise. But you can't make a career of doing nothing. Freddie Fulcrum weighed everything too carefully. He would say, "On the one hand ... but then, on the other," and his arguments weighed out so evenly he never did anything. When Freddie died, they carved a big zero on his tombstone. If you decide to fish—fine. Or, if you decide to cut bait—fine. But if you decide to do nothing, you're not going to have fish for dinner."
©United Technologies Corporation, 1982

"All things come to those who wait ... If they work like hell while they wait!"
author unknown

"The self-renewing man is versatile and adaptive. He is not trapped in techniques, procedures or routines of the moment.

He may be a specialist but he has also retained the capacity to function as a generalist.

The self-renewing man is highly motivated and respects the sources of his own energy and motivation.

He knows how important it is to believe in what he is doing.

Enthusiasm for the task to be accomplished lifts him out of the ruts of habit and customary procedure.

Drive and conviction give him the courage to risk failure. And not only does he respond to chal-lenge, but he also sees that challenge where others fail to see it.

For the self-renewing man the development of his own potentialities and the process of self-discovery never end."
John Gardner

The Busy Man's Creed

"I believe in the stuff I am handing out, in the firm I am working for, and in my ability to get results. I believe that honest stuff can be passed out to honest men by honest methods. I believe in working, not weeping; in boosting, not knocking; and also in the pleasure of my job. I believe that a man gets what he goes after, that one deed done today is worth two deeds tomorrow, and that no man is down and out until he has lost faith in himself. I believe in today and the work I am doing, in tomorrow and the work I hope to do, and in the sure reward which the future holds. I believe in courtesy, in kindness, in generosity, in good cheer, in friendship and in honest competition. I believe there is something doing, somewhere for every man ready for it. I believe I'm ready—right now!"
Elbert Hubbard

"My grandfather once told me that there are two kinds of people: those who do the work and those who take the credit. He told me to try to be in the first group; there was much less competition there."
Indira Gandhi

"I use not only all the brains I have but all I can borrow."
Woodrow Wilson

Quality

Quality Memos

Quality Is the Product of Everyone

We are embarking on a program of improving the quality and reliability of the products and services that we render to our customers so that we may continue to deserve their business. Too often, the quality of our product is associated only with the workmanship performed in the manufacturing operation. Because quality is inherent in all of our jobs, from the general manager on down, I have addressed this letter to all Communications Division Motorolans and their colleagues in our subsidiary companies, Motorola Communications and Electronics Inc. and Motorola Communications International Inc. Thus, it includes Motorolans in sales, marketing, engineering, purchasing, production and accounting.

A customer's order must be taken courteously, written up accurately, typed without error and scheduled for shipment in accordance with our ability to produce it. The product must be designed well, the components must be of the highest quality and they must be where they are supposed to be when needed in the manufacturing process. The product must be wired, soldered, assembled, tested and packed correctly, then shipped at the right time to the right place.

It must be installed without fault and maintained in the field with competence. **If we do all these things properly at a fair price, then, and only then, can we expect customers' continued support in the way of new orders.**

Most of us know these things well. But it is not enough just to talk about quality in general. We must do something about it. We are. I said before that all our departments play an important part in the quality picture. Therefore, we must have programs in all departments. These programs already have been or will soon be implemented. They involve evaluations of our engineering techniques, a review of our component parts quality, an evaluation of our manufacturing procedures, tools, fixtures and training. Our field sales operations, factory scheduling, purchasing and material control procedures are likewise being studied.

The maintenance of high standards of quality is like the strength of the proverbial chain. It is only as strong as its weakest link. A poor operation, anywhere from the salesperson taking the order to the person installing the equipment, will produce a poor result for the customer.

Programs have been and are being implemented, and tools and facilities improved. But tools, programs and facilities can only create the environment that makes quality possible. They do not themselves produce quality. Individual awareness, skill, determination and dedication produce quality. I am asking everyone to pay particular attention to the maintenance and improvement of our proud standards of quality. I ask that each of you rededicate yourselves to the quality philosophy. I ask that each of you help by searching out and being alert to those things that can be improved or those things that are causing problems. Report these to your supervisor with your recommendations for improvement. Not all ideas can be evaluated

"No matter how small the undertaking, do it as well as you can. You can't afford to do anything but your best.

Don't get into the way of thinking, 'Oh, this is such a small and unimportant job that it makes no difference how sketchily I do it.'

If you are not reliable in small things you can't be trusted with big things.

Never be afraid of doing a little bit more than you are actually called upon to do.

The employee who is always afraid that he will do too much will never amount to anything."
Dr. Wallace C. Abbott,
founder, Abbott Laboratories

simultaneously or all implemented because of various reasons. But all will be given proper evaluation.

Motorola Communications products have set the world standard for quality and reliability. We do not wish to merely maintain that standard. We want to raise our level of performance to an even higher point, so that we continue to set the pace in the marketplace for fine products, excellent service and unapproachable quality. To do this requires the wholehearted effort and support of every person in our organization, regardless of his or her area of operation. I know that each of you will do your part.

I thank you for your continuing contributions to maintaining our position of leadership in the eyes of the real boss, the customer.

BW

March 15, 1984

Quality of Performance — High Expectation Levels

I'd like to start this memo by thanking all of you for your contributions, and for your continued effort to achieve our objectives and goals.

From time to time you have received philosophy memos from me that included various quotes that agreed with our company's philosophy or made a specific, timely point. I would now like to speak to you more directly about the things we must do to achieve our goals, and the level of expectation we must set for the quality of our performance.

It is our objective:

To be the worldwide leader in all of our businesses, and to ensure their continued growth by supplying products, systems and service to our customers with greater value than our competitors, in all respects.

To do this profitably.

To share the profits of our endeavors with our stockholders and our employees who have contributed to the achievement of our objectives.

In asking myself whether every step in this objective is achievable, I can unequivocally answer yes, even after the most searching analysis. Our markets are growing rapidly. We have the technological ability and talent to do the job. We have good people who can be counted on to meet the constant challenges of growth. We have a management attitude that supports whatever is necessary to do the job, and we have integrity of purpose and deed that governs the way we handle ourselves.

"The goal is zero defects. It is difficult. But we have to get rid of the idea that we can permit some leeway simply because total elimination of defects is so difficult. We should not speak of this issue in percentages. For instance, if a consumer comes across a defective product which happens to be 0.01 percent of all the goods produced at the factory, as far as that customer is concerned there is a 100 percent defect record. **Masaharu Matsushita,** president, The Matsushita Company

As we move through 1984 and face the challenges of our objectives, it is appropriate that we take the time right now to reconsider what we are doing every day to achieve our goals. In the heat of problem-solving, we sometimes get so involved in the details of specific situations that we overlook, or don't take the time to operate by, the basic philosophies of management that we all know so well. **But it is strict adherence to basic philosophies in attacking all problems and opportunities that determines success or failure.** In applying those basic tenets, you cannot go overboard and put all your emphasis on any one to the neglect of the others, nor vacillate from one to the other. They must be applied evenly and regularly.

How, then, will the quality of our performance be measured, and how can we achieve the high level of performance that we must have? I would like to break that down into four basic measures. I think these four measures apply, whether you are a salesperson, a line wirer, a purchasing agent or an engineer. The only difference is the specific unit of measure. These measures are:

1. Accomplishment. Did we do what we said we would do, everything we said we would do, and did we do it well?
2. Timing. Did we do it on time? Not a day, or a month, or a year late, or 90 percent of it on time—but all of it on time?
3. Cost. Did we do it for the proper cost just as we had planned, and not missing it by 5 percent, 10 percent or 20 percent?
4. Was the objective or goal, no matter how well it was executed, the right one?

For example, was the result of a perfectly executed product plan a product that the customers really needed and wanted more than those offered by our competitors? If this is true, will the product be delivered on time, when they need it, at a price they can afford, and with a cost that allows Motorola to make a fair profit? Not achieving all of these conditions consistently will soon lead to failure.

To achieve the results we need, it is first necessary to believe that it is possible to lay out a workable plan and meet it fully. **In other words, you must believe that 100 percent achievement is possible.** I do. Lesser results must only be acceptable as steps in a timed program of getting to 100 percent achievement.

What are some examples of the things that we must do in order to meet our corporate goals?

1. We must make careful selection of the new products we introduce and the new business areas we enter.
2. We must have newly designed products go into production with no changes required later.
3. We must plan for, buy, bring in and handle our materials with unquestioned accuracy.
4. We must have zero defective units go out the shipping door, and to do this we must wire, solder, assemble and test our equipment without fault.
5. We must meet productivity standards, whether in the factory or the field, and whether it is the production line rate or the budget of a sales or marketing department that is the standard.

I know it is easy to say these things and not always so easy to achieve them, but they are achievable. More important, they must be achieved in all departments by all people regardless of how small the operation. The whole is the sum of all of its parts. Ninety percent achievement by each group in a series operation, whether it is in producing our products or selling them, results in a compounded effect that many times yields only 50 percent overall performance.

How do you go about getting 100 percent achievement?

Review the basics of your responsibility in detail. What are you expected to do, when and for how much? Do you know? If not, find out fast. Do your people know what each one of them must do, in detail? Do they all know the required results of their group or department, and how their performance affects it and all of us, right out to the customer? If not, better tell them fast. Work with your people to be sure they know these things, and that they have the tools and guidance from you, or anyone else they need to do their job. Solicit their suggestions as to how to do the job. They are a fountain of knowledge. Then set high expectations. Ask them to achieve those results, and ask them regularly. When they don't, help them to achieve by training, or modifying techniques or procedures. Don't accept substandard achievement.

I believe that 99 $^{44}/_{100}$ of the people will do a fine, professional job if they know what is expected of them and they are given the atmosphere, guidance and tools to do the job.

In short, become involved with your people—not one hour a day, but most of the day. You think you don't have the time to become involved? There is nothing more important to occupy your time! Study your own activities. How can you rearrange your own schedule to make the time? Where can you delegate activities or get help from someone else that frees you up? The most important job that you as managers and senior professionals have is to work with, motivate and build people, because people do the job. With the proper spirit and "gung-ho" attitude, average people move mountains. Without it, geniuses fall flat on their faces. Everyone wants to contribute and wants their contribution appreciated. **The efforts of thousands of hard-working, spirited people is unbeatable.** The reward for success is continued leadership, pride, sense of accomplishment, personal promotion, increased compensation and profit sharing.

"*Efficiency is doing things—not wishing you could do them, dreaming about them, or wondering if you can do them.*"
Frank Crane

Obviously, we have had problems created for us by the outside influences of inflation, the economy, the competition, etc. There will always be problems. Only the names will change from time to time. Equally important is the fact that opportunities stem from the problems, and new opportunities abound. All of you are working diligently to improve our performance. I, for one, am not ready to settle for less than the best quality of performance by saying that we can't do anything about a situation because it was created outside the company, or outside a particular department. Settling for less than the best performance eventually means loss of leadership, followed quickly by lesser profits and lesser rewards for all of us. I don't think that you will settle for less than the best either.

May I ask, then, that each of you carefully make a searching review of your own activities and those of your people. Review them against the basic philosophies and goals of your own organization. If necessary, reorient your thinking and procedures so that you concentrate on the really important things that will ensure meeting the highest level of expectation in the quality of your performance—100 percent of the time.

BW

April 16, 1984

Small Errors Are Not Always Small

A number of you have written to me asking if the incorrect dating of the Quality of Performance—High Expectation Levels memo, dated 1983,* was a test to see how many of you would catch the error. Obviously, those who have written have passed the test. Unfortunately, it was not a test, and therefore is illustrative of the fact that mistakes can be made that shouldn't be. **While it may seem unimportant on this particular memo, if this were a customer order or a piece of correspondence used as evidence in litigation, it would have been a very serious mistake.**

Those of you who wrote to me were correct in "calling me" on it. It's a lesson in the importance of 100 percent performance. I encourage you to continue to speak to me or anyone else in the organization who does not maintain the appropriate level of performance, or who creates mistakes that you catch.

BW

*This memo is in the immediately preceding pages, dated March 15, 1984.

I cut the attached article from the Chicago Daily News *the other day. It is a good discussion of some of the problems faced by businesses today, and they happen because businesses let them happen. I am not advocating uncontrolled use of the "stick," but I do advocate the idea that we must hold our employees responsible for a quality job at reasonable costs, done in the proper time period. We must continue to ask our employees for the kind of performance we expect, and not rationalize that good people are hard to get, and we must live with whom we can get. Almost every time we have asked the employees to measure up to our standard of quality and treated them fairly, they have gotten the job done correctly and demonstrated higher morale as well.*

Prosperity and Laziness

by J. A. Livingston

*Quality
Articles*

Four examples of prosperity:

1. An auto owner was overjoyed when the service station manager said, "Yes, your car is ready—motor checked, wheels rotated, everything in order."

   The customer thought, "Well, that's one place that keeps its promise."

   A few days later, his wife put some groceries in the trunk, and saw a void. Where, oh where, was the spare tire?

   No, it wasn't stolen?

   It was at the service station. "Sorry," said the manager-owner, "that was a bad one." The motorist pondered uneasily: "Was the rest of the work done so haphazardly? Did no one check the job?"

2. A couple went into a concession-chain restaurant noted for its quick, on-the-road service, picked out a table for two, and waited and waited and waited. Finally, the man beckoned the hostess.

   Before he could say anything, she said, "How did you get here at this table?"

   "We just sat down."

"Why didn't you wait in line 'till I could get to you?"

"There was no line, and we didn't see you."

Grudgingly, she handed over two menus and told a waitress to attend to them. But the service was terribly slow. The waitress had too many tables. The hostess didn't care.

3. In a supermarket, three long queues crawled toward the cashiers at the checkout counter. Five minutes, 10 minutes—little progress. Finally, two customers, in exasperation, abandoned the carts they had so painstakingly filled and walked out. Time lost, sales lost.

4. The silverware (steelware would be more precise) in this cafeteria is set in receptacles marked teaspoons, knives, forks and soup spoons. But the soup spoon container holds teaspoons as frequently as soup spoons. Could it be that the busboys can't read? Or is the cafeteria short of soup spoons?

Readers, I'm sure, can match these examples of frustration. The skirt from the department store comes shortened instead of lengthened. The laundry delivers shirts minus buttons. The china, lovingly selected, arrives as a jigsaw puzzle—all broken up because of poor packing.

Cause: Too much carrot, not enough stick.

Look at the help-wanted ads. Column after column of them. In proportion, the situations-wanted ads are negligible. Jobs are looking for people, rather than people for jobs.

Wages go up. Organizations offer bonuses to employees who bring in candidates for employment. People switch positions with ease for higher income.

Result: No stick. No penalty for indifference, incompetence and ineptitude. No wonder this is called "The Age of the Goof-Off."

Prosperity has become so diffused that people—and this means organizations—have become careless as to the literal meaning of the word. A subordinate who knows he can walk across the street to a competitor and get another job is impervious to reproof.

A company won't scold or dock an employee who is discourteous or inefficient. The danger of losing an employee is greater—and the consequences more costly—than losing a customer. Every "body" counts in a period of shortage.

In those far-away and long-ago days of the industrial cycle, unemployment—the danger of losing a job—was the stick that supplemented the carrot. The prospect of unemployment or the loss of business was the penalty for shoddy, get-by and indifference.

But recessions are socially unacceptable in the Great Society. To suggest that unemployment has an economic function is ...

Sorry. My fingers hit the wrong keys. I shouldn't have typed such an antisocial notion. But in the age of Goof-Off, what does it matter?

October 15, 1973 and May 7, 1987

Accuracy is a Winner's Policy

by Evan Hill

Excerpted with permission from "Accuracy is a Winner's Policy," *Reader's Digest*, October 1973. Copyright ©1973 by The Reader's Digest Assn., Inc.

The electrician wiring my new house worked swiftly and efficiently. But I asked him, "Couldn't you put those outlets in closer to the floor? Six inches down, perhaps, where they won't be so conspicuous?"

He shook his head. "No," he said, "it's the code—the electrical code. They've got to be this height."

"State law?" I asked.

He nodded. "Town, too."

Next day I made a few telephone calls. Our state building code did not specify anything about the height of outlets. Our little town did not even have a building code. What the electrician referred to must have been just a local contractor's custom.

What difference did it make, six inches up or down? Not much, perhaps. **Still, the electrician had been inaccurate about a matter in which he should have been expert, and so he undercut my trust in him.** If he made an obvious error like that, that I could see, what might be hidden behind the walls where I couldn't check? And what about the accuracy of the bill?

Our safety and sense of well-being—our lives, in fact—depend on the degree to which we can trust the accuracy of the people we deal with. For example: in July 1971, a jumbo 747 jet was damaged on takeoff in San Francisco. Fortunately, no one was killed, although there were serious injuries. Later, the pilot testified that the flight dispatcher had told him his runway was 9,500 feet long, which it was. However, mostly because of construction work, only 8,400 feet were available. This led to a miscalculated takeoff speed and the accident. Investigators thus came down to the use of incorrect takeoff speed, resulting from a series of irregularities, tiny pieces of misinformation, or lack of information. Every day thousands of passengers stake their lives on the gamble that bits of information vital to their safety will be transmitted with absolute, scrupulous accuracy.

Inaccurate or imprecise language can lead to diplomatic incidents, or, conceivably, even to war. The English diplomat Sir Harold Nicolson decried "the horrors of vagueness." He wrote, "The essential to good diplomacy is precision. The main enemy is imprecision."

The charge of the Light Brigade, the famous 19th century disaster, has been attributed to vague and misunderstood orders. Lord Raglan's aide may have compounded the confusion when he transmitted the order to Lord Lucan and gestured vaguely as to which guns were to be attacked. As a result, the Light Brigade rode into the very center of the Russian army rather than against a redoubt where the Russians, in disarray, were removing their guns. Whatever the reason, of the 609 British cavalrymen who made the charge, only 198 returned.

When my Uncle George remarked that a man "kept a dull ax," that was about as severe a condemnation as he could muster. And he applied that phrase to others besides woodsmen. I thought of Uncle George's saying when I worked on a newspaper with a photographer who labeled a picture of the White Mountains of New Hampshire as the Canadian Rockies.

He laughed when he said it was just an error. Some error—
3,000 miles. I suspected I'd have to check every picture identification, and I was right.

Few executives consider accuracy a special virtue—they
just expect it. **The makers of loose and exaggerated statements
may seem to get more attention, but the habit of accuracy casts
a long shadow ahead.** Its users are trusted, relied on, and so
become obvious candidates for responsibility. After all, if you
have a choice between a guess man and a fact man, which do
you trust?

How can we develop the art of accuracy? Here are some
pointers.

1. **Fact:** Do Your Homework. We live in a time of the instant
   opinion, the prefab argument and the pseudo-statistic.
   Facts are not always known or easy to interpret. But we
   must do our homework so we at least know what the facts
   are thought to be. Further, we must give proper weighting
   to all the relevant facts, not "picking our cases" and ignoring
   those that weaken our position.

2. **Precision:** Develop the Reference Book Habit. Accuracy is
   not just a matter of facts; it is also correct spelling, punctua-
   tion, grammar, measurement, context, relevance—in a word,
   precision. I learned this from my first city editor, who taught
   me that a door is not a doorway; that "no injuries were
   reported" does not mean "there were no injuries;" that a
   man charged with burglary is not necessarily a burglar.

As Dr. Richard Asher told aspiring medical writers in the
Journal of the American Medical Association, "Look up everything you quote. You may be certain there is a book called
Alice in Wonderland, and that it mentions a 'Mad Hatter;' that
there is another book called *Alice Through the Looking Glass;*

that Sherlock Holmes said, 'Elementary, my dear Watson;' and that in the Bible story of Adam and Eve, an apple is mentioned. In all five cases you are wrong."

Similar situations occur all the time. And to discover the facts then requires that we carefully weigh conflicting evidence and build one observation on another. This takes discipline, as well as a healthy skepticism. **The accurate person will more often withhold his judgment than hazard a wild guess. He is more willing than most to say, honestly, "I do not know."**

At its best, accuracy is a painstaking, caring, patient and reasonable faculty of mind. And, ultimately it is creative, too. For it not only looks up facts, it discovers them in the first place.

February 15, 1977

*Submitted by Joe Tucker, National Telephone Sales Group,
Communications Division, Schaumburg.*

The Making of a No. 1 Spud

Reprinted from *Telephony* magazine.

Consistency is perhaps the most important element in producing first-class results. That holds for telephone work or just about anything. Even potatoes. There are four grades of potatoes—the cull, the No. 3, the No. 2 and the most valued prize of all, the No. 1. Every farmer tries to produce as high a percentage of the profitable No. 1's as possible. And the secret of doing so is the same as that in producing other successes.

Potatoes are prepared and planted equally in the field—same day, same way, same place; they receive the blessings of the same soil and sun. The element that varies is water, which, in the spud's life, is parallel to the need for effort in our own. As soon as water hits the "eye" from which the potato plant grows, it sprouts and puts out leaves and roots; then perfect, oval potatoes begin to form. **How well they develop depends upon how well the irrigation water is applied—just as the value of each of us and our work depends upon the consistency of our application of effort.**

In potatoes, the cull is a worthless, discarded reject because of soft spots, rot, cuts and sun-green ends. These faults are caused by too much water too often, which rots part of the tuber and exposes other parts, causing sun scorches and cuts. Too much misdirected effort can be very costly.

The No. 3 spud is a right healthy specimen, but it has bumps, knots, knobs and other deformities which result from the plant getting small spurts of water—enough to stimulate growth, but not enough to fulfill it. A No. 3 is used as cattle feed and brings a very low price.

The No. 2 is almost a No. 1, but not quite. It started out right and was watered consistently until just about the end of the season. But the farmer got behind and missed watering; the potato began to taper off and stop growing. A narrow neck formed at its stem. Then the farmer caught up and shot an ample amount of water to the plant. It drank thirstily and the spud began to grow again, only it ended up with an hourglass configuration without good market appeal. It is worth half as much as a No. 1.

The No. 1 spud brings top dollar and is always in demand. How does it get there? From the day it was placed in the growing environment it was watered regularly, on schedule, with the right amount of water. Consistency was the thing that made the difference. The same thing applies to people and work. Too many have ample knowledge and access to the right tools, but apply them erratically and finish second or third or worse. **Most of these mediocrities could be a No. 1 grade product if they would just take a lesson from a good potato farmer.**

November 10, 1992

Competitive Success Requires Participation, Teamwork and Quality

Presented to the MIT Sloan School of Management, Senior Executive Program.

Quality Speech

I'm going to start today by setting the stage for three key points. Over 40 years ago, when Motorola was making monstrously large mobile radio telephone units with big klunky stepping switches, a group of engineers had a vision—or at that time, really, a dream. The dream was this. We believed that when a person made a telephone call, they wanted to talk to another person, wherever that person was, not just when he or she was in a vehicle. Therefore, sometime in the future whenever a baby was born, he or she would be given a miniature portable telephone and assigned a personal telephone number for use anywhere in the world. If you dialed that number and it rang six times without being answered, you could assume that the party being called was dead!

A wild dream to have in those days. We knew then that it was not currently possible and had no idea when it would be. All sorts of research and development and invention had to occur to make it so.

But that vision was a driving force for 40 years to work constantly for miniaturization, to design for lower current to reduce battery drain and extend operating life, and to reduce weight. And so we did—for years. **Over the years, we developed whole lines of radio pagers, and Handie-Talkie® units and pack sets for public safety and business organizations — each line of products becoming smaller and lighter, and working longer on its built-in batteries.**

Among these products was a radio pager that allowed you to be paged anywhere in the United States, a wristwatch in combination with a pager, and recently a credit-card-sized pager for complete U.S. coverage. About 10 years ago, Motorola introduced the Dynatac® portable cellular telephone, which was the first part of the dream coming true—but still briefcase-sized and with cellular coverage only in major metropolitan areas. Three years ago, the MicroTAC® portable cellular telephone, the flip phone, was introduced, which really did fit in a pocket. Then came the MicroTAC® Lite™ and just a couple of months ago, the MicroTAC® Ultralite™, weighing only 5.9 ounces.

And then in 1990, Motorola announced the Iridium™ Satellite system, which will really make that crazy original dream come true. **Sixty-six satellites in nonsynchronous orbit, 400-plus miles above the earth, integrated with today's terrestrial cellular systems, will provide cellular-type coverage literally to every place on the globe.** Iridium™ is a $4 billion program with satellite launch starting in 1996 and the whole system in commercial service in 1998. The portable units themselves are today the size of our original Dynatac® units, but will eventually resemble the MicroTAC® pocket-sized unit.

Our vision over 40 years ago, no matter how general and crazy it may have seemed at the time, was an important driving force for technological development. But in order to pull off the realization of that vision—a successful worldwide Iridium™

cellular system—there are three other required ingredients. They are the three points that I am going to cover today. Let me telegraph them to you very directly.

> Mandatory for Iridium™ success—and for that matter, any commercial success today—is perfect quality. We can't have failures in space or in portable units operating in the African jungle. We have a good start on this with no failures in any of the Motorola equipment that has been on all U.S. space shots, and with Malcolm Baldrige Award quality in our current cellular portables.

> Because of high development cost and high subsequent operating cost, we must have maximum efficiency in design, manufacturing and operating the system. This means cooperation and teamwork within and between very diverse types of organizations.

> To win competitively, we must have highly motivated people contributing their best effort all the time.

Those are my three major points for today. Now let me tell you the story in a little more detail. In Motorola's growth from a $500 investment in 1928 to over $11 billion in sales in 1991, we have regularly practiced aggressive renewal. We have tried to continually improve our processes and functional skills. Over the years, we have changed from a totally domestic U.S. automobile radio manufacturer to a broadly diversified, high-technology, global electronics company. Our sales are split approximately 50-50 between the United States and the rest of the world, with about 44 percent of our employees outside of the United States. We operate 76 major facilities in 22 countries, not counting sales and service offices throughout the world.

With all of our history of renewal and change in the past, in the late '70s we recognized that we needed to change our historical way of doing things in many places at a much faster rate if we were to survive. The catalyst for that conclusion was substantially increased competition by Japanese and other foreign competitors. The result of that increased competition forced us to make a deep introspective analysis—to challenge everything that we were doing that prohibited us from serving the customer better than anyone else in the world and also to reduce cost at the same time.

For government organizations, while the causes for such an introspective evaluation may be different, the result is about the same. Recession, inflation, drought, real estate failures, bank problems and budget balancing all create a difficult economy, one that does not yield the historical level of revenues to governments. At the same time, demands are being made for increased performance to solve a growing set of complex problems. **Dramatic improvements in efficiency and quality of service achieved through *totally new* approaches become absolutely mandatory.**

No doubt you have all heard the saying, "If it ain't broke, don't fix it." An article from the February 1987 *Machine and Tool Blue Book* takes issue very successfully with these sayings. It says:

"When viewed in the light of a nation's industrial capability, if taken at face value, they are utter nonsense, damaging, and a block to the country's growth and productivity. In every country something needs fixing and tampering, and we need to work hard at it.

If we hadn't tampered with success, we would still be an agrarian society. Many countries were successful nations in the early 19th century. A bunch of "malcontents" had to tamper with the lovely farm country and develop steam engines, machine tools, and railroads, to say nothing of the social and cultural tampering in areas like health, education, social services and work design. Such tampering changed one type of successful country into another type of success.

We must break, smash, revise, fix, tamper and destroy everything that stands in the way of our becoming the most competitive business force in the world. Better products, better service, lower costs. It will take guts and hard work and not little slogans."

This philosophy is captured very well in newspaper ads run recently by the Cigna Insurance Co. They say, "If it ain't broke, fix it. Take fast and make it faster. Take smart and make it brilliant."

One key factor in improving performance is attitude. In my opinion, where competitive or better-than-competitive performance does not exist in this country, it is because we do not accord an appropriate sense of urgency and priority to that issue, have not set high enough expectation levels and have not committed 150 percent to their achievement. In those places, we have not set unmatched customer satisfaction as the superordinate goal, and meant it. We in the United States are not dumb. We are not incompetent. We are not lacking in creativity, determination and commitment. **When we understand a problem or an opportunity, and when we accord it the appropriate sense of urgency, we are quite capable of achieving superior results.**

We at Motorola concluded many years ago that we were in a battle for survival. The most important result of that conclusion was a deepened determination and commitment to win the competitive battle. Winning fundamentally means that first, and most important, we long ago committed to just plain running our business better than the competitors ran theirs. It means delivering to every customer better products, quality, service and value than any competitor. By the way, when we say "win," we don't mean "we win" and the competitor disappears. As a matter of fact, with multinational companies, we are at the same time customers, suppliers, licensors, licensees and competitors to each other. Among developed industrial nations, that means that each must remain viable and strong.

In the late 1970s, our company made a major strategic decision. We decided that we had to be successful in penetrating the domestic Japanese market, which was relatively closed to foreign companies. **We concluded that if we could compete successfully against our Japanese competitors in Japan, we could do it anywhere in the world.** With the help of the U.S. and Japanese governments, we were given the opportunity to design and build a radio pager for NTT, Nippon Telegraph and Telephone Company, which we believe is one of the most demanding customers in the world. NTT had five Japanese suppliers—no foreign ones. The product specs were tough to meet, the delivery requirements were worse. Our Communications Sector with the help of our Semiconductor Products Sector designed and delivered 150 prototype paging units in 15 months. In 1980, we were given the first production contract ever given by NTT to a foreign communications supplier. The five existing Japanese suppliers and Motorola each shared one-sixth of the volume. Our quality and field reliability consistently placed first or second among all suppliers. In fact, our pager has a mean time between failure of about 100 years. Over the 12 years through 1991, since we became NTT's first foreign communications supplier, we have delivered well over 1 million pagers to them. American companies can do the job!

I talked to a large group of our employees after they had just completed and delivered the first prototype radio paging units to NTT. They had the highest morale of any organization I had ever been exposed to, even though many of them had worked 70- and 80-hour weeks for months on end—culminating in 20-hour days—in order to meet the delivery commitment. My speech was literally interrupted a dozen times by applause and cheers. I have never had the spontaneous reaction that I had that night. The message is clear. No one wants to be a loser. They want to win. They want to work hard and be *personally involved* in achieving that objective.

People want to be proud of their performance, proud of their activities and proud of their personal contribution to the success of their organization. **Each individual, no matter how small a cog in the operation, must feel that he or she is important to the success of the organization.** We try to make production line workers in our Land Mobile Radio Sector believe that they fight crime every time they make a perfect solder joint in a Handie-Talkie® unit—that the quality of their personal work may save a police officer's life someday when he or she calls for help over that radio.

In the late 1960s, Motorola recognized the necessity of getting the maximum contribution from every one of our people. Long before Japanese quality circles were the "in" thing, we started a program whereby teams of people worked together to solve problems or take advantage of opportunities. That program has developed over the years into what we call our participative management process (PMP). We had to literally teach people how to be participative—teach managers how to encourage the participation and suggestions of their subordinates, and teach every employee who had not been used to involvement and participation how to do it. People didn't know how to speak up—or worse, were afraid to. Many managers felt threatened. Some were trying to save the company from its senior managers who implemented such a "stupid" program. The process was successfully implemented only after continually working with the people, auditing and disciplining the results, and sometimes changing our managers.

PMP is different from the Japanese quality circle because it involves all levels of the organization, from the production line right up to the officers. It is horizontal as well, involving all functional departments. As improvements are made in quality, delivery, productivity, inventory, market penetration and other items that yield a higher return, a cash incentive is paid. Though we have had PMP in operation for over 20 years, we continue to be amazed by the improvements that occur when the management and all of the employees really unite in a PMP group with a single focus. PMP is today yielding great improvement in productivity, efficiency, cost reduction and service to our customers.

If we truly have involved, motivated people, if we and they together set very "reach out," high expectation goals, then they'll make certain that everything else occurs. Product designs will be outstanding, the best tools and equipment will be put in place, and the customer will be served better than anybody else can do it.

One of the purposes of this school of business is to further train senior managers. Every time we get a group of our managers together, we re-emphasize management's basic job. The most important job of leaders and managers is to create the environment and the atmosphere in which every person can contribute to the maximum of his or her capability. The book *Managers for Tomorrow*, by Rohrer, Hibler and Replogle, puts it as follows:

"The challenge to the manager of tomorrow is to find ways by which each individual can be given opportunity for self-realization and will be valued for himself. Every person within an organization should have the opportunity to grow; the purpose of management is neither to tend nor to tame men, its purpose is to realize the power of men."

Though written in 1965, this statement is even more true of the future today and is a good description of our participative culture.

In the late '70s, we concluded that the only acceptable goal is perfect performance in everything we do, the products we make and the services we provide. We made a commitment to achieve perfect performance. While I suspect that we all buy the desirability of perfect performance philosophically, converting it to actuality on our part is another story. We find it hard to set the very high expectation levels necessary to yield the desired results. We haven't believed that perfect performance is achievable, or even desirable. At Motorola, we've found that the most significant hurdle to jump in achieving perfect performance is getting everyone's mental attitude to be correct. **Once people believe, truly believe, that this is really an issue of survival and that perfect performance is achievable, you'd be amazed at how many individuals and organizations can achieve it.**

But very important, over and above the philosophical reasons for perfect performance, improving quality turns out to shorten the time needed to do any task and, therefore, lowers the cost. Conversely, as we shorten the time cycle allowed, we have no time to do things over. They must be done right the first time, which also results in lower cost.

In his book *Quality is Free*, Phil Crosby decisively proved that the true cost of poor quality products and service for an industrial company was shockingly running around 10 percent or more of total sales dollars. Once our managers really understood that improved quality meant that substantial dollars could be recovered and then be reinvested in sorely needed additional activities, great impetus was given to our drive for it. We passed out hundreds of copies of *Quality is Free* to our management team. By the way, we believe that a somewhat similar cost of poor quality exists in the government sector, and in the education field, too.

In 1979, Motorola embarked on a quality-improvement program that required changes across the board in the standards we set and in the way we did things. In 1981, our corporate policy committee began by setting a goal for a *10-times* improvement in *five years* in the quality of all our products and services — an improvement from whatever absolute level any given division was running, even if it was the quality leader in its field in the world. We set an expectation level to which we, the senior managers, were absolutely committed. From then on, we monitored, reviewed, coached and *insisted on* results — and we got them.

Part of the secret of our success was setting a really reach-out, "10 times in five years" goal. A more normal 10 percent improvement per year goal might have been achieved by ordinary methods, but the 10 times goals could not be, thus forcing totally new approaches to be developed. Very high expectation levels must be set and there must be a relentless commitment to and belief in the fact that these reach-out goals must be achieved. When attitudes and expectation levels are correct, there is no physically possible job that can't be done in superior fashion.

We know from experience that changing our expectation levels, setting higher standards and then achieving them is not a short-term, quick-fix job. It many times requires a total culture change that takes years in large organizations. There is no single panacea. **Much like the war on drugs, it takes action on a broad range of fronts simultaneously — none can be neglected because they are all interrelated. Above all, it takes the true belief and daily example of management at all levels. This is not delegatable!**

By 1986, we had achieved our "10 times in 5 years" goal in most hardware product areas. In 1987, we set tougher goals — a tenfold improvement in quality in two years and 100-fold in four years, on the way to achieving what we call Six Sigma™ in 1992. At Motorola, Six Sigma™ Quality is one of our five key customer-service initiatives. In statistical terms, Six Sigma™ translates into 99.9997 percent perfect products or service. We once measured defects in parts per thousand. Now we measure them in parts per million, and in some areas, parts per billion. Motorola was honored to be recognized by President Reagan in 1988 when he presented to us the very first Malcolm Baldrige National Award for quality achievement.

Six Sigma™ goes beyond manufacturing. The principles can be applied to every facet and discipline of the business, including service, delivery and all support functions. **Because high-quality companies still waste about 10 percent of sales dollars because of less-than-perfect quality, the potential for financial improvement, as well as improved customer satisfaction, is enormous.**

At Motorola, we know that we cannot achieve our fundamental objective of total customer satisfaction necessary to win the competitive battle unless we ourselves become world-class customers. This means that we must demand world-class performance from the companies, governments and educational institutions that supply us with material and services. We are requiring all of our eligible suppliers to apply for the Malcolm Baldrige National Quality Award. Going through the Baldrige application and evaluation process forces a deeply introspective review and is extremely helpful in further improving all phases of a company's operations.

In our quality-improvement efforts, we learned that designing for quality manufacturing and being good at serving the customer does not require black magic. But it does require a zealous attention to detail. There is no innate cultural advantage available to our foreign competitors. Notwithstanding all that has been said and written, neither the Japanese nor anyone else has a unique culture that preordains their success. But in many places, the past business attitude to perform "good enough" does require change—and that change is a major one in operating culture.

Also in the mid-1970s, we determined that a large factor in increased design time, cost, quality and reliability was the lack of team design of a product. We had too many functional areas where products were passed in series from organization to organization without the appropriate involvement of all of them in design. The result in many cases was a costly and difficult manufacturing process or poor service to our customer. What we did was change the fundamental method of product and service design to a team-design technique. Team design meant that one person of every functional skill from marketing, engineering, purchasing, manufacturing and all other departments became part of the team designing a product. They had to work together from conception until the product was being successfully delivered to customers.

We believe that 99 $^{44}/_{100}$ percent of the people want to do the right thing because it's easier and causes less problems. But the processes, the systems and the culture that we had in place inhibited the ability for everyone to get involved as part of a team early on. Teamwork among functional skills that normally reported to different places was the key to achieving substantially improved results. But we learned that in order to work as a team, we had to break down barriers between organizations that had existed de facto for years.

At the end of a five-day training program in our Motorola University for our managers of managers, we give our middle managers a mandate to go back to their various organizations and challenge everything that we do that does not allow us to provide total customer satisfaction far better than any competitor. We encourage them to reach out and take risks. **But we say to them that there are certain things that are not subject to change at Motorola. The first is our fundamental objective — everyone's overriding responsibility — total customer satisfaction. The second is our key beliefs; how we will always act, today, tomorrow and forever, in that pursuit.** We will always act with uncompromising integrity, honesty and ethics, and with constant respect for people and for the dignity of the individual.

Our dynamic world is constantly changing, and for any given generation of management not all the proposed directions will be determined. Carefully thought-out strategic adaptation to the long-term trends with quick tactical reaction in the short-term is mandatory. Failure to recognize, adapt to and, in fact, help shape the major long-term trends—while taking advantage of the big impact events—will make us as extinct as the dinosaur. **But a continual sensing of the environment, analyzed appropriately, in a culture that encourages reach-out decision-making and change, will ensure control of your organization's destiny, and thus a consistently successful future.**

If you are to be a successful executive you need to demonstrate creativity and technological flair and have a good understanding of the world's markets and political and economic forces. If you are or will be in a commercial company you can be expected to help weld together a team that satisfies very specific customer needs with super quality at a reasonable cost. The team may include technologists, product designers, production managers, accountants, marketeers and administrators. You must help create an environment that enables your team to succeed and that will attract the best and brightest people.

You may also exert a positive influence beyond your company—in your community, in your profession and on your government. If you are not in an industrial company, you must be supportive of business and industry in general, and of the policies that are needed to foster successful competition.

Whatever the many unforeseen changes that will be required as we go into the future, one thing is certain in my mind. We as a nation must embrace a perfect performance culture if we are to maintain our standard of living in today's highly competitive world. If we are to be successful, whether in business, government or education, we must believe that perfect performance is the responsibility of every individual. We all must be involved, participate strongly and work cooperatively as part of a cross-functional team. **But we must not only do our own jobs in superior fashion, we must also demand perfect performance from the people who sell to us or serve us.** Only when all of us do so will we raise the overall performance level in our organizations and our country. The resulting culture will yield stronger, more profitable companies, more effective public services, a stronger nation and a better world. There really is no other alternative—and each and every one of you, as the present and future leaders, must assume the personal responsibility for championing this effort.

BW

Quality Quotations, Poems & Lists

"Excellence is never granted to man but as a reward of labor."
Joshua Reynolds

"No great man ever complains of want of opportunity."
Ralph Waldo Emerson

Excellence
You can recognize it.

It's more than pretty good.
It's not just better than average,
  or even better than all the rest.
Excellence is its own standard.
  Good enough just isn't
  good enough.

The search for excellence isn't
  a competition.
It's a way of life.
Excellence is the goal, not
  the prize.

Excellence.
Look for it in yourself and in your
  organization.
Expect it, and it will be there.

Excellence.
You'll recognize it.
Philosophy statement of the
Recognition Division of **Jostens**
headquartered in Memphis, Tenn.

"The reward of a thing well done is to have done it."
Ralph Waldo Emerson

"Success, as I see it, is a result, not a goal."
Gustave Flaubert

"Men judge us by the success of our efforts."
Charlotte Elizabeth

"You will invariably be working for somebody. Part of your job is to make your supervisor look as good as possible. Don't worry about a supervisor hiding your talents because word about a good man will spread fast, both laterally and vertically."
Biesele

"Success is easy to sustain if you recognize the contributions of others and occasionally thank them for their efforts."
author unknown

"The person who advances is not the one who is afraid to do too much; it is the one whose conscience will not permit him to do too little, the one whose driving desire is to give the best that is in him, even though it may seem at times like casting bread upon unreturning waters."
B.C. Forbes

"Luck is what enabled others to get where they are. Talent is what enabled us to get where we are."
author unknown

"The world advances by impossibilities achieved."
Ralph Waldo Emerson

"It is one's duty to make the most of the best that is in him."
Duncan Stuart

"Search for a single, inclusive good is doomed to failure. Such happiness as life is capable of, comes from the full participation of all our powers in the endeavor to wrest from each changing situation of experience its own full and unique meaning."
John Dewey

"We must not judge of a man's merits by his great qualities, but by the use he makes of them."
La Rochefoucauld

"Success is finding, or making, that position which enables you to contribute to the world the very great services of which you are capable, through the diligent, persevering, resolute cultivation of all the faculties God has endowed you with, and doing it all with cheerfulness, scorning to allow difficulties or defeats to drive you to pessimism or despair. Success consists of being and doing, not simply accumulating. The businessman or enterprise that aspires to win the highest recognition for success must distinguish himself or itself, not by the magnitude of the profits, but by the value of services performed."
B.C. Forbes

"Anything that is worth doing at all is worth doing well."
Earl of Chesterfield

What is Responsibility?

1. Responsibility means accepting the importance of the job we do. Work that we value is the only work that is valuable.
2. Responsibility means seeing things from a point-of-view big enough to include the people and the organization around us.
3. Responsibility means taking criticism as it is intended: an attempt to improve the quality of our efforts, without disparaging us as people.
4. Responsibility means accepting the little, essential disciplines that go with any team operation—punctuality, neatness, safety.
5. Responsibility means realizing that the situation at work is like the situation at home—every single thing we do affects someone else, for better or worse.
6. Responsibility means accepting problems and difficulties as a normal part of any job. If we had no problems, we would win no victories, and without victories, life would be pretty drab.
author unknown

"We sometimes speak of winning reputations as though that were the final goal. The truth is contrary to this. Reputation is a reward, to be sure, but it is really the beginning, not the end of an endeavor. It should not be the signal for a let-down, but rather, a reminder that the standards which won recognition can never again be lowered. From him who gives much—much is forever after expected."
Alvan Macauley

"Quality. We receive what we will accept."
Rear Admiral Frank Collins, United States Navy

"Better is the enemy of good enough."
Chief of Naval Operations, USSR

"It is a funny thing about life; if you refuse to accept anything but the best you very often get it."
Somerset Maugham

"There's never time to do it right, but always time to do it over."
John Mestimer.

Be the Best of Whatever You Are

We all dream of great deeds and high positions, away from the pettiness and humdrum of ordinary life. Yet success is not occupying a lofty space or doing conspicuous work; it is being the best that is in you. Rattling around in too big a job is worse than filling a small one to overflowing. Dream, aspire by all means; but do not ruin the life you must lead by dreaming pipe dreams of the one you would like to lead. Make the most of what you have and are. Perhaps your trivial, immediate task is your one sure way of proving your mettle. Do the thing near at hand, and great things will come to your hand to be done.

If you can't be a pine on the top of the hill,

Be a scrub in the valley—but be the best little scrub by the side of the rill;

Be a bush if you can't be a tree.

If you can't be a bush be a bit of the grass,

And some highway happier make;

If you can't be a muskie then just be a bass—

But be the liveliest bass in the lake!

We can't all be captains, we've got to be crew,

There's something for all of us here,

There's big work to do, and there's lesser to do,

And the task you must do is the near.

If you can't be a highway then just be a trail,

If you can't be the sun be a star;

It isn't by the size that you win or you fail—

Be the best of whatever you are!
Douglas Malloch

Customers

Customer
Memos

October 13, 1967

The other day, Denny LaBud of our financial organization sent me a little squib that discussed a subject I think you might be interested in. It speaks to why the boss, our customer, stops buying from a particular company. I was impressed, and its first effect on me was to be a lot more pleasant and concerned when I answered my telephone. Obviously, the ramifications of the comment go well beyond the telephone stage, covering all contacts with the customer and all contacts with any other internal or external organization with which you may deal. I am, therefore, attaching a copy of this brief note so that you may reflect upon it.

Where Do They Go?

What happens to a customer when he quits buying from a company?

The Canadian Manufacturers Association conducted a survey in many corporations to answer the question. Out of every 100 lost customers, they found:

One was lost because of death.

Three were lost when their salesperson left the company.

Five left to buy from a friend or relative.

Nine left because they found they could buy at lower prices.

Fourteen quit buying from the company because of unadjusted complaints.

And 68 quit buying from the company because employees of the company were indifferent and showed a lack of interest in the customer.

To have more than two-thirds of the ex-customers lost through lack of interest, indifference or just plain rudeness makes you wonder, doesn't it?

April 11, 1988

Satisfied Customer

Bill Nitschke, marketing manager, International Operations, Cellular Infrastructure Division, sent in the following bit of information:

"According to a Wharton study, a satisfied customer will tell three others about your quality and service. An unhappy customer will tell 15 other people. Wharton says about 90 percent of your customers who were dissatisfied will again buy from you as long as their complaints are quickly resolved."

How easy it would be for us to increase our business by showing our customers more attention and interest, and by satisfying them regularly.

BW

"Once you have sold a customer, make sure he is satisfied with your goods. Stay with him until the goods are used up or worn out. Your product may be of such long life that you will never see him again, but he will sell you and your product to his friends."
William Feather

"Whether you are the biggest corporation in the world or the smallest individual, the only thing you can offer for sale is satisfaction."
author unknown

July 29, 1987

I thought you would be interested in a service performed for a Motorola customer of long ago. Notwithstanding the fact that this particular customer may not be a current one, the goodwill generated by her will reach out broadly beyond our expectations.

Total customer satisfaction is mostly a matter of attitude on our part. It is generally not an issue of competence or cost. If we all had the attitude displayed by Gini Jewett, office manager of the Motorola Semiconductor Sales Office in Orange, California, there is no way the competition could come close to us.

Customer Articles

That's the Tone

A 91-year-old California woman who has "kept the faith" all these years had her aged Motorola radio repaired. And her plants are doing just fine, thank you.

The woman wrote Motorola Company, Phoenix, Arizona, and perhaps it was her notation: "This is important" that prompted the post office to make sure the letter reached Motorola.

The woman explained that her Motorola radio, "had played for about 19 years, whenever I've turned it on, and yesterday it stopped." She gave the model and serial number and asked where she could get it fixed.

After giving her address, the woman wrote, "I've lived at this address 22 years and I'm going on 91 years this year. I always enjoyed the music. I'd like to have this one repaired, instead of buying a new one. I even play it while I'm gone somewhere so my plants won't be without music."

The letter was forwarded by Sector Marketing to Gini Jewett in the Motorola Anaheim sales office. Although Motorola has been out of the radio business for years, Gini can't tolerate a dissatisfied customer. So she made arrangements to personally pick up the radio, have it repaired at Motorola's expense, and return it to the woman.

"I found a Motorola radio and TV repairman in the yellow pages," Gini explained, "and he was so excited to see such an old radio that he waived the initial service charge. He had kept a schematic of the radio in his attic all these years, and was able to make the repairs."

Gini added that when she delivered the radio and plugged it in, the woman tuned in her favorite rock station and exclaimed, "That's the tone." She had borrowed a replacement radio, and it didn't sound as good.

The woman continued, "All my friends said I couldn't get my radio fixed. It's amazing how writing a little letter works when you're dealing with the right company."

The attached article came across my desk. I think it explains in very concrete terms a philosophy that should be Motorola's.

Memo to Management: Love Your Customer!

by Stew Leonard
Mr. Leonard is founder and president of Stew Leonard's, the world's largest dairy store, in Norwalk, Connecticut.

My wife, Marianne, and I risked everything we owned in the world when we opened our small dairy store back in 1969. About a week after opening day, I was standing at the entrance when a customer came up to me and angrily said, "This eggnog is sour." I took the half-gallon carton, opened it, and tasted it. It tasted all right to me, so I said, "You're wrong, it's perfect." Then to prove the customer was really wrong, I added, "We sold over 300 half-gallons of eggnog this week, and you're the only one who's complained." The customer was boiling mad. She demanded her money back and said, "I'm never coming back to this store again!"

That night, at home, I couldn't get the incident out of my head. As I carefully analyzed, I realized that *I* was in the wrong. First, I didn't listen. Second, I contradicted the customer, and third, I humiliated her and practically called her a liar by saying 300 other customers had not complained.

Chiseled in Stone

This incident has had a great impact on our business. I learned two important lessons that have been chiseled into a 6,000-pound rock next to the front door of our store in Norwalk, Connecticut, where our 100,000 customers can read it each week. We call it our "rock of commitment." It states:

Our Policy

Rule 1—The customer is always right.

Rule 2—If the customer is ever wrong, re-read rule 1.

It's chiseled in stone because it's never going to change. These rules are the main reason why we built our business from a 1,000-square-foot "mom-and-pop" store into a 100,000-square-foot "world's largest dairy store," with annual sales now approaching $100 million.

Now we're actually *glad* when customers complain. We feel they're our friends because they care enough to give us the opportunity to improve. **The customers you have to worry about are not the ones who complain, but the ones who don't—because they don't come back either!**

We begin to instill our spirit of customer service the moment an applicant sits down for a job interview. The main thing Jill Tavello, our director of personnel, looks for is a good attitude—above experience, skills, training, education or appearance. If applicants have a good attitude, we can do the rest, give them extensive training, send them to business seminars, give them audiotapes and books, and set an example by our actions. But if they have a bad attitude to start with, everything we try to do seems to fail. Usually, Jill has to interview 15 to 25 applicants to find the exact person she's looking for.

Chickens to Go

Tom Leonard is in charge of what will someday be our second store: a farmer's market in a circus tent in Danbury, Connecticut. He has a customer suggestion box which he often opens two or three times a day. In so doing, he's taking our customers' pulse.

At about 6 p.m. one evening, Tom found a note that had been written only half an hour earlier. "I'm upset. I made a special stop on my way home from work to buy chicken breasts for dinner, but you're sold out and now I'll have to eat a TV dinner instead."

As Tom was reading the note, Les Slater, our Norwalk front-end manager who lives in Danbury, stopped by on his way home to say hello. Just then, the big white Perdue chicken truck backed into the loading dock to make a delivery. Tom and Les got an idea. Five minutes later, Les was in his car taking a little detour. You can imagine the smile on the customer's face when he answered the door at 6:20 p.m. and found Les Slater with a complimentary two-pound package of fresh Perdue chicken breasts—just in time for supper!

Think "YES"

The moral of this story? Customer service cannot be a sometimes thing. That's why we use the acronym, "Think YES."

The Y in YES stands for you. We tell employees, "Pretend you are the customer. Put yourself in his or her place. How would you like to be treated?"

The E stands for encourage. We encourage the customers to talk about their problems relative to the store's products, services or employees. The more we listen, the better the customer will begin to feel and the more we'll learn about the cause of the complaint.

The S stands for support. Management will support its employees. We should never let a customer leave the store unhappy because we look at each customer as a potential $50,000 asset. An average customer spends $100 a week on food shopping. That's more than $5,000 a year, and more than $50,000 over ten years. Customer service is big business when you look at the long-term picture.

Here's an example at how our "Think YES" program works. At five minutes before closing one Sunday night, a customer said to cashier Betsy Mucci, "We've just returned from vacation and are so happy you're open. Our refrigerator is empty, and we needed this bread and milk for breakfast and the kids' school lunches tomorrow." When the total was rung up, the customer panicked, "Oh my gosh, I forgot my wallet. I don't have any money!"

Betsy just smiled and said, "That's okay, just give me your name and address." She wrote the information down, put a void slip in the register drawer, and added, "Don't worry, the next time you're in the store, you can pay for your groceries." The customer asked, "Do you have the authority to let me walk out without paying for all these groceries?" Betsy said yes, but the customer still wasn't convinced and asked to see the manager.

When the manager appeared and the customer explained the problem, he said, "When it comes to keeping our customers happy, we have no hard and fast rules. Each of us has the authority to use our own best judgment and treat every customer the way we'd like to be treated ourselves."

1 versus 999

Two weeks later, I ran into a friend at a local restaurant. He came up to me all excited and said, "Stew, you won't believe this story!" He proceeded to tell me how his wife had been the customer who forgot her wallet, and how she had been telling the tale to everyone she met. "But what I don't understand," he said, "is how you can afford to do it. Aren't you afraid cashiers will use poor judgment and you'll lose money?"

I responded, "How can we afford *not* to do it?" Ninety-nine percent of the people in our store at any given moment are repeat customers. They're back because we satisfied them the last time they shopped with us. **Our attitude is that everybody's honest. If we occasionally run into someone who isn't, we just take it on the chin.** But the important point is that 999 out of 1,000 customers *are* honest. We simply refuse to let the one dishonest customer determine how we are going to treat the other 999.

"Pushing" Employees up the Ladder

We give the responsibility of customer satisfaction to the people on the firing line, because we are training them for future management positions. I once had the opportunity to meet the chairman of a large chain of supermarkets. I told him I admired his organization but wondered why there often were long lines at the registers in his stores. He said, "I can't afford to keep all of the registers open just to eliminate lines. Some of our cashiers have been working at the registers for 15 years straight and by now are earning $20 an hour. We have to control our labor costs, even at the expense of customer service."

I wondered how he could keep someone on staff for 15 years without training them and promoting them to a job equal in value to their earnings. To this day I don't understand it. It seems to me that everybody involved loses. The cashiers resent being in the same job all those years, and you can be sure their resentment comes across to customers. The company loses because of the inefficiency at having to pay $20 an hour strictly on the basis of tenure, not contribution. The customers lose because they have to wait in long lines, waste valuable time, and become frustrated.

Good leaders look for growth potential in their people. They want to be surrounded by people who want to better themselves and get ahead. When we hire employees, we should ask ourselves about each one, "How would I like to work for this person?" Then, when some day they're being paid $20 per hour, they'll be worth every penny.

The people who start at the bottom and work their way up to the top are the backbone of any business. They make good managers because they know what it's like to be on the firing line. A big sign hanging in our employee cafeteria reads, "If you're training someone to do your job as well or better than you, you're one of the most valuable people in our company — and one of the most likely to be promoted."

Attitude is the Secret

The longer I'm in business, the more I'm convinced that our real secret of success is our attitude towards customers. The bottom line is that "like attracts like." If you treat the unreasonable customer the same way you treat the reasonable one, it's amazing how often you can turn a frown into a smile.

Marion Murphy works at our customer service desk. A very angry customer came up to her and slammed two cases of empty soda cans on the counter and said, "Look, lady, I'm not going to put these 254 cans in those automatic can refund machines of yours, one at a time. I want my money back ... now!"

"Sir, this is not the can return department," Marion replied, "and we don't take cans here. But I can see that you're in a hurry, so let me give you your refund out of my pocketbook. I'll put the cans in the machine on my lunch hour and get reimbursed." The customer's expression changed. He asked, "You'd do that?" Marion answered, "It's no problem, that's my job, to make customers happy." The man blushed and said, "I can't let you do that for me. If you've got the time, I've got the time."

November 21, 1988

The following article by George T. Selin, president of Selin Corp.,
an Atlanta-based human resources and organization development
consulting firm, deals with the subject of customer satisfaction
and fits right in with our programs to totally serve our customers.

That Extra Mile or Your Competitors Will

Reprint permission granted by *Transportation & Distribution*
magazine, July 1988.

A 30-second decision or interaction by one employee with only
one customer can cost a company hundreds of thousands of
dollars. Providing top-quality customer service is viewed as an
expense by some companies. Unfortunately, most don't get
beyond the lip service stage when it comes to improving how
they take care of their customers. They simply don't understand
the lifetime value of a customer to their business.

Each time an employee interacts with or makes a decision
on behalf of a customer, he or she is putting the lifetime value
of that customer at risk. And the impact of those interactions
and decisions, if not handled properly, can be very costly indeed.

To determine the lifetime value of one customer to your
business, use the following formula:

Average monthly sales	= $ _____
x 12 months	= $ _____
x number of years customer stays with company	= $ _____
x5 (number of referrals by each customer per year)	= $ _____

An average monthly sale to one customer of only $3,000 (when that customer stays with your business for 10 years) can mean $1,800,000! One employee inadvertently can cost your company megabucks in a very short time.

Service improvement is not an expense—it's an investment. It's an investment in maintaining the future business of your customers—which means the success and possibly the survival of your business.

The secret to making service your competitive edge for achieving increased profits is to convince each employee that service is everyone's business. They must understand that their jobs and the health of the company depend on making and keeping customers satisfied.

The traditional approach is one in which service is promised during the sales pitch, but gets little attention after the sale. This attitude must be replaced by the reality of each employee treating your customer as if you'll lose them tomorrow. **Service isn't something that's promised then forgotten—it's the basis of a long-term relationship, and should be particularly emphasized after the sale.**

The key is to determine what your customers perceive as critical to their satisfaction. Then go beyond that expectation. Merely meeting their expectations neither will attract new customers nor retain them. To get and keep customers you must identify and provide value-added services that clearly exceed their expectations.

These value-added aspects of service should be identified for each level of customer interaction. Regardless of whether the interaction occurs during the sales process or at the time of invoicing, your people must strive to perform better than your competitors. Look for ways to make the customer's job easier.

Most organizations spend a considerable portion of their budgets trying to acquire new customers. Yet they do little to focus on retaining the customers they have. This is backwards, and very cost-ineffective. Studies have demonstrated that it costs five times as much to acquire a new customer as it does to keep one you have.

Consistent quality service must be developed at all levels of customer interaction throughout the organization. Once this attitude is translated into action and service becomes every-one's business, your value-added service approach should be positioned as part of your marketing strategy. Stop and give it serious thought: customers deserve that level of attention. They will cast their vote with their checkbook. Your challenge is to make sure your company—and not your competitors— deposits that check.

Customer Quotations and Poems

"Business exists to serve customers, and unless it does that, it fails."
William Feather

"It is our job to make things simple so that they fit the reality of the consumer, not the ego of our engineers. I've long ago learned that when most manufacturers say 'quality,' they use the engineer's definition, which is: Something that's very hard to make and costs a lot of money. That's not quality, that's incompetence."
Peter Drucker

Impressions
"A corporation may spread itself over the entire world ... employ one hundred thousand men ... yet the average person will form his judgment of the corporation through his contacts with one individual. If this person is rude or inefficient, it will require a lot of courtesy and efficiency to overcome the bad impression. Every member of an organization who in any capacity, comes in contact with the public, is a salesman!"
author unknown

A customer is ... the most important person in any business.

A customer is ... not dependent on us—we are dependent on him.

A customer is ... not an interruption of our work—he is the purpose of it.

A customer is ... doing us a favor when he calls—we are not doing him a favor by serving him.

A customer is ... a part of our business—not an outsider.

A customer is ... not a cold statistic—he is a flesh-and-blood human being with feelings and emotions like our own.

A customer is ... not someone to argue or match wits with.

A customer is ... a person who brings us his wants—it is our job to fill those wants.

A customer is ... deserving of the most courteous and attentive treatment we can give him.

A customer is ...the fellow that makes it possible to pay your salary whether you are a truck driver, plant employee, office employee, salesman or manager.

A customer is ... the lifeblood of this and every other business.
author unknown

The Good Guy ...

I'm the fellow who goes into a restaurant, sits down and patiently waits while the waitresses finish their visiting before taking my order.

I'm the fellow who goes into a department store and stands quietly while the clerks finish their little chat.

I'm the fellow who drives into a service station and never blows his horn, but lets the attendant take his time.

You might say that I'm the good guy. But do you know who else I am?

I'm the fellow who never comes back.

It puzzles me to see business spending so much money every year to get my business—when I was there in the first place.

And all they needed to keep me coming back was to give me some service and extend a little courtesy.

author unknown

"It is not an employer who pays wages, he only handles the money. It is the customer that pays wages."

Henry Ford

You Are P.R.

Publicity is what we say about ourselves.

Reputation is what others say about us.

Or put another way: "What you are speaks so loudly, I cannot hear what you say."

We have a dress code at Motorola. It is not stringent but it does offer guidelines. All of us are in sales—if nothing else, we're "selling" ourselves. No matter what our function, we must be attractively packaged.

Many times the public judges Motorola by one telephone call, a telephone response at the switchboard, or through a printed piece or letter. You may be the only contact an outsider will have with Motorola and the impression you made will be the lasting one. There might not be a second chance.

author unknown

Customers like to do business where they are treated right. When they're neglected or get a raw deal they take their business somewhere else. They also spread the word among their friends. That's why employees who are customer-conscious are so valuable to their company. Their good work helps protect everybody's paycheck.

Many employees never meet, see or speak to a customer from one year to the next. Some of them lose sight of the customer completely—the only important things in their lives are their own department, their own particular jobs and their own convenience.

They forget that the customer, in the final analysis, pays the bill for every bit of work done by everyone in their company. Each employee, by doing his or her job well, has an opportunity to give customers good value for their money. If one doesn't do a good job, the customer receives poor value.

They also forget that you don't have to meet customers face-to-face to please or displease them. A late or mixed-up delivery, a poorly typed letter, a faulty or slipshod piece of work, a mistake in billing—things like these can make customers a thousand miles away blow their tops.

Customers bring us their needs and wants. Our job is to fill them profitably—to them and to us.

Customers are affected by the way each of us does his or her work—no matter how far away they may seem.

Customers' good opinions of us and our work are our most valuable asset. Anything we can do to improve their opinions of us is important.

Customers' good opinions cannot be bought—they are freely

given in response to good value and good service.

Customers expect value for the money they spend with us. If we don't give them good value, they'll go elsewhere to get it.

Customers are the bosses behind our bosses. If we serve them well, they'll be glad to pay us well. If we don't, nobody's paycheck is safe.

Customer-conscious employees are always better employees. They recognize what the business is all about.

author unknown

Don't Promise What You Can't Deliver

"I'll have your parts in two weeks." Four weeks later the parts arrive.

"I'll put it in your hand the minute you walk in the door." But all you get when you walk in is a handshake.

"Dinner will be at 6:00." But as you dip your spoon in the soup, the clock strikes 7:45.

"The doctor will see you in five minutes." Thirty-five minutes later you're greeted cheerfully: "And how are we today?"

Avoid a lot of grief and inconvenience for the people you deal with. Think before you announce how long something will take— and then deliver what you promised. On time.

© **United Technologies Corporation, 1986**

"It is the customer and the customer alone who casts the vote that determines how big any company should be."
Crawford H. Greenewalt

Business & Economics

*Business &
Economic
Memo*

How fully do your people understand that their jobs and futures depend on making a profit?

The purpose of our business is to honorably serve the needs of the community by providing products and services of superior quality at a fair price; to do this so as to earn a fair profit, which is required for the total enterprise to grow; and by doing so provide the opportunity for our employees and shareholders to achieve their reasonable personal objectives. In order to do this, any business must make a fair profit. And if it doesn't make a fair profit, it will soon go out of existence.

One of the keys to good management is to keep everyone connected with an organization alert to this simple fact. Profits go to the profit-minded. When people don't see how their work is related to the company's profit or loss—or think it really doesn't make much difference—a lot of potential profits go right down the drain.

It's hard for a lot of people to see how their jobs are related to company profits. **Some feel their individual effort is so small it doesn't matter ... others can't see how they affect profits anyway—that's something that's handled in the accounting department.**

Yet the plain fact is that everybody affects profits — through good work or bad, being careful or wasteful with time and materials, being present or absent, late or early, thinking of better ways to do his work or just resting on his oars. The profit account — or loss — is merely the sum total of all these individual performances.

How do you sell this attitude to subordinates and employees? **First, by being eternally profit-minded yourself. Second, by constantly explaining the relationship of everything you and they do to company profits. Third, by recognizing and praising their cooperation in this direction.**

The message can be sold. When it is, the results are obvious. It can improve the operation of a work crew, a department or a whole company.

author unknown

Average profit percent to sales for all industry ranges between 4 percent and 8 percent. A poll of Motorola employees taken throughout the corporation in 1972 revealed that in their opinion, a fair profit was 8 percent. In the 4th quarter of 1974, Motorola, Inc.'s profit was 1.3 percent. **BW**

April 17, 1972

It seems to be in fashion in the United States today to be anti-business and anti-technology. I am deeply concerned that unless many of us are willing to stand up and speak out, "the baby will be thrown out with the bath water." I wrote the following article for a book for college students who want to enter the business world.

While the article specifically addresses the student, the comments apply generally to the subjects of social progress, technology and business.

Business &
Economic
Articles

"Every right implies a responsibility; every opportunity an obligation; every possession a duty."
author unknown

Social Progress and Business

by Bill Weisz
Published by Triton College, River Grove, Illinois.
Reprint permission granted.

It is my purpose in this letter to talk to you about business, its contribution to our society, and the very important part that you will play in the future growth of that society. It is my opinion that increased social progress has a cost, that this cost must be funded and that it only can come from increased productivity, which is derived from successful, ethical, profitable business growth. The student of today has a tremendous desire to make a contribution to the improvement of society. This desire speaks well for the student and for the American way of life and the society that produced the student. But we must work to improve things, not just talk. The big ideals of freedom, peace and prosperity can only be achieved if everyone has important personal traits like the simple ones of honesty, integrity, perseverance, loyalty, the willingness to work hard, and all of those things that are the underpinnings of the big ideals. Because the whole is purely the sum of the parts, we can only achieve the very lofty ideals spoken about every day, almost everywhere, if lots of people down at the grass roots practice those lofty ideals in every little way, every day. Accomplishment of the simple, personal ideals leads to the accomplishment of the big ones.

Our fantastic increased standard of living was no accident—it was the result of technological achievement made practical and delivered to the public in an affordable manner, by business, down through the ages. If social problems are to be solved, it must be done within the relevance of the society that exists. Therefore, each of you will play a major role, not merely in the continued growth of the free enterprise business system, but in the improvement of man's lot.

You all know the Law of Conservation of Energy—you can't have perpetual motion. You can't get something for nothing. This same theory applies equally as well in the field of economics. It is stated by the American Economic Foundation in this way:

"Nothing in our material world can come from nowhere or go nowhere, nor can it be free; everything in our economic life has a source, a destination and a cost that must be paid."

"They who give have all things; they who withhold have nothing."
Hindu proverb

"It is one of the most beautiful compensations of life that no man can sincerely try to help another, without helping himself."
John P. Webster

The improvement of society must be paid for in some way. But where does the money come from? Take government aid funds, for example. They come from taxes, which come from the people. It is money—taken from the people directly or from business who collects it from its customers as part of the selling price—that is then returned to the people, minus the government's cost of administering the funds. Thus, to support direct or indirect programs of social welfare, money must be earned and spent. People and businesses must earn more in order to afford such programs. To earn more money, they must produce more. There must be increased gross national product. There must be increased business growth. Without it, the funds to support social and cultural progress are not forthcoming. There is no shortcut. Successful business is the source of the funds and affluence that support social and cultural progress. Without successful business, there would be no growth in other areas.

Technical innovation, creating new processes and products, techniques and services, is the major source of business growth. Now, if you accept my first thesis that business is the provider for social and cultural progress, then it follows that technological innovation and change is what really funds social and cultural progress. The first prehistoric man had to spend all of his time just worrying about eating, sleeping, clothing and protecting himself. It was only technical innovation—fire, the wheel, the bow and arrow—that gave him the time to spend on other things, such as painting and building the prehistoric version of the Great Society.

It is true that without scientific achievement, progress cannot occur, but a state-of-the-art invention or discovery is absolutely no good if it cannot be turned into something practical and usable for people. It must not only be designed well and be economically feasible, but it must also be manufactured properly, merchandised and distributed well, and taken care of, if necessary, after it is in use. Thus, engineering is but one partner in a successful business venture. Each partner is absolutely essential.

The disturbing part of many students' comments today is that so many of them appear to think that business does not contribute to society. The comments of college students are filled with sayings like, "business exploits the public," "pollutes the air," "enslaves the employees;" "business doesn't encourage individual creativity," "the employee is lost in a large corporation," "in business, it's wealth, connections, religion and race that count," and so on.

It would be ridiculous for me to say that some or all of these conditions don't exist somewhere. They probably do in some business establishments, just as they do in some universities, hospitals and government agencies.

But the good businesses have always been people-oriented and have always been addressing themselves to social concerns like safety, health, and service to the community in the same way that the good private citizen has. In fact, the social ideals that so many students feel cannot be served in or by private business can be realized only through economic growth, which in the United States means the expansion of private business.

Thus, my thesis really speaks to how to be successful in business. What are the basic requirements for a successful business? Let's examine these in a little more detail.

Our chairman, Bob Galvin, defines the purpose of a business to be, "to honorably serve the needs of the community at a profit." In my company's case, our products not only provide entertainment, but help fight crime, work for industry, support the national defense and lead scientific breakthroughs. We think that we are good corporate citizens in all the communities in which we live around the world. Our people work hard in community affairs. We educate our employees, support the local schools, work for social welfare and contribute financially to many areas of the community. We do almost everything that any good private citizen can be expected to do. The very fact that we do all these, create jobs and turn out useful products at real value is in itself a major contribution to society which far too few people understand.

Now, what about the words, "at a profit." Profit is probably one of the most misunderstood and maligned words in our vocabulary. To some foes of the American system it has become a dirty word. To those who really understand why the United States has achieved a standard of living superior to all others, it is a very important concept.

"The core values that have sustained our society over many generations are three: (1) the urge to excel, (2) the acceptance of change, and (3) spiritual concern for our fellow man. The survival of our civilization depends on their sure transmission from one generation to the next.

The urge to excel is the heart of the sometimes disparaged Puritan work ethic, which converts millions of the individualists into a competitive society.

The acceptance of change, with all that it entails in hazard and loss, makes a competitive society dynamic. Spiritual concern for our fellow man makes a competitive society compassionate and channels the pursuit of excellence to beneficial and humane needs. For excellence or competition alone can be antisocial; concern for our fellow man alone can result merely in sympathy without sustenance."
Gabriel Hauge

"The best index to a person's character is (a) how he treats people who can't do him any good, and (b) how he treats people who can't fight back."
Abigail Van Buren

You

*You cannot bring about prosperity
    by discouraging thrift*

*You cannot strengthen the weak
    by weakening the strong*

*You cannot help the wage earner
    by pulling down the wage payer*

*You cannot further the brother-
    hood of man
    by encouraging class hatred*

*You cannot help the poor
    by discouraging the rich*

*You cannot establish sound
    security
    by spending more than
    you earn*

*You cannot build character
    and courage
    by taking away man's initiative
    and independence*

*You cannot help men permanently
    by doing for them what
    they could and should do
    for themselves.*
Abraham Lincoln

Let me read you a quote: *"The worst crime an employer can commit against the worker is to fail to make a profit."* That statement was not made by a big businessman. It was made by Samuel Gompers, founder of the labor union movement in America. What did he mean?

Profit is important not simply because a company greedily wants to make money, but profit is important because of what it does for people. Profit gives a company, which is, after all, basically a conglomeration of people, the ability through the distribution of that profit to raise the standard of living of the people associated with the company. Whether it is in salaries or profit sharing to the employees, in dividends to the stockholders or the increasing price of stock on the market that only occurs if a company is successful and profitable; whether in educational assistance, or suggestion payouts or patent awards, the source is always profits. Without the earning of profit we could have none of these. But equally important, out of that profit, we must invest continuously in new plans, tools, materials and receivables in order to maintain our share of the business or grow. If a company starts losing its share of the business and doesn't make these investments, it starts losing position ever more rapidly. The companies who do increase their share, at the losing company's expense, can now make lower-cost products because of their volume. They can invest more in engineering or improved services to make their company step out in front. It is a snowballing situation where soon the company that does not make a profit and reinvest much of it in the business in order to serve the customer, will have to shut its doors and put all its people out of work. Obviously, a company that sustains a loss may substantially hasten this final result. Business history is replete with these situations. And so, Samuel Gompers knew that in our competitive society to protect the jobs of the working people, companies must operate efficiently and be profitable.

Thus, simply said—and worth repeating—for people to share in a company's profits and thus achieve a better personal life, the company must make a profit. To make a profit, it must be successful in competition with other companies that are in similar businesses. The success of a company is in the hands of the customers, despite the horror stories of many who believe, and continually spout, that businesses dominate and exploit the customer. The customer must be served with good products or service at a fair value or he will simply take his business elsewhere or stop buying.

To be successful, the company must have people who do the absolutely best possible job. They must always try to make their company number one in every field in which it participates. The success of the individual and of the company, which is really only a vehicle for its people, are completely intertwined. We cannot have success for one without success for the other.

The book *Managers for Tomorrow* says:

"The challenge to the manager of tomorrow is to find ways by which each individual can be given opportunity for self-realization and will be valued for himself. Every person within an organization should have the opportunity to grow; the purpose of management is neither to tend nor to tame men, its purpose is to realize the power of men."

The most important job of management is to create the environment and the atmosphere in which each and every person can contribute to the maximum of his or her own capability.

In a people-oriented company, people should be real gung-ho fireballs about the importance of their jobs, the company, and their opportunity to reach out and grow with it. Given such spirit, average people can do fantastic things. Without it, excellent people turn in second-rate performances.

Here's a prize-winning recipe for success. Mix these ingredients generously:

Honesty in our every action
Appreciation of our employees
Pride in our "Quality Products" image
Participation in community affairs
Youth-oriented management

New modern facilities
Experienced friendly supervision
Waste and pollution concern

Yearly growth and expansion
Excellent benefits program
Affirmative-action support
Regard for human rights of all
Add that special ingredient "You" and the result is unbeatable!
author unknown

People want to be proud of their company's activities, and proud of their personal contributions to the success of those activities.

The challenge to us as managers is to find the ways to ensure that all of our people can feel that pride in whatever they personally do, and in the achievements of their organization, regardless of who did it.

The individual has a responsibility, too. He or she must put forth his or her very best effort. They must seek and work to grow. They must also realize that such growth is tied intimately to the success of the enterprise as a whole.

We can only have successful businesses by ensuring that they are concerned about people. Such a business will operate with integrity and honesty, will develop good and high-quality products and will be properly concerned about its role in contributing to every phase of the public welfare.

Now, let me forge the last link in the chain. Who makes the successful person? Who creates the technological revolution? Who raises the standard of living? My answer is that it is those individuals or groups of individuals who take the initiative, work hard and honestly, not only to better people in general, but to better themselves personally. They make significant increases in all phases of our society, and, I might add, I don't define "better one's self personally" to be only in the financial realm. Initiative by the individual, based on personal pride and ambition, and the incentive that each person will be rewarded according to the fruits of their own labor, stimulate success.

Well, now I've laid the philosophical foundation. How does all this philosophy affect you as individuals? Obviously, you are the creators of the future. It is your creative work, properly conceived and properly merchandised by a successful business, that will be the key to whether we will truly see a great society or not. Business should be established as one of our most respected occupations because it has, in fact, provided all the things we enjoy today—not just money, but stimulus, challenge, free time and the proper atmosphere that has allowed progress in social and cultural areas.

The business world is exciting, challenging, dynamic and rewarding, not just financially, but personally. In fact, it's fun.

You, as young people and students, have the power to determine the future course of our society. If you really want to contribute to social and cultural progress, you must work toward it by contributing to economic and business expansion. We don't necessarily have to personally fight disease in order to feel our involvement in improving the health of the public. In our company, we feel a very direct involvement and know the importance of what we do every time we ship a high-quality two-way radio system to a hospital for instantaneously finding and alerting doctors, or for radioing a heartbeat from a remote area to the hospital location of the expert cardiologist. We contribute to pollution control every time we ship a high-quality pollution monitoring system.

"The society that scorns excellence in plumbing because plumbing is a humble activity, and tolerates shoddiness in philosophy because philosophy is an exalted activity, will have neither good plumbing, nor good philosophy. Neither its pipes nor its theories will hold water."
John Gardner, former Secretary of Health, Education and Welfare

If you agree that increased productivity is necessary to support increased endeavors in social welfare, then you must contribute to it by continuing technological advancement, which can best be brought to people through successful business. If you believe that individual initiative and hard work should be rewarded by increased participation in the fruits of that hard work by the people responsible, in proportion to their contribution, then I feel confident that continued increase in our standard of living and continued increase in social progress are inevitable. The world of tomorrow will be of your making. You stand in the forefront of the quest for the great society.

March 15, 1982

Submitted by Dolores Porter, Government Electronics Division, Communications Operation, Scottsdale, Arizona.

The Ten Pillars of Economic Wisdom

Reprint permission granted by the American Economic Foundation, Cleveland, Ohio.

1. Nothing in our material world can come from nowhere, nor can it be free: everything in our economic life has a source, a destination and a cost that must be paid.

2. Government is never a resource of goods. Everything produced is produced by the people, and everything that government gives to the people, it must first take from the people.

3. The only valuable money that government has to spend is that money taxed or borrowed out of the people's earnings. When government decides to spend more than it has thus received, that extra unearned money is created out of thin air, through the banks, and, when spent, takes on value only by reducing the value of all money, savings and insurance.

4. In our modern exchange economy, all payroll and employment come from customers, and the only worthwhile job security is customer security; if there are no customers, there can be no payroll and no jobs.

5. Customer security can be achieved by the worker only when he cooperates with management in doing the things that win and hold customers. Job security, therefore, is a partnership problem that can be solved only in a spirit of understanding and cooperation.

6. Because wages are the principal cost of everything, widespread wage increases, without corresponding increases in production, simply increase the cost of everybody's living.

7. The greatest good for the greatest number means, in its material sense, the greatest goods for the greatest number, which, in turn, means the greatest productivity per worker.

8. All productivity is based on three factors: 1) natural resources, whose form, place and condition are changed by the expenditure of 2) human energy (both muscular and mental), with the aid of 3) tools.

9. Tools are the only one of these three factors that man can increase without limit, and tools come into being in a free society only when there is a reward for the temporary self-denial that people must practice in order to channel part of their earnings away from purchases that produce immediate comfort and pleasure into new tools of production. Proper payment for the use of tools is essential to their creation.

10. The productivity of the tools—that is, the efficiency of the human energy applied in connection with their use—has always been highest in a competitive society in which the economic decisions are made by millions of progress-seeking individuals, rather than in a state-planned society in which those decisions are made by a handful of all-powerful people, regardless of how well-meaning, unselfish, sincere and intelligent those people may be.

Social Progress, the Business World and the Student

Presented to the Rotary Golden Anniversary Meeting
Beatrice, Nebraska.

Business &
Economic
Speeches

These days, too much is being said to glamorize all kinds of dissent or to find fault with all sorts of American ideals, and not enough is being said about the facts of life that back up such ideals. Dissent is important and necessary, but a true understanding of the problem is also necessary in order for dissent to be proper and meaningful. Tonight, I'm going to take up the philosophical cudgel and talk about our insatiable demand for more social and cultural progress, which so many people seem to think can be achieved by violent dissent. I'm going to give you my opinion about the proper way to achieve such progress and the roles that we all must play in order to get it. I'm going to throw some opinions at you, and also put before you what I contend are facts—no, not mere facts—possible laws of nature.

It isn't necessary to be a Ph.D. or a psychologist to talk about the problems of social progress. Everybody does it. But it does take a lot of understanding to solve these problems.

A number of things I have observed these past few years have been bothering me, and maybe you, too. There is a trend developing that is so dangerous, it threatens the very foundation of American world leadership because it attacks the basic philosophies that made America what it is, and believe me, with all of our problems, we're a long way ahead of whoever is in second place in terms of living standards and freedom for our people. And what is this trend? In a series of advertisements, Warner & Swasey, a Cleveland machinery company called it the "pie-in-the-sky" philosophy. It's the "something for nothing" philosophy. Whether you camouflage it with pretty-sounding phrases or call it that bluntly, you've all seen examples of it. It is espoused in the name of social progress. Warner & Swasey's ad goes on, "More wages for less work seems such a pleasant idea. It looks so easy to pass a law to give everyone everything he likes."

Fortune magazine carried a series of articles that spoke to this same general attitude. "The government of any Lower Slobbovia can declare the abolition of poverty to be a national goal, but attaining it requires increasing gross national product which has to be produced, not just declared."

Now the abolition of poverty is a worthy goal, and might well be achievable if we attack the problem correctly.

You probably all know the Law of Conservation of Energy, which says that you can't have perpetual motion. You can't get something for nothing. This same theory applies equally as well in the field of economics. It is stated by the American Economic Foundation in this way, "Nothing in our material world can come from nowhere or go nowhere, nor can it be free: Everything in our economic life has a source, a destination and a cost that must be paid."

Take federal aid, which seems to be free of cost to the people. After all, it's government money. But where does the money come from? It comes from taxes, which come from the people. It is money, taken from the people directly, or from businesses that collect it from its customers as part of the selling price, and is then returned to the people, minus the government's cost of administering the funds. **Without arguing the pluses or minuses of federal aid, it is clear that in order to support it, or any other social progress program, money must be earned and spent.** People and businesses must earn more in order to afford such programs. To earn more, they must produce more. There must be increased gross national product. There must be increased business growth. Without it, the funds to support social and cultural progress are not forthcoming. There is no shortcut.

Therefore, my fact No. 1 is that business is the source of the funds and affluence that support social and cultural progress. Without successful business, there would be no growth in other areas.

But what is the prevailing attitude toward business today in the colleges that are the main source of our future business leaders? In the same issue of *Fortune* there was an article titled "The Private World of the Class of '66." In it, various students were interviewed regarding their opinions about, and attitudes toward, business and economic growth. Let me give you some direct quotes from these college students:

"Business isn't where the action is."

"In a university laboratory you can pursue whatever interests you. In business, mostly you crank out answers for some pharmaceutical company."

"I had a summer job with a corporation — every morning 150 guys arriving at the same office, all carrying briefcases and wearing neckties."

Here's a good one:

"I know when I've got it good. I'd like to stay right here."

Fortune *said that the general theme running through every discussion was "a concern with doing something significant."*

Said one student:

"I've given thought to business only as a last resort. Business and the sale of products are what make the United States what it is. But what I'd like to do is improve the lot of people. I'd like to say I've made a change no matter how small, in the United States, Africa or somewhere."

The desire to make a contribution to society speaks well for the students and for the American way of life that produced and supports them. They are very concerned about freedom, very concerned about the fact that if they join an organization like a corporation, there will be a subjugation of their freedom. **There is a certain spirit abroad in this generation that freedom represents independence to the point of casting oneself adrift. They don't realize that if they are to solve a social problem they must do so within the relevance of the society that exists.**

When they speak of ideals, they mean the big ideal. They want to accomplish the ideals of freedom, peace, prosperity, etc., not realizing that one has to have important personal ideals like hard work, perseverance, loyalty, honesty and morality. All of these things are the underpinnings of the big ideals. **Accomplishment of the simple, personal ideals leads us to the accomplishment of the big ones.**

The disturbing part of the students' comments is that so many of them appear to think that business does not contribute to society. The comments of college students today are filled with sayings like, "Business doesn't encourage individual creativity;" "Business isn't interested in making society a better place;" "The employee is lost in a large corporation;" "In business, it's wealth, connections, religion and race that count;" and so on. It would be ridiculous for me to say that some or all of these conditions don't exist somewhere. They obviously do in some business establishments, just as they do in some universities, hospitals and government agencies. I guess not too many of them exist in my own company or I'd still be a junior engineer today. I view the subject from a different point of view than do most business people and students.

Most criticism of modern business comes from articles, books and people whose views of business have been formed from the outside looking in rather than from a broad experience within the business world. **It is becoming dramatically evident that both business and the student suffer from a lack of understanding of each other's views, way of life and importance on the American scene.** In addition to any other problems, we certainly have a lack of good communication. Good communication between objective people leads to understanding, which spurs problem-solving and/or viewpoint-changing. Most people want to do the best possible job objectively. Disagreement may be, in large part, due to misunderstanding.

We in business have been addressing ourselves to ideals like safety, health, community service and all the things that each of our companies engage in daily. The students' present freedom from economic pressures and concerns—the very fact that they've "got it so good"—results from the high standard of living that Americans enjoy, and that business contributed to so greatly. And as *Fortune* puts it, "Moreover, the social ideals that so many students feel cannot be served in, or by, private business can be realized only through economic growth which in the U.S. means, the expansion of private business."

Because we have a successful private business economy, our friend in college was able to make the statement that he's "got it so good" and that he'd like to stay there. If everybody stayed there, there would soon be a situation where no one could stay there.

As a matter of fact, the business world is just the opposite of what the *Fortune* students think it is. It is exciting, challenging, dynamic and rewarding, not just financially, but personally. In fact, it's fun.

My second fact is that technical innovation—creating new processes and products—is the major source of business growth. Now if you accept my first thesis that business is the provider for social and cultural progress, then it follows that technological innovation and change is what really funds social and cultural progress. The first prehistoric man had to spend all of his time just worrying about eating, sleeping, clothing and protecting himself. It was only technical innovation—fire, the wheel, the bow and arrow—that gave him the time to spend on other things such as painting, and building the prehistoric version of the Great Society.

But before all the engineers break their arms patting themselves on the back, let me hasten to add one very important statement. **It is true that without scientific achievement, nothing else can occur, but a state-of-the-art invention is absolutely no good if it cannot be turned into something practical and usable for people.** It must not only be designed well and be economically feasible, it also must be produced properly, merchandised and distributed well, and taken care of, if necessary, after it is in use. Thus, engineering is but one partner in a successful business venture. Each partner is absolutely essential.

Well, now I've laid the philosophical foundation. How does all this philosophy affect us as individuals? Obviously, we are the creators of the future. It is our creative work, properly conceived and properly merchandised by a successful business, that will be the key to whether we will truly see a Great Society or not. Instead of being viewed with disdain by the student, business should be established as one of our most respected occupations because it has provided all the things we enjoy today—

not just money, but stimulus, challenge, free time and the proper atmosphere that has allowed progress in social and cultural areas.

So what can you do as an individual? Well, you can live and breathe this philosophy every day of your life. You can teach by example and by advising the young people you come in contact with. Should they remain in college because that's where the good life is? At the risk of offending the educators, I'm going to answer that question no. After getting a good education, my advice to the student is to go out in the world because, believe me, that's where the action really is.

Most students want to start at the top, impatient and disbelieving that they can have an impact at lower levels. This is a fine objective, but wrong, especially from the student's own selfish point of view. **If they've got the stuff, they'll be big wheels soon enough, but he or she has got to start at the bottom.** They've got to start by doing the work that so many of our students in the *Fortune* article refer to as menial and useless. But why? Is it not truly menial and useless? No! A young student right out of school can and does make significant contributions. But the reason for starting at the bottom is not because there is an intent to subjugate or to treat the student unfairly. The student starts there because he or she has to learn. The student has to experience the actual on-the-job situation, so that later as an executive, he or she has a "feel" for the problems that can be gained in no other way but by personal experience. This is true whether you're a doctor, lawyer, engineer or salesperson.

In my own case, for example, it meant the dirty work of installing two-way radio equipment in cars and trucks, accidentally drilling a hole in the chief engineer's gas tank, and consequently learning the importance of designing the radio equipment right in the first place to minimize such an occurrence. It meant learning the problems on the bench and in the field that are inherent in radio frequency channel-splitting, so that today, many years later, when I'm participating with top government and industry leaders in radio spectrum utilization discussions, I know what it means to the equipment and the user. I understand the practical, everyday problems that will occur and that could make the whole program a failure if not solved, no matter how good the technical solutions are on paper.

Instead of the thought that the early years are years of wasted work beneath the good student's capabilities, they must be viewed as opportunities for gaining indispensable experience and practical knowledge that can't be gained any other way.

Today, because of the shortage of good people in industry, government and education, the danger is not one of being forgotten in the masses. **The danger is being pushed ahead too fast and too soon before one has gotten enough experience to successfully carry out increased responsibilities, without catastrophic mistakes both for the person and the organization.** Ladies and gentlemen, there is no shortcut to the top—not because that's the way the world runs today, but because there is no substitute for personal experience. You just can't be successful at the top without having gone through the intermediate steps that give that experience, and that is my fact No. 3.

Now let me forge the last link in the chain. Who makes the successful person? Who creates the technological revolution? Who raises the standard of living? My answer is those individuals or groups who take the initiative and work hard, not only to better people in general, but to better themselves personally. They make significant increases in all phases of our society. I might add, I don't define bettering oneself personally to mean only financial betterment. Initiative by the individual, based on personal pride and ambition, and the incentive that each person will be rewarded accordingly, stimulate success.

Now let me state at this point that I'm not against federal aid, Medicare or motherhood. They all have their proper place in proper balance. I am, however, against the philosophy that everyone is entitled to the same degree of happiness because they were born on the earth, and for no other reason. **If I may paraphrase the novelist Ayn Rand, everyone is not guaranteed happiness, they are only guaranteed the free and equal opportunity to pursue happiness—and there's a big difference.** I am dead set against the philosophy that the non-contributor is entitled to the same standard of living as the hard-working contributor. The results of such a philosophy are that the ranks of the non-contributors grow rapidly. If everyone were to share equally in the results of the hard work of others, even if they sit around all day and do nothing, then what incentive is there for the few who do the work? Why shouldn't they decide to be one of the sitters instead of the workers? Why shouldn't they recognize that they've "got it so good" that they needn't really work hard? What happens when all the workers quit working and sit with the sitters? Now who are the providers? The result, of course, is complete economic collapse. If you'd like a dramatic picture of this, I recommend that you read *Atlas Shrugged* by Ayn Rand.

My fourth fact of life is this, then. If you restrict reward for initiative and hard work, if you eliminate incentive, if you put limits on doing the best possible job because it would be unfair to the less competent person, if you decide that we are all entitled to happiness and good living just because we were born, without any relationship to effort—then we shall soon see the cessation of technological innovation, business expansion, economic progress and, consequently, social and cultural progress. Let me assure you that the fall of the Roman Empire will look like a kindergarten play compared to the catastrophic results of such a course to our society. It might not happen this year or even this decade, but it will happen just as surely as 2 plus 2 equals 4.

We have it within our power to determine the future course of our society. If we really want to contribute to social and cultural progress, we and the students must work toward it by contributing to economic and business expansion. In our company we don't have to wrestle a thief to the ground in order to feel our involvement in the war on crime or the ideal of law enforcement. We feel a very direct involvement, and know the importance of what we do, every time we ship a high-quality, two-way radio system to the local constabulary. As a matter of fact, that brave, wonderful guy who walks the beat is helpless today without two-way radio communications.

If you agree that increased productivity is necessary to support increased endeavors in social welfare, then you must contribute to it by continuing the technological advancement that can be brought to people through successful business. If you believe that individual initiative and hard work should be rewarded by increased participation in the fruits of that hard work by the people responsible, in proportion to their contribution, then I feel confident that continued increases in our standard of living and social progress are in sight for all. **The world of tomorrow will be of your making. You stand in the forefront of the quest for the Great Society.**

If you and I work at it and work at it hard, if we insist that everyone else do the same and we provide the opportunity for them to do so, then the free pie in the sky won't turn out to be lemon, very sour and expensive indeed. Instead that pie in the sky will be right down-to-earth, well-earned and very tasty.
BW

March 2, 1976

Inflation and the Management of a Business

University of Notre Dame 1976 Finance Forum
South Bend, Indiana.

While there is some small minority of people who think a little bit of inflation is OK, I think most will agree that it's almost like being a little bit pregnant. Maybe a little inflation can be characterized as one of my Motorola colleagues did the other day as, "at least better than a sharp stick in the eye." I am not here to discuss all the root causes of inflation or how to eliminate them. If you have 10 competent people in a room, you're likely to get 15 opinions on the subject. **I am here to talk about how a business manager must operate in order to cope with inflation, because while we all dislike it, and will do our best to reduce or eliminate it, we nevertheless must live with it while it's here, and that may be a long time.** We must first know some basics about the causes of inflation in order to live with it. While I'll talk just a little about that, in the words of many of my old college texts, that is mostly "left as an exercise for the student."

The recent reports coming out of Washington and other world capitals indicate that the rate of inflation has been reduced substantially in some places from the double-digit extremes of the past couple of years. If this is so, why worry about it now? Well, there is little question that it remains too high and still has the potential for getting worse. Only three or four years ago, most economists projected long-run rates of inflation of 3 percent to 4 percent. Now projections of 6 percent or higher are in vogue. This carries with it the implication that a significant rate of inflation is now embedded in the economy. History says that inflation generally doesn't stay stable too long. It is either accelerating or slowing down. **Most inflations of the past, in the United States and elsewhere, were associated with other wartime periods, and were short-lived when the wars were over.** Other occasional bursts of inflation were associated with poor harvests or sudden increases in the money stock, such as gold discoveries in the 19th century. These, like war-induced inflations, were never long-lasting. Although the aftermath of World War II did not experience a typical postwar depression and deflation, prices did stabilize. In the period that followed, through the mid-1960s, and including the Korean War, which produced a typical wartime inflation and subsequent deflation of raw material prices, there was little evidence of a secular drift in the inflation rate. In fact, prices in the early 1960s were rising at a lower rate than in the late 1950s. Since 1965, however, there has been a steady acceleration of price increases. While there have been some apparently autonomous factors like the poor harvests of 1972 and the OPEC action in 1973 that aggravated the situation, there is increasing evidence that the main source of present-day inflation lies within the economic, political and social system itself.

There are examples of things happening in our society that support the thesis that this higher level of inflation is embedded in the system. There are escalation clauses in labor and other contracts; social security and some welfare and pension benefits have their payment schedule tied to increases in costs;

health-care and casualty insurance are the same way. Contracts are being written for shorter periods of time, or with provisions to reopen negotiations. Some major national figures are even suggesting indexing. All these techniques are supposedly designed to help us cope—to live with inflation. But by doing so, they actually reduce the social and political pressure to end inflation.

If we agree that there is a chance that higher inflation is here to stay and not just a temporary phenomenon, or when it is low can recur, then the first thing we need to do is understand the fundamental issues that caused it. Higher prices, government deficits, increased wage demands, reduced productivity—all of these are part of the reason. Beyond these, I think many people would agree that there are a number of fundamental changes that have taken place in our economic structure.

In the United States, there has been a marked shift in priorities from the goal of economic growth to a more specific focus on the redistribution of output and income. This change in priorities has manifested itself in numerous ways. First, the rapid expansion of government budgets over the past decade. Second, the emphasis on social and environmental goals, all the way from racial and sexual equality to better welfare and social security. Pollution controls and safety regulations, both of which pre-empt capital from more productive uses, have played an increasingly dominant role in business capital spending in the past decade.

The reprioritizing of expenditures and income by itself is not bad. The problem is how to pay the tab. We can all agree that every human being is entitled to a minimum standard of living. We can all agree that an improved environment is important. We can all agree that improved consumer safety is important. What we seem to have trouble agreeing upon is that a country's economy is no different than a family's or an individual's. None of them can live beyond its means for very long without paying the price. In the case of a country, its creditors are the other countries that will call their loans or value their currency in proportion to their belief in its worth.

We cannot do everything at once, as we have tried to do, because it creates deficits and inflation. If we try to solve all the problems of society overnight, some of which were actually virtues in the past, like automobile size and horsepower, we not only have deficits but we also redirect the application of capital. Funds that would be saved and later invested in capital goods designed to improve productivity, provide jobs and generate more national income, are diverted to current expenditures, the net result being that more resources are spent pursuing the same amount of goods and less is spent in developing additional goods.

Another fundamental factor that will determine the course of inflation and real growth in the U.S. economy over the next decade is recognition of, and reaction to, the growing economic and financial interdependence among the nations of the world and the mechanism for transmitting inflation among countries. No country is a closed economy—that is, subject only to its own economic forces and policies. **Although recently more attention has been given the world as an integrated economy, there has been little recognition given to worldwide phenomena in setting policies and in projecting domestic inflation.**

The increase in the rate of inflation in the last five years has been a worldwide phenomenon. Although the United States has been responsible for transmitting inflation to other countries through its balance of payments deficits and the response of its trading partners to these deficits, much of the generation of inflation has its roots in basic worldwide supply-demand imbalances and reactions to these imbalances. At the end of World War II, the United States was clearly the dominant force in the world's economy. Since then, significant economic progress in Western Europe and Japan has narrowed the economic gap between the United States and these countries. In addition, these developing countries have made impressive strides in the last two decades. The resulting increase in effective world demand has put pressure on existing world supplies of natural resources. This is particularly true in the case of food and other basic commodities, as exemplified by the substantial increase in oil prices.

In the early 1970s, official free-world monetary reserves expanded at an unprecedented rate, primarily as a consequence of the large U.S. balance of payments deficits and the accumulation of dollars by its trading partners. The Eurodollar market grew at an extraordinary rate, with net Eurodollar deposits growing to $220 billion by 1974, from $22 billion in 1967, a tenfold increase. Often referred to as "stateless money" because Eurodollars are not counted in the money supply of any nation, this new source of money was responsible for an explosion of global reserves greater than ever before.

This impact was a very significant one, as demonstrated by the correlation between world inflation and the world money supply during this period.

Certain basic techniques for fighting inflation can be agreed on by all. We can elect fiscally responsible people to public office. We can insist on living within our means. We can improve our productivity. We can exercise restraint. But any lofty ideals must be lived by everyone, not just our politicians. **Achievement of results at a national level, or at any high level, is only accomplished by everybody at the lowest levels doing things and acting in accordance with those ideals every day in every way.** As an example, if we want to stop police corruption, the private citizen must obey the laws and stop trying to fix parking tickets.

Therefore, learning to operate successfully in the inflation environment—a matter of survival for the business enterprise—must be accomplished at every level of organization.

Inflation is complicated, not simple. Its bad effects are insidious. They may be hidden from view, yet continually deteriorate the business. If the business person is not capable of taking them into account in the areas in which they operate, some day he or she may wake up to find that he or she can't afford to stay in business.

There is no single way, no simple report that you can get once every few months, to allow you to cope with the problem. The inflation rate can vary widely from one sector of the economy to another. Oil prices went sky-high, but semiconductor prices actually went down. **The technique of living with inflation must be built into the everyday culture of running the business.** There are countries where inflation has been continual—indeed violent at times—yet business enterprises have successfully adapted. They have achieved good results in these environments. Countries as diverse as Brazil and Israel are examples. So that no one gets the wrong idea, let me repeat again that stable economic growth with no inflation is far preferred to living with any inflation.

We in the United States are primarily concerned with our inflation, and other countries with theirs. While certainly this is the major area where a private citizen sees and feels the problem, because of the large amount of international trade and interdependent situations, inflation in many countries affects many others. For the business that is multinational in nature— that builds products any place and ships to anywhere in the world, that buys and sells anywhere in the world, that employs people around the world—the problem of worldwide inflation is very real.

Inflation levels are different in every country. Not too long ago the United States had 8 percent, the United Kingdom 12 percent, France 18 percent, Japan 25 percent, and so on. Government approaches to fight inflation are generally different in every country. There are frequent changes of government regulations on such things as taxes, import duties, exchange rates, wage and price controls, non-tariff barriers, money supply, interest rates and export incentives. Due to the time lag between implementation of any of these and their interaction with other elements, the results are not easily predictable.

As I enumerate all the variables, it would be easy to say that the problem defies solution. Luckily, business people, like most other people, don't throw in the towel. We don't look at Mt. Everest and say, "My God, it's so high we'll never be able to climb it." Rather we say, "The way to climb Mt. Everest is to put your left foot in front of your right one and then your right foot in front of your left and pretty soon you're half way there." That's how I'd like to tackle this problem with you—by looking at the basic fundamental business operations and what must be ingrained in the culture of managing a business. Once it is so ingrained, we are prepared to handle varying rates of inflation, short of catastrophic proportions.

To understand what goes on in a typical manufacturing business, let's look at the business transaction cycle. It consists of a number of specific actions that may overlap somewhat, but primarily follow one another in time sequence.

If it is a new product, first market research is conducted before product design. Then the product is designed.

A factory may have to be designed, built and equipped, and people hired and trained.

The price must be set.

The customer must be quoted a price for his unique requirements.

We must get the order.

If we are quoting off-the-shelf delivery or a relatively short delivery of four to six weeks, we may have ordered material very much earlier in this cycle because it takes anywhere from six to 16 weeks or more to get most materials. The materials may be received and the product built before we quoted the price to the customer, or on the other hand, we may have to buy all the material after we get the order and add the labor content after that.

We must deliver the product and bill the customer.

Finally, we must collect the money.

This whole process can take years on a new product, and months on a current product.

During this whole cycle, we are subject to changes that can occur at any time, which affect the profit earned on the sale and the worth of the profit to pay dividends or to invest in the future of the enterprise. **Other than the normal business management and competitive factors, inflation—the change in the value of money occurring with time—is the key factor in success or failure.**

Let's tick off what happens as the worth of money decreases.

1. Money and monetary assets we owe, and liabilities owed to us, are continually losing value over time.
2. The market uncertainty increases, and the marketplace, meaning customers, competitors and regulators, may not adjust rapidly enough to this fact.
3. International transactions—purchases, sales, borrowings— may be impacted by changing exchange rates, devaluation or revaluation, all of which change the value of cash received from the amounts originally anticipated.
4. International investments are changed in value as exchange rates vary.
5. Comparison of current business results with prior years' contains significant distortion, both in profits and fixed assets, due to the changing value of the monetary unit of measure.
6. Budgets and forecasts, both long- and short-range, are very difficult to establish, and they degrade rapidly with time. This is accentuated in countries with floating exchange rates or potential step function currency exchanges.

7. Depreciation charges are too low to provide adequately for replacing assets at the higher inflated prices, and in addition, cause the payment of too much in taxes or increased tax rates.

8. Profits may be overstated and cause too high a dividend payout, while in reality they may be too low to meet both investment needs and the need for additional working capital that continually grows in local currency, even when the business does not grow in real terms.

Well, that's a mouthful of potential catastrophes. Mt. Everest, here we come! What do we do?

In general, we must plan better, even though planning horizons are shortened, because predictability is difficult. **We must learn some new tricks, control more tightly and react more quickly.** That's the general answer. Now what does that mean in the specific?

First of all, it means that the day-to-day management control in an inflationary environment must be decentralized as much as possible to each country of operation. Because the rules, conditions and inflation rates may be different, it requires greater local in-country knowledge about, and faster response to, local government, economic, market and social conditions. Business managers must become increasingly knowledgeable of economic trends and economic policy moves by governments, and not just concerned with making and selling a quality product. Higher level management overview is also necessary to ensure that local managers are not only doing the things they have to do to cope with inflation in their own country or business, but also to ensure that the interrelation-ships among countries in a multinational enterprise are adequately considered and coordinated.

Second, working capital must be kept to minimum levels through:

a) minimum cash and monetary investments;

b) strong control over receivables collection;

c) low inventories, and

d) maximum utilization of local borrowing and supplier credit consistent with reasonable debt-equity ratios.

But don't get fooled into ridiculously high borrowings now, payable back later in cheaper currency. In simultaneous inflation-recession periods like the last one, the loan interest and principal payments coming due in periods of poor business and reduced or no profits may require selling of good assets to raise cash, or even force bankruptcy.

Third, great emphasis must be placed on improving productivity of labor and capital equipment. Increased wages can only be afforded by increasing productivity.

Fourth, high-level attention must be constantly focused on the pricing of goods and services. Pricing must be continually and aggressively maintained in real terms. Long-term sales contracts must be protected against losses due to inflation-caused increased costs, which can be significant. Therefore, terms of sale should contain down payments, linkage features and interest charges on late payments if inflation is high and where business conditions permit. But there is a major danger here, too. If it is too easy to raise prices, the pressure on reducing costs and improving productivity is removed. Senior management must make astute judgments balancing these issues.

Fifth, the normalizing of business data is required, whether that is by some form of official price level accounting or whether specific correction factors are always utilized, when reviewing both historical and future time series data.

Sixth, profit margins must be higher to compensate for increased risk and continual depreciation of assets.

Seventh, international transactions and investments must be protected against losses through currency exchange rate shifts:

   a) Transactions should be linked. For example, a foreign sales contract involving substantial imported materials should have a price-protection clause in the event of the devaluation of local currency.

   b) Investment exposure must be neutralized by: 1) the use of local borrowings, 2) forward currency contracts, 3) investment of excess funds in tangible assets, and 4) offsetting anticipated gains in one country by anticipating losses in another.

Eighth, employee-compensation practices must be reviewed more frequently to avoid unfair compensation, dissatisfaction and loss of key people.

Ninth, periodic reviews must be held of profit-and-loss statements and balance sheets, in local currency and in constant prices, in addition to dollars. Budgeting and forecasting must be done more frequently, concentrating on shorter time intervals.

Tenth, flexible contingency planning is mandatory. The astute business person of the future will have developed a series of alternate plans for operating actions to be taken in the event certain conditions develop. They will be based on a range of possibilities.

That's quite a mouthful, and easier said than done. Lots of people can reach the right conclusions and determine the right course of action, but what counts is the successful, timely implementation of the decisions made and the policies set. **All the good intentions in the world count for nothing if the results are not there.** To give the best probability of achieving results, here are some things that must be done.

1. Good people are the key, but that's not enough. Good business managers in a stable environment may flunk the course in a situation where the rate of inflation is changing rapidly. Therefore, the first mandatory requirement is that everyone believe and understand the seriousness of inflation as a problem and be committed to doing something about it.

2. Managers must recognize that some of the previous rules cannot apply any longer. Particularly, they should not underestimate the complexities and differences among countries.

3. Wherever possible, managers who have successfully coped with the inflation problem should be moved into areas of the business where this experience doesn't exist. There is no substitute for experience!

4. For many businesses in countries with high inflation, it may be necessary to appoint an experienced manager just to handle the whole subject of pricing and terms, and assign authority to back him or her in this complex area.

5. Management systems for control and forecasting that take into consideration all the elements of the dynamic inflationary economic environment must be installed, so that they pervade the organization at all levels.

After going through the previous discussion, some of you may think it's easier to control the inflation than learn to cope with it. I don't believe that. I do believe that we can cope with a limited inflation situation, because many of the items with which we must deal are within our own control, as long as governments don't artificially restrict our ability to manage. I also believe, however, that the most serious problem we face is the control of inflation on a continuing basis. While we seem to be doing better these days, getting that culture inculcated is the surest way to guarantee the survival of our business enterprises if and when another inflationary cycle begins.

I read a statement the other day that I'd like to read to you. "For who is so insensitive and so devoid of human feeling that he can be unaware or has not perceived that uncontrolled prices are widespread in the sales taking place in the markets and in daily life in the cities."

Inflation is as old as history. That statement was made when across-the-board wage and price controls were instituted in Rome by Emperor Diocletian in 310 A.D.

I like to think that I am basically a pragmatic optimist. I'm not exactly sure how we will solve every problem, but I do know that with real determination, proven by history, we will do it overall. You can see how vitally important it is to have correct financial information in real time, and to have astute financial management analysis of the facts and the trends. Each of you here today will be a major factor in the "how." Having been exposed to students like you around the country, I have no concern about the "if."

BW

Business & Economic Quotations

"Business without profit is not business any more than a pickle is candy."
Charles F. Abbott

"The worst crime an employer can commit against the worker is to fail to make a profit."
Samuel Gompers

"When business policies undergo economic obsolescence, they in effect degenerate into business prejudices."
John McLean

You Can't Legislate Economics
Economics is just Human Nature in action.

People will always buy more of the good product whose price is fair.

There will always be employers who will hire the man or woman who produces the most.

Mounting debt will always eventually destroy a man or a government.

You can only have what you produce—nothing is ever truly "free," nor for long.

High taxes restrict the standard of living of everyone; high productivity increases it.

The worker who steadily learns more will always earn more.

The safe (and happy) family or nation is the one which spends less than it earns.

And all the government regulations in the world can never change a single one of these basic rules of living.
Reprinted with permission from
Giddings and Lewis, Inc.

"Every time you step on someone to further your own cause, you dig your own hole a little deeper."
author unknown

"A company is known by the men it keeps."
author unknown

"Behind an able man there are always other able men."
Chinese proverb

"There is a time to speak and a time to keep quiet. There are things to tell and things not to tell. But it is an excellent rule to practice frankness in all dealings and associations with others, whether in business or socially. The frank person treads a firm bridge crossing a river, while the secretive person charily steps from stone to stone."
B.C. Forbes

"The real price of everything, what everything really costs to the man who wants to acquire it, is the toil and trouble of acquiring it."
Adam Smith

It is unwise to pay too much.
It is unwise to pay too little.
When you pay too much,
   all you lose is a little money—
   that is all.
When you pay too little,
   you lose everything—because
   the thing you bought was
   incapable of doing the thing
   you bought it to do.
If you deal with the lowest
   bidder,
it is well to add something for
   the risk you run.
And if you do that, you'll
   have enough to pay for something better.

John Ruskin

"There are two ways of being
happy; we may either diminish
our wants or augment our means.
Either will do, the result is the
same. And it is for each man to
decide for himself, and do that
which happens to be the easiest.
If you are idle or sick or poor,
however hard it may be for you
to diminish your wants, it will be
harder to augment your means.
If you are active and prosperous
or young or in good health, it
may be easier for you to augment
your means than to diminish
your wants. But if you are wise,
you will do both at the same
time, young or old, rich or poor,
sick or well. And if you are very

wise, you will do both in such a
way as to augment the general
happiness of society."
Benjamin Franklin

"Method is the very hinge of
business; and there is no method
without punctuality."
Richard Cecil

"One worthwhile task carried to a
successful conclusion is worth half
a hundred half-finished tasks. On
the football field you cannot score
a goal unless and until you have
forced the ball between the posts.
It is the same in the business field.
Concentrate. Be a finisher."
B.C. Forbes

Backing into the future

"If, in conclusion, I may give for
what they are worth the impres-
sions of a brief visit to Washington,
I believe that there is much devot-
ed and intelligent work in progress
there, and that the fittest ideas
and the fittest men are tending
to survive. In many parts of the
world the old order has passed
away. But of all the experiments
to evolve a new order, it is the
experiment of young America
which most attracts my own deep-
est sympathy. For they are occu-
pied with the task of trying to
make the economic order work
tolerably well, while preserving
freedom of individual initiative

and liberty of thought and
criticism.

The older generation of living
Americans accomplished the
great task of solving the technical problem of how to produce
economic goods on a scale adequate to human needs. It is the
task of the younger generation to
bring to actual realization the
potential blessings of having
solved the technical side of the
problem of poverty. The central
control which the latter requires
involves an essentially changed
method and outlook. The minds
and energies which have found
their fulfillment in the achievements of American business are
not likely to be equally well
adapted to the further task. That
must be, as it should be, the fulfillment of the next generation.

The new men will often appear
to be at war with the ideas and
convictions of their seniors. This
cannot be helped. But I hope that
these seniors will look as sympa-
thetically as they can at a sincere
attempt—I cannot view it otherwise—to complete, and not to
destroy, what they themselves
have created."
John Maynard Keynes
The New York Times, June 10, 1934

It's true in football—and I suspect the same is true in business—that your own mistakes are going to hurt you more than your competitor does. You observe your competitor and you may learn from him. But your problem is your performance—the thing that you can control.

You never quit trying to improve and you never can quit trying to improve, because when you think you've arrived, you're starting downhill. You always have shortcomings, and if you want to be the best, you work on your shortcomings.

It's human nature to go out and do the things you do best. But those who work on their shortcomings and make them their strengths are the ones who are going to have the edge that makes them the best.
Chuck Noll, former coach,
Pittsburgh Steelers
Reprinted with permission from
IndustryWeek, November 1976.
Copyright©, Penton Publishing, Inc.
Cleveland, Ohio.

"We must have courage to bet on our ideas, to take the calculated risk, and to act. Everyday living requires courage if life is to be effective and bring happiness."
Maxwell Maltz

"If we would have anything of benefit, we must earn it, and earning it become shrewd, inventive, ingenious, active, enterprising."
Henry Ward Beecher

"Business is like riding a bicycle. Either you keep moving or you fall down."
John David Wright

Contributors

The following is a listing of contributors. They represent people from all over the world, all levels of business and all age brackets; most of them are, or have been, Motorolans. Their contribution has challenged, strengthened and molded the vision of The Philosophy Memos.

A

Joel Adams
Fred Anrod

B

Mike Babka
Bill Bakrow
Ed Bales
Dave Bartram
Bill Bang
Maggie Beard
Barry Bedard
John Bennett
Jim Bernhart
Bert Bertolozzi
Bob Bigony
Stan Bobowski
Ben Borne
Warren Bornhoeft
Kathryn Bowman
Carlton Braun
John Breckline
Bob Brown
Earl Brown
Karl Burgess
Chuck Burnside

C

Jim Caile
Jerry Cain
Michele Caple
Bob Cecil
Ron Chapman
Chuck Crider
Dexter Collard
Richard B. Comport
Marty Cooper

D

A.P. Davies
Dick Day
Jack Dean
Marie DeMaggio
Ray Dempsey
Akemi Denda
Toni Dewey

Maria Dickmann
Bill Drake
Tom Draper

E

Chuck Eichelkraut
Paul Elmer

F

MaryAnn Fahrberger
Ed Falls
Ray Faye
Don Foecking
Jim Fogle
Brent Fox
Bob Frantz
Gloria Fruin

G

Bob Galvin
Frank Gast
"Red" Gentry
Dick Gilley
Rose Giurato
Helmut Goerling
Al Goldstein
Eric Goleas
Chuck Granieri
Lee Gualano

H

Fred Hamm
John Hathway
Frank Havlicek
Bob Hawkins
Larry Heavey
Roger Hekhuis
Ron Henry
Jack Hickey
Ingrid Holmer
Ken Hooton
Shirl Hunter
Jim Hyatt

J

Ken Jahns
Ray Jenks

Gini Jewett
Arnie Johnson
Ken Johnson
Joe Jordan

K

Norm Kazyk
Larry Keller
Phil Kenny
Bob Killackey
Allan Kirson
Dick Kovarik
George Kuharsky

L

Denny LaBud
Bruce Ladd
John Lahet
Frank Lambrecht
Jack Larsen
Marty Levy
Steve Levy
Carl Lindholm
Jack Lloyd
Dave Long
Dorothea Love
Norm Lovett
Chuck Lynk

M

Grant Malchow
Bill Mahoney
John Maloney
Peter Manson
Homer Marrs
Bruce Martin
Ed McLellan
Bill McMurry
Bill Meehan
Roger S. Meiners
Art Merims
Dave Metz
Jim Mikulski
Ron Miller
Wally Miller
David Minter

Jerry Moch
Bob Mohler
Jim Moncada
Steve Morgan
Joanie Moshis
Hal Mumma
Art Murcott

N

Carl Nierzwicki
Bill Nitschke
Kathleen Nitschke
Dan Noble
Bea Novak
Marianne Nyberg

O

Tom Ochal
Barney O'Conner
Pat O'Malley
Jerry Orloff

P

Bill Parrish
Dick Passmore
Woody Peres
Doni Peterson
Larry Peterson
Ed Porrett
Dolores Porter

R

Deke von Reischach
Roy Richardson
Jon Rodgers
Tom Rollins
Bob Rosenberger

S

Curt Schultz
Walter Scott
Virden Scranton
Bill Seefeldt
Phil Shuman
Al Siebert
Pete Simonis
Dick Skinner
Norma Smith

Jim Sorenson
Ed Staiano
Paul Stancik
Bob Stephens
Jack Stewart
Ted Stewart
Ken Stork
Kathy Sullivan
Bob Swift

T

Wayne Talbot
Ernie Tate
Frank Todd
Sam Tomas
Bill Tomlinson
Jim Torrence
Gail Triplett
Joe Tucker

U

Gen Ulm

V

Ed Valaskovic

W

Art Waslicki
David Weisz
George Weisz
Bill Welk
Jerry Werner
Ken West
Ed Wieczkiewicz
Marilyn Williams
Hugh Willson
Beckey Winter
Jim Wright
Phil Wright
Joyce Wolfsmith
Ted Woods

Z

Ray Zack
Herb Zeller

"The value of publications is in the sharing of knowledge and ideas. There is something both challenging and liberating about putting knowledge and ideas on paper. The authority of the written word helps to carry our thoughts more effectively to our associates.

As each of our roles in life mature, it is even an increasing credit to all of us that we have things sufficiently worthy to say that they be shared in this disciplined and creative way."
Robert W. Galvin